Contemplative Social Research:
Caring for Self, Being, and Lifeworld

Fielding University Press is an imprint of Fielding Graduate University.
Its objective is to advance the research and scholarship of Fielding faculty, students
and alumni around the world, using a variety of publishing platforms. For more information, please contact Fielding University Press, attn. Greta Walters, 2020 De la Vina
Street, Santa Barbara, CA 93105. Phone: (805) 898-2924. Fax: (805) 690-4310. On
the web: www.fielding.edu.

© Fielding Graduate University, 2016
Published in the United States of America by Fielding University Press

Library of Congress Cataloging-in-Publication data
Contemplative Social Research: Caring for Self, Being and Lifeworld
1. Education systems – higher learning.

CONTEMPLATIVE SOCIAL RESEARCH: CARING FOR SELF, BEING, AND LIFEWORLD

Edited by
Valerie Malhotra Bentz, PhD, Fielding Graduate University
Vincenzo Mario Bruno Giorgino, PhD, University of Turin

Casandra D. Lindell, M.Div., MA,
Associate Editor

Table of Contents

Preface by Harry Moody.. 6

Preface by Sander Tideman.. 10

Introduction by Vincenzo Giorgino and Valerie Bentz......... 16

PART ONE: CONTEMPLATIVE KNOWING AND BEING

Zack Walsh, *The Social and Political Significance of Contemplation and its Potential for Shaping Contemplative Studies*.. 27

Valerie M. Bentz, *Knowing as Being: Somatic Phenomenology as Contemplative Practice*.. 50

Doug Porpora, *Critical Reason and Spirituality*.................. 80

Donald McCown, *Inside-Out: Mindfulness-Based Interventions as a Model for Community Building*.................................... 98

Xabier Renteria-Uriarte, *Contemplative Science and the Contemplative Foundation of Science: A Proposal of Definitions, Branches, and Tools*... 129

Vincenzo M. B. Giorgino, *Contemplative Knowledge and Social Sciences: Close Encounters of the Enactive Kind*.............. 163

PART TWO: CONTEMPLATIVE RESEARCH AND PRACTICE: APPLICATIONS

Krzysztof Konecki, *Meditation as Epistemology. How Can Social Scientists Profit from Meditation?*............................ *193*

Annabelle Nelson, *Contemplative Psychology and Imagery*... *239*

Luann Drolc Fortune, *Retracing the Labyrinth: Applying Phenomenology for Embodied Interpretation*...................... *261*

David Casacuberta, *Toward Embodied Digital Technologies*... *276*

E. Christopher Mare, *Designing for Consciousness: Outline of a Neurophenomenological Research Program*...................... *300*

About the Series Editor and Associate Editor *335*

About Fielding Graduate University *336*

Preface

The Varieties of Contemplative Experience

By Harry "Rick" Moody
Distinguished Visiting Professor, Fielding Graduate University,
Santa Barbara, California, United States

Let's begin with the word "contemplation" and let's begin with its history. If we were considering the word "contemplation" in the year 1000 or 1500 A.D., it would have a very different meaning from its meaning in the 2000s. In the past generation, the idea of contemplation—and its cousins "contemplative studies" and "contemplative science"—have undergone a revival, partly because of a new appreciation for the idea of "mindfulness." The vogue for mindfulness, and debates about its meaning, are everywhere today: in business, health care, neuroscience, everywhere we look. Evidently, in our hyper-rational information society, there is a hunger for something else, and that "something else" turns out to be named "contemplation."

But is this the same contemplation we would have known in the year 1000 or 1500 A.D.? Yes and no. In medieval Christian tradition, the contemplative life was understood in contrast to the active life—in the New Testament the difference between the sisters Mary and Martha. The contemplative life, often anchored in monasticism, was a life directed at silence and inwardness, at something quite different from the lure of social media, big data, and hyperactivity that dominates our world today.

What about contemplative social science? What's wrong with the social sciences we have known? Misgivings have arisen, doubts about the positivist hegemony that rules the social along with the natural sciences. Those doubts and misgivings have found their place, as the authors of this book recognize, in perspectives such as phenomenology, ethnography, grounded theory, appreciative inquiry, and qualitative research. The list goes on; the misgivings are many.

Then why "contemplative" social science? Are we aspiring to refashion social science on a medieval model? Not at all. The articles in this book do not read in the least like a text from a medieval university. (Trust me, I was trained in medieval philosophy). Quite the contrary. In terms of style, argumentation, and intellectual discourse they are all written at the high level of excellence we would expect in an academic treatment of a distinctive field of knowledge.

Yet this distinctive field of knowledge does not exist or does not yet quite exist. "Contemplative social science," as called for by the authors in this book, is a field that wants to exist, that needs to exist, and that may well come into existence. The discourse of contemplative social science might offer a home to those with misgivings about prevailing methodologies. As someone who has used qualitative research methods for my own endeavor in biomedical ethics and aging, I can only applaud this venture. I hope that it inspires more practice along these lines in years to come.

Let me focus on a single word in my last sentence: namely, "practice." If we go back to the meaning of "contemplation" in the year 1000 A.D., we will see that, above all, it points to a way of life, a kind of practice. Paradoxically, this practice (e.g., contemplative prayer) aspires to "*theoria*," the original Greek term for vision. What we see is more than what we hear, and "seeing is believing," isn't it? Thus, we can imagine a form of social science that carries out the Husserlian mandate "to the things themselves." Indeed, one of the authors in this volume actually makes the correlation between *epoché* and yoga. The difference is that yoga, like Zen meditation or Sufi *dhikr*, is part of a wisdom tradition, a tradition of practice extending over hundreds, even thousands of years. In other words, forms of meditation practice are not a variety of academic discourse. The wisdom traditions have always been a means of going beyond our conventional state of consciousness, our ego-centered consciousness, in favor of something else: of directly "seeing" what is before our eyes yet is (paradoxically) invisible. As the Sufis say, "The path is long because thy foot delays; were it not so, the road to Him is but a single step." It is not talking, but doing and seeing, that are at stake in spiritual practice.

I make this point because the book you hold in your hands is, for the most part, not at all a "cookbook" intended to give social scientists a way to practice the contemplative approach to their field. It could not be such a thing. It may be that no book could ever be such, because practices are learned in a different way, as Michael Polanyi, a chemist, argued long ago (*personal knowledge*). There's a strange thought: chemistry—like cooking, natural childbirth, or public speaking—can only be learned by *doing*, perhaps also *guided* by a living model who transmits elements of practice that can never be pinned down in words.

Yet books, and theoretical statements such as those found in this book, have their value. They are a call to action, which is what the practices of the wisdom traditions have always been. The primary practice, meditation, is a path to transcending, even in part, the domination of the ego. In the case of social science, what this means is a radical transformation of what we call "the observer." Contemplative social science, as propounded by the authors of this book, means overcoming and transforming ourselves: becoming a different kind of person. This is exactly what the contemplative tradition in Christianity, as in Kabbalah, Sufism, Zen, and Vedanta, has always been about. And until the observer changes, contemplative vision will be beyond our reach.

The observer, in social science, is the instrument for seeing. What we learn from the natural sciences is that instruments are essential. Until the microscope and the telescope were invented, it was not possible to see worlds that were always available but invisible to the eye. In the case of the social sciences, we will not see what can be seen until the instrument, the observer, is changed and enlarged. Contemplation is the means of doing this.

I conclude with reference to a book that made a profound impression on me, as it has on thousands of other readers: *Zen and the Art of Archery*, by Eugen Herrigel. Herrigel's story is the account of a man who wanted to learn a form of practice (archery), yet was told by his teachers to act in many small ways far removed from shooting an arrow at the target. Herrigel had to spend long hours simply learning how to stand in position, how to hold a bow, how to pull the string back, and so on. Only after undergoing all this effort did he discover, miraculously, that he was able to hit the target with the arrow every time. Patience in practice was the key to success.

Anyone who has practiced the ancient arts of meditation will understand the point here. To repeat a mantra (sacred syllable), to pay attention to breathing or body position, to focus the mind without regard to purpose or outcome—meditative practice underscores the importance of patience, as Eugen Herrigel learned and as each of us must learn. Contemplative practice, in any of the great wisdom traditions of the world, is the means to transform the practitioner (the observer).

The book you hold in your hands is a call for such a transformation of social science into a form of practice that will allow us to see the world in unexpected ways. But all books, all theories, are only the preface to doing, in the same way that my words are a preface to this book, a book that can enlarge your vision and invite you to see the world in new ways.

Harry "Rick" Moody, PhD, recently retired as Vice President and Director of Academic Affairs for AARP in Washington, D.C. A graduate of Yale (1967), he received his PhD from Columbia University in 1973. He is currently Distinguished Visiting Professor at Fielding Graduate University in Santa Barbara, California. He is the author of more than 100 scholarly articles, as well as a number of books. His most recent book, *The Five Stages of the Soul*, has been translated into seven languages worldwide.

Preface

The Need for Contemplative Social Science

By Sander Tideman, PhD
Managing Director at Mind & Life Europe, The Netherlands

Science is the dominant framework for investigating the nature of reality, and the modern source for knowledge that can help improve the lives of humans and the planet. Yet, for understanding mind, inner experience, and reality, the dominant approach of science is rather incomplete. Whereas science relies on empiricism and "objective" observation of phenomena, understanding "subjective" experience will benefit from well-refined contemplative practices and introspective methods. These can, and should, be used as equal instruments of investigation.

The field of *contemplative science* offers fresh perspectives on our subjective experience of life, our "inner reality" or the first-person perspective, which complements our understanding of "outer" phenomena—that is, the second- or third-person perspectives. Contemplative science not only makes science itself more humane but also ensures that its conclusions contribute to human and societal flourishing by providing a "fuller" picture of the mind and its potential. It also reveals the effects of contemplative practices on cultivating the qualities that lead to human well-being. In other words, contemplative science is not limited to the "inner" perspective; it incorporates the inner perspective into an overall understanding of reality. From this viewpoint one can say that contemplative science *by nature* is part of social science. Why, then, does this book call for contemplative *social* science?

One reason is cultural. Rick Moody has already described how contemplation has historically been regarded as something solitary and removed from society. Another reason may lie in the more modern history of contemplative science, especially in the emergence of mindfulness. One of the pioneers working at the intersection of science and contemplative practice was Jon Kabat-Zinn (1990), a medical scholar who made mindfulness a household name in the field of pain and stress management. Another successful scientist in this domain was neuro-scientist Francesco Varela who, together with H. H. the Dalai Lama and Adam Engle, co-founded the Mind & Life Institute. Varela introduced into neuroscience the concepts of neurophenomenology, which combined the phenomenology of Edmund Husserl and Maurice Merleau-Ponty, with "first-person science" (Varela, Thompson, & Rosch, 1992). Neuroscientist Richard Davidson, by showing that meditation causes measurable change patterns in the brain, caused a revolution in scientific thinking about the power of contemplative practice (Davidson & Begley, 2012). These pioneers were followed by countless others in the field of neuroscience, psychology, and clinical science.

For these professions it was natural to focus research on the effects of contemplative practice on individual brains. Henceforth, contemplative science has become associated with studying individuals engaged in reflective practices of introspection. While in itself this work is critically needed, as a side effect it has reinforced the apparent dichotomy between the "inner" and "outer" aspects of reality, and between the individual and social dimensions of life.

If contemplative science is to fully live up to its promise, this perception has to change. Contemplative science is not *only* about the individual and his brain. It is quite obvious that in order for humanity to solve today's growing social, economic, and ecological challenges, we will have to upgrade our capacity of mind. Since many of the modern challenges have been created on the basis of our mind-sets and worldviews—the way we see the world (for example, as an unlimited resource for our own consumption), there is an urgent need to cultivate new mindsets and worldviews (especially those that recognize the fundamental sacredness and interconnectedness of life). How can we cultivate these minds? This will require a shift in culture, not merely the study of the individual brain. In such a collective undertaking, the

11

separation between inner and outer aspects of reality is not so helpful.

There is no logical reason why this is not possible. Take, for example, the phenomenon of neuroplasticity. Neuroplasticity quite literally means that brains are "plastic"; that is, they can be changed through practices such as meditation and reflection. In other words, negative patterns in the brain such as selfishness and short-term thinking can be transformed into positive patterns such as altruism and long-term thinking. If this applies to human brains, it should logically follow that plasticity must also be true for organizations, because they are made up of human beings with brains. If beings can be transformed, so should organizations and political/economic systems. Said differently, organizations and political/economic systems are social constructs. If humans can be changed, social constructs can be changed.

A dichotomy between inner and outer is not tenable on a deeper experiential level either. Anyone engaged in contemplative practice will at one point discover that the mind cannot be "found" inside our head, or at any specific location. The mind is an emergent experiential phenomena allowing internal and external reality to become manifest. For the mind there is no distinction between inner and outer. Daniel Siegel (2009, 2013) describes the mind as a process that is both embodied and interpersonal, which means that it is shared through relationships with others and with the world. Contemplative practice in fact entails a process of recognizing one's natural interconnectedness with the world. Our minds determine our relationships and the ways we perceive the world. The world cannot be known except through the lens of one's own mind, or one's "worldview."

The promise of contemplative science lies herein: human beings have the capacity to transform their relationship with the world, and, in this way, change the world. However, we are still lacking an intellectual framework for this exciting view. How can we understand it in an academic discourse that typically separates the natural sciences from the social sciences, the individual from the collective, and the inner from the outer?

The Dalai Lama (2002), speaking from the Mahayana Buddhist tradition, defines the purpose of meditation as the cultivation of positive mental qualities, leading to a responsible and proactive attitude toward all of life. While mediation may bring stillness and tranquility of mind, this is not considered the endpoint of the contemplative path. While in the Buddhist context mind-training has a specific spiritual goal, the Dalai Lama (2013) has stressed the importance and the possibility of cultivating the mind in a secular context so as to become a better human being who is more effective in the world. The principles of mind-transformation operate equally in a spiritual and secular context. Thus the inner-outer dichotomy is transcended; contemplative practice allows us to transform both our inner and outer reality.

What are these principles of mind transformation? As they span both inner and outer dimensions, can these principles be used for philosophically defining contemplative social science?

I find the best reference for this in the Mahayana Buddhist ideal of the Bodhisattva. A Bodhisattva is defined as someone who decides to take the path of developing his mind while engaging with the world (Shantideva, 1997). Throughout Asian history and up to today, the Bodhisattva ideal has inspired many leaders such as statesmen, merchants, scholars, and artists (Loizzo, 2006; Thurman, 1997). The Bodhisattva's main practice is the development of wisdom and compassion. In the Buddhist view, wisdom is the correct understanding of how the outer and inner phenomenological worlds exist and operate, namely as an interconnected and interdependent system (Dalai Lama, 2002). In view of the interconnected nature of reality, the Bodhisattva does not make a distinction between self and others, or inner and outer. While his principal focus is the development of his own mind, the Bodhisattva is equally concerned with the world around him. Given that we and others are interconnected and interdependent, and that our happiness in the ultimate sense relies on the happiness of others, compassion is considered a natural state. A Bodhisattva, therefore, works on his mind to develop wisdom while practicing compassion in finding ways to diminish the suffering of others. His qualities of wisdom and compassion will need to be supported by a powerful, determined, and focused mind, brought about by meditation.

In view of the fact that modern political, societal, and economic reality—or any social system for that matter—is driven by the principles of increasing interconnectedness, and the Bodhisattva model is rooted in the same principles of interconnectedness, it can serve as an appropriate model for contemplative social agency and leadership (Tideman, 2016). The Bodhisattva model and its underlying philosophy transcending the inner and the outer aspects of reality may provide inspiration for the emerging field of contemplative social science.

Along with the views expressed in this excellent book, I hope this brief introductory analysis can help us to see that contemplative science is not merely focused on individuals engaged in contemplative practice, but that it can play a role in transforming relationships, organizations, and larger social fields, and even our political/economic system. Contemplative social science is needed to understand how humanity can cultivate the mind capacity needed to address the unprecedented complex and collective challenges of our time.

References

Dalai Lama. (2002). *The meaning of life from a Buddhist perspective.* Boston, MA: Wisdom Publications.

Davidson, R. J., & Begley, S. (2012). *The emotional life of your brain: How its unique patterns affect the way you think, feel, and live—and how you can change.* New York, NY: Hudson Street Press.

Kabat-Zinn, J. (1990). *Full catastrophe living: Using the wisdom of your body and mind to face stress, pain, and illness.* New York, NY: Bantam Books.

Loizzo, J. (2006). Renewing the Nalanda legacy: Science, religion, and objectivity in Buddhism and the West. *Religion East & West, Journal of the Institute for World Religions, 6*, 101-121.

Shantideva (1997). *A guide to the Bodhisattva way of life.* (V. A. Wallace & B. A. Wallace, Trans.). Ithaca, NY: Snow Lion.

Siegel, D. (2009). *Mindsight: The new science of personal transformation.* New York, NY: Random House.

-------. (2013). *The developing mind: How relationships and the brain interact to shape who we are.* New York, NY: Random House.

Thurman, R. (1997). *Inner revolution: Life, liberty, and the pursuit of real happiness.* New York, NY: Riverhead Books.

Tideman, S. G. (2016). Gross National Happiness: Lessons for sustainability leadership. *South Asia Journal for Global Business Research, 5*(2), 190-213.

Varela, F., Thompson, E. T., & Rosch, E. (1992). *The embodied mind: Cognitive science and human experience.* Boston, MA: The MIT Press.

Sander Tideman, PhD, is Managing Director at Mind & Life Europe and serves on the faculty of the Rotterdam School of Management, Erasmus University, where he directs research on sustainable business models, strategy, and leadership. He began his career in international law and then international banking before transitioning into strategy and leadership development, with a focus on creating sustainable organizations. He has co-authored many articles and books, including *Compassion or competition: Business as instrument for positive change*, with H. H. the Dalai Lama.

Introduction: Opportunities for Human Potential in the *Great Transition*: An Embodied Perspective at Work

By Vincenzo M. B. Giorgino, University of Turin, Italy, and Valerie Malhotra Bentz, Fielding Graduate University, United States

Contemplative scholars from Europe and North America, and from a variety of social science disciplines, have contributed to this book. Their work extends and broadens the social and human sciences, pushing the boundaries between disciplines and cultures. Our aim is to give voice to an existent array of research and practices that have in common a contemplative vision within a social and human science approach.

A dialogue between contemplative knowledge and sciences has already started in other disciplines, such as in physics (Capra, 1975; Zajonc 2003, 2004), neuroscience (Wallace, 2007; Walach, Schmidt, & Jonas, 2011; Menon, 2014, Schmidt, & Walach, 2014), and life sciences (Varela, Thompson, & Rosch, 1991; Varela & Shear, 1999). It has begun more recently in the human and social sciences: in education; (Barbezat & Bush, 2014; Gunnlaugson, Sarath, Scott, & Bai, 2014; Renteria-Uriarte & Giorgino, 2016); economics (Kolm, 1982; Schumacher, 1973; Zsolnai, 2006; 2014a; 2014b); sociology (Bentz & Shapiro, 1998; Giorgino, 2014, 2015; Immergut & Kaufman, 2014; Pagis, 2010a, 2010b, 2015; Preston, 1988; Schipper, 2012); and in organizational studies (Nonaka & Takeuchi, 1995; Senge, 1990; Senge, Schwarmer, Jaworski, & Flowers, 2005).

From the traditions of wisdom, whether religious or philosophical, we have inherited a legacy that can be pragmatically translated in secular terms to address the quest for meaning expressed in the current age by post-modern humans. We hope to contribute to the construction of a new paradigm of contemplative social sciences that can be grounded in an embodied and nonindividualistic model of knowledge.

16

Recent attempts to assess the meanings and uses of metaphors of the self (Davis, 2011) benefit from the redefinition of experience and the introduction of the "no-self" concept (Immergut & Kaufman, 2014; Kolm, 1982; Zsolnai, 2014c; Zsolnai & Ims, 2006) intended as the inescapable companion of the human search for a wiser approach to life.

So far, contemplative based inquiry has recognized the deep oneness of humanity. It requires embodied awareness as well as openness to the transpersonal dimensions of human experience. In recent decades, scholars have included the body as well as emergent communities, or lifeworlds, in social research (Bondebierg, 2015; Fourcade, 2010; Waskul & Vannini, 2012). Contemplative inquiry focuses on emerging understandings of being, questioning existing theories of self, mind, culture, and society. The researchers in this book demonstrate the contributions of various forms of contemplative practice to ways of knowing and being.

Vincenzo M.B. Giorgino was inspired to initiate this book after the third conference he promoted October 15, 2015 at the University of Torino for the International Day of Happiness. This was called the "Economies of Becoming".[1] In particular, the idea was shared with Valerie Malhotra Bentz, who has similar interests. This led them to include in this book authors who attended the conference or who share the same orientation toward a contemplative approach in social sciences. This is the first volume of the initiative, and the second volume, expected in Spring 2017, will be focused on radical approaches in economics and technologies in dialogue with contemplative social sciences.

No single discipline can deal with vital emergent issues such as the consequences of climate change, growing social inequalities, or extraordinary opportunities to modify and create life artificially, as well as the social impact of new digital technologies. We propose a transdisciplinary approach, intended in its wider sense, across the academy and beyond it (Nicolescu, 2008).

This volume intends to contribute to what has been called the

"Great Transition" in world societies. The term originally referred to the changes occurring with dramatic speed and impact in the environment resulting from climate change, and the necessity of modifying our behavior and lifestyles to reverse the process. After the 2007-8 financial crisis, it assumed a wider meaning: scholars from across the social and human sciences disciplines concluded that underneath the economic crisis of 2007-8 and 2012 lies a structural and cultural crisis and the search for new forms of social order. This has led to a growing field of literature (Bonaiuti, 2014; Coote & Goodwin, 2010). An irreversible change in our social and economic system also emanates from the technological revolution: a new society and economy in which traditional hierarchical organizations are made obsolete by new networked peer-to-peer organizations (Benkler, 2006; Castells, 1996; Rifkin, 2014).

Also relevant is the individualization process to which little attention is usually given. Its disruptive strength makes much easier to understand why the individual is at the center of possible whirlpools for which our culture – including our institutions – seems unable to offer safe harbors (Beck & Gernsheim-Beck, 2001). In an experiential dimension, the continuous changes in everyday life that we have to deal with in almost any sphere exert an enormous pressure on sentient beings. Too frequently, institutions are failing to provide safe harbors from these changes.

Contemplative social sciences are intended to help us be aware of our prejudgmental attitudes and to have a more open-minded approach for the benefit of all. Contemplative social sciences place these processes at the core of their inquiry: a wise and pragmatic methodology to develop and nurture a fresh approach to social interactions.

We can integrate the traditions of wisdom with social sciences under the umbrella of contemplative research and practice. This implies the understanding and transcending of religious contexts in which contemplative knowledge is usually born and cultivated. We look to contemplative practice as a way to explore ways of approaching the crises of understanding brought about by the continued fragmentation of learning. We are taking the first steps in an uncharted land in which actors are invited to dismiss their certainties and be open to unexpected solutions. The production of knowledge, as Polanyi (1958) wrote, is neither subjective nor objective, but a commitment characterized by "dwelling in." A contemplative approach to knowledge is able to create islands of change-oriented open and democratic social and economic ties.

A mindful approach to knowledge begins within the consciousness of the researcher (see Bentz & Shapiro, 1996). Research thus becomes a way of being within the lived experiences and lifeworlds in which it occurs.

Part One focuses on conceptualizations of knowing and being. Zack Walsh broadens mindfulness practice beyond various cultural, religious, and disciplinary perspectives. He seeks to avoid reducing its power by making it simply a product in the services industry marketplace. To Walsh, contemplative practice is an important source for social and political change, as well as beneficial to individual practitioners. His approach has historical roots in Buddhist and Christian traditions, associating contemplation with ethical action.

Valerie M. Bentz addresses the essentially contemplative nature of phenomenological inquiry, which is a way of being as well as a way of knowing. From Edward Husserl's great vision, phenomenology is transformative, a way to get "back to the things themselves." It involves a practice of *epoché*, through which prior judgments and categories are suspended so that one's vision opens to what is occurring. Phenomenological practice offers ways of healing stress in persons, organizations, and the environment. There is congruency between phenomenology and findings in neuroscience regarding core consciousness and autobiographical consciousness. Bentz shows how these principles were already basic in the ancient and current Vedantic texts.

Doug Porpora's "critical realism" reclaims the spiritual realm as necessary to ground moral and ethical action. Porpora argues against the viewpoint of positivism that eliminates the spiritual from inquiry. He refutes social constructionism—that the spiritual level is unreal, a mere construct with no ontological significance.

Donald McCown recaps the benefits of mindfulness-based interventions (MBIs), structured as nonhierarchical groups of friends. This focus avoids the labeling in typical medical model-based programs, where even in an MBI the power is still with the "expert" who labels the "client" or "patient" with a "diagnosis" and "prescribes" the treatment. Such practices further isolate and humiliate the patient. Instead, McCown turns this model inside out, looking to the group or community as a rich context in which all can contribute and thrive. The end is not a "cure" or "resolution" but shared contemplation, co-produced in a context forming an ethical space.

Xavier Renteria-Uriarte views contemplation as the basis for all knowledge systems throughout human history. Contemplation provides a pivot point for heuristically approaching all research throughout the natural and human sciences. He addresses the existing gap between the contemplative knowledge of the traditions of wisdom and contemplative science. He ends by suggesting a new contemplative economics that would prioritize enlightened humans co-creating worlds of mutual care and wisdom.

Vincenzo Giorgino argues in favor of a balanced point of encounter between contemplative knowledge and social sciences. Although the Westernization of Asian contemplative practices has been successfully accompanied by an unexpected secularization, the latter remains unfinished and also has to deal with the consequences of its own achievements. Giorgino proposes that the enactive approach proposed by neurobiologist Francisco Varela, and the related debate so far, seem a necessary starting point for the transformation of the same social sciences.

Part Two presents applications of contemplative research and practice.

Krzysztof Konecki maintains that consistent meditative practices enhance the ability of social scientists to see beyond the concepts and categories that may constrain their research. Meditation is a powerful epistemology. These practices involve opening up self-concepts to a form of emptiness that allows for deep change.

Annabelle Nelson shows that contemplative psychology, along with advancements in knowledge of the brain, allow for a fundamental transformation of the mind. The experience of alpha waves opens the door to spiritual imagery, which leads to a spacious and wise mind. In her own practice this has led her to work with children in indigenous cultures facing oppressive obstacles.

Luann Fortune describes her experience using the somatic and meditative practice of labyrinth-walking as a tool for opening up her interpretation of data about her participants' experiences. She shares how this embodied practice enhanced her insights and increased the depth of her research and her satisfaction with the results.

David Casacuberta demonstrates that the current software design for smartphones and computers—now pervasive ways of connecting—developed from a hierarchical and power-based mode of connectivity. He suggests an alternative enactive design based on Buddhist principles such as nonattachment. Such a design could turn communicative networks into contemplative spaces for shared experience.

Christopher Mare takes contemplative practice deeper into neuroscience and broader into environmental design. By practicing deep meditation, he accesses spatial centers of the brain prior to walking in the environmental spaces to be designed. The result is villages designed for the enhancement of consciousness.

There is a sense of astonishment that captures us when we put ourselves in a position of openness toward those kinds of social practices and see them for what they really are designed: to transform ourselves, overcoming the set of patterned values and behaviors that characterize our *selves*. This is a marvelous gift, a surprising social invention to desocialize and resocialize through previously unseen "breaches in the wall" of social research. Within the emerging framework of contemplative social research, we may deal effectively with economic and social suffering, and promote wise social innovations, which will liberate human potential and enhance well-being.

Endnote

[1] This is 20 March each year, as the UN established in 2013. Since its declaration in Torino, there have been four meetings. The reader interested in a contemplative approach to coproducing and designing technologies and economies at urban and community levels can find more information at www.wiseandsmartcities.eu/.

References

Barbezat D. P., & Bush, M. (Eds.). (2014). *Contemplative practices in higher education: Powerful methods to transform teaching and learning.* San Francisco, CA: Jossey Bass.

Beck, U., & Beck-Gernsheim, E. (2001). *Individualization: Institutionalized individualism and its social and political consequences.* London, England: SAGE.

Benkler, Y. (2006). *The wealth of networks. How social production transforms markets and freedom.* New Haven, CT: Yale University Press.

Bentz, V. M., & Shapiro, J. J. (1996). *Mindful inquiry in social research.* Thousand Oaks, CA: SAGE.

Bonaiuti, M. (2014). *The Great Transition.* London, England: Routledge.

Capra, F. J. (1975). *The Tao of physics: An exploration of the parallels between modern physics and Eastern mysticism.* Boulder, CO: Shambala.

Castells, M. (1996). *The rise of the network society.* Oxford, NY: Blackwell Publishers.

Coote, A., & Goodwin, N. (2010). *The Great Transition: Social justice and the core economy*. London, England: NEF.

Dalai Lama. (2011). *Beyond religion*: *Ethics for a whole world*. New York, NY: Houghton Mifflin Harcourt.

Davis, J. E. (2011). The shifting experience of self: A bibliographic essay. *The Hedgehog Review*, *13*(1), Spring.

Fourcade, M. (2010). The problem of embodiment in the sociology of knowledge: Afterword to the special issue on knowledge and practice. *Qualitative Sociology*, *33*(4), December.

Giorgino, V. (Ed.). (2014). *The pursuit of happiness and the traditions of wisdom*. Dordrecht, The Netherlands: Springer.

Giorgino, V. (2015). Contemplative methods meet social sciences: Back to human experience as it is. *Journal for the Theory of Social Behaviour*, *45*(4), 461-483.

Gunnlaugson, O., Sarath, E. W., Scott, C., Bai, H. (Eds.). (2014). *Contemplative learning and inquiry across disciplines*. New York, NY: State University of New York Press.

Husserl, E. (1954/1970). *The crisis of the European sciences and transcendental phenomenology*. (D. Carr, (Trans.). Evanston, IL: Northwestern University Press.

Immergut, M., & Kaufman, P. A (2014). Sociology of no-self: Applying Buddhist social theory to symbolic interaction. *Symbolic Interaction*. *37*(2), May.

Kolm, S. (1982). *Le Bonheur-liberté. Bouddhisme profond et modernité*. Paris, France: PUF.

Menon S. (2014). *Brain, self and consciousness. Explaining the conspiracy of experience*. Dordrecht, The Netherlands: Springer.

Nicolescu, B. (Ed.). (2008). *Transdisciplinarity: Theory and practice*. New York, NY: Hampton Press.

Nonaka, I., & Takeuchi, H. (1995). *The knowledge-creating company: How Japanese companies create the dynamics of innovation*. Oxford, England: Oxford University Press.

Pagis, M. (2015). Evoking equanimity: Silent interaction rituals in Vipassana meditation retreats *Qualitative Sociology*, *38*(1), 39-56.

-------. (2010a). Producing intersubjectivity in silence: An ethnography of meditation practices. *Ethnography*, *11*, 309-328.

-------. (2010b). From abstract concepts to experiential knowledge: Embodying enlightenment in a meditation center. *Qualitative Sociology*, *33*, 469-489.

Polanyi, M. (1958/2015). *Towards a post-critical philosophy.* Chicago, IL: University of Chicago Press.

Preston, D. L. (1988). *The social organization of Zen practice: Constructing a transcultural reality.* Cambridge, NJ: Cambridge University Press.

Renteria-Uriarte, X., & Giorgino, V.M.B. (in press). Towards an ontological underpinning of practical wisdom's business suitability: Ancient philosophies and modern contemplative social sciences. In W. Kupers and O. Gunnlaugson (Eds.), *Wisdom learning: Perspectives on wising-up*. London, England: Waterstones.

Rifkin, J. (2014). *The zero marginal cost society. The Internet of things, the collaborative commons, and the eclipse of capitalism.* New York, NY: Palgrave MacMillan.

Schipper, J. (2012, June). Toward a Buddhist sociology: Theories, methods, and possibilities. *The American Sociologist*, *43*(2), 203-222.

Schmidt, S., & Walach, H. (Eds.). (2014). *Meditation: Neuroscientific approaches and philosophical implications*. Dordrecht, The Netherlands: Springer

Schumacher, E. (1973). *Small is beautiful: A study of economics as if people mattered.* New York, NY: Vintage Books.

Senge, P. (1990). *The Fifth Discipline. The art and practice of a learning organization.* New York, NY: Doubleday.

Senge, P., Schwarmer, C. O., Jaworski, J., & Flowers, B. S. (2005).

Presence: Exploring profound change in people: Organizations and society. London, England: Nicholas Brealey Publishing.

Varela, F. J. (1999). *Ethical know-how: Action, wisdom, and cognition.* Stanford, CA: Stanford University Press.

Walach, H., Schmidt, S., & Jonas, W. B. (Eds.). (2011). *Neuroscience, consciousness, and spirituality.* Dordrecht, The Netherlands: Springer.

Waskul, D., & Vannini, P. (2012). Introduction: The body in symbolic interaction. In D. Waskul & P. Vannini (Eds.), *Body/Embodiment: Symbolic interaction and the sociology of the body.* Aldershot, UK: Ashgate Publishing.

Zajonc, A. (2003). *Investigating the space of the invisible collective: Arthur Zajonc in conversation with Otto Scharmer.* Retrieved from http://www.collectivewisdom.org/papers/zajonc_interv.htm.

-------. (2004). *The new physics and cosmology: Dialogues with the Dalai Lama.* Oxford, England: Oxford University Press.

Zsolnai, L. (2014a). *Beyond self: Ethical and social dimensions of economics.* Oxford, England: Peter Lang.

-------. (Ed.). (2014b). *The spiritual dimension of business ethics and sustainability management.* Dordrecht, The Netherlands: Springer.

Zsolnai, L., & Ims, K. J. (Eds.). (2006). *Business within limits: Deep ecology and Buddhist economics.* Oxford, England: Peter Lang.

Part One

Contemplative Knowing and Being

The Social and Political Significance of Contemplation and Its Potential for Shaping Contemplative Studies

By Zack Walsh
PhD Candidate, School of Theology,
Claremont School of Theology, United States

Abstract

In today's highly individualistic culture, expressions of religion and spirituality have been largely restricted to the inner sphere of one's private life. Yet despite the oft repeated belief that contemplation is about individual subjective experience, rather than social experience, contemplation has always had a strong relationship to ethical action. This chapter will argue for a shift away from the focus on individualized, privatized forms of contemplation, and it will argue instead for the importance of socialized and politicized forms of practice and discourse. First, I examine the evidence for contemplation as a powerful mechanism for social and political transformation by using Buddhist and Christian sources to give a historical demonstration of contemplation's social and political effects. Then, I argue in favor of democratizing the field of contemplative studies, so that more individuals may speak from a diversity of social locations and religious traditions. Overall, this will help set the framework for determining the practical goals of a contemplative social science.

Psychological Interpretations of Contemplation

The history of contemplation's social and political effects has become obscured by the progressive privatization of religious and spiritual experience. Today, people generally conflate the terms "spirituality," "mysticism," and "contemplation" with personal experiences without recognizing their association to religious tradition, community, or specific historical contexts (Lanzetta, 2005, p. 28). Popular books on spirituality also reiterate this general tendency to remove individuals from their social relations by treating contemplation as a private experience with the transcendent (Jantzen, 1995, p. 21).

This privileging of individual, subjective experience in the study of contemplation is largely a modern phenomenon, beginning with William James' seminal study *The Varieties of Religious Experience*, in which he defined religion as "the feelings, acts, and experiences of individual men [sic] in their solitude, so far as they apprehend themselves to stand in relation to whatever they may consider divine" (James, 1982, p. 31). Since James popularized the study of contemplation in Western academic circles, a long lineage of scholars have focused on the individual rather than social dimensions of religious experience (Taylor, 2007, p. 31). Despite disagreements among individual scholars, the academic community as a whole has generally upheld James' characterization (Jantzen, 1995, p. 7), while attempting to find in contemplation a pre-linguistic or 'pure' consciousness that transcends material and social contexts (McIntosh, 1998, p. 137).

In their effort to conform to the demands of modern science, contemplative scholars have often objectified and venerated contemplative experiences, despite contemplatives warning "against seeking any 'experiences' whatsoever" (McIntosh, 1998, p. 137). Scholars have largely ignored the fact that Buddhists and Christians alike view the attachment to higher states of consciousness as obstacles, and thus scholars' chiefly psychological metaphors for describing contemplation have failed to reflect what contemplatives consider most important to themselves.

In light of historical accounts of contemplative experience, it is evident that the modern reduction of contemplation to an individual's isolated experience is a historically and socially constructed phenomenon. As Beverly Lanzetta (2005) writes, "It was not until the end of the Middle Ages that the term 'mysticism' moved toward the highly individual, subjective meaning involving a purely private, inner experience prevalent today" (p. 30). Grace Jantzen (1995) explains the reason for today's distortion of contemplative wisdom by asserting that "much of the modern construction of mysticism derives from an attempt to circumvent Kantian strictures on epistemology, strictures whose effect would be to render veridical religious experience impossible" (p. 7). Whereas Kant believed knowledge is derived from the perception of an object's appearance, understood solely in terms of categories of perception, scholars who discussed mysticism in terms of intense psychological states, which exceed conceptual or linguistic understanding, could assert that it was still possible to attain direct knowledge of objective reality.

Despite being an historical anomaly, today's psychological understanding often claims to be universal. This claim that contemplation possesses certain universal characteristics has effectively led to both a lack of historical and social awareness and an uncritical adoption of social norms, irrespective of the suffering that they entail. Under such false pretenses, contemplation becomes a mechanism for improving personal psychological well-being, without a critical social awareness to "address the question of where the stresses of life originate" (Jantzen, 1995, p. 19). If the stress arises out of unjust social conditions, then contemplation ends up reinforcing the structures of injustice that generate stress (p. 20), while also deflecting attention away from peoples' real needs (p. 18). So long as contemplation flourishes within this "secret inner life," then "those who nurture such an inner life can generally be counted on to prop up rather than to challenge the status quo of their workplaces, their gender roles, and the political systems by which they are governed" (McIntosh, 1998, p. 137). To make matters worse, within a capitalist society, this complacency perpetuates misery not only for oneself, but also for others, when stress is implicated in larger structures of oppression that undermine people's wellbeing or "the life-sustaining capacities of the earth" (Jantzen, 1995, p. 20-21). In these times, contemplation functions as little more than a palliative, sublimating anxieties and alleviating distress, while providing a "private religious way of coping with life, whatever the external circumstance" (p. 20). It becomes identified with a tendency toward passivity and sedation, even though notable contemplatives like Thomas Merton emphatically state, "Contemplation is no pain-killer... It is not mere passive acquiescence in the *status quo*" (Merton, 2007, p. 13). Contrary to the desires of a therapy industry invested in maintaining psychological evaluations and prescriptions, Merton insists "there is really no adequate *psychology* of contemplation. To describe 'reactions' and 'feelings' is to situate contemplation where it is not to be found" (p. 6). Inevitably, the limitations of an exclusively psychological view of contemplation invites critique.

Currently, the field of contemplative studies is experiencing a critical backlash precisely because it has not yet confronted the implicit problems of maintaining such an ahistorical and apolitical view of contemplation. As the explosion of interest in mindfulness garners public attention, the widespread appropriation of contemplative practices risks alienating people, because it lacks social and political awareness (Wylie, 2015). Today, the fact remains that presenting contemplation as a therapeutic palliative does not require it to recognize moral concerns, and unless personal psychological well-being is affected, contemplation simply has nothing to do with politics and social justice. Nor does it recognize how particular social and political contexts determine which individuals have access to contemplative practices or which individuals are recognized by society as proper contemplatives (Jantzen, 1995, p. 5).

This widespread indifference to social and political concerns among contemplative scholars and practitioners has produced a stalemate in debates between advocates of mindfulness and their critics. Generally, this represents a breakdown in contemplative studies (Walsh, in press), which Ronald Purser and Edwin Ng have said is a result of mindfulness proponent's "bad faith," expressed as a general disregard for critics' legitimate social and political concerns (Purser & Ng, 2015). Yet, regardless of one's opinion on the validity of critics' concerns, much of popular culture's appropriation of mindfulness is driven by forces situated within a much larger historical context.

In part, the fact that contemplation came to be seen as a private, not public matter reflects the separation of religious and political life over the course of modern history. In institutionalizing the separation between church and state and in separating sacred and secular knowledge, liberalism limited the role of religion to the spiritual life of private individuals without critically questioning their relation to economic and political systems. Though liberalism allowed critical reasoning to challenge religious orthodoxy, it tended to conform to the economic and political life of the society in which it was embedded (*Sölle, 1990*). Jantzen (1995) argues that today "there is little indication that mysticism and spirituality have anything to do with politics and social justice" (p. 20). And yet, a cursory understanding of contemplative traditions shows that wisdom and compassion are inseparable—two sides of the same path. In light of this history, it thus behooves contemplative scholars and practitioners to recognize how contemplative action may challenge today's uncritical acceptance of the status-quo.

Wisdom and Compassion

In general, the contemplative experience rejects the popular notion that contemplation is associated with "nonaction, hiding from the world, and a detachment from social change" (Lanzetta, p. 32). The fact is that contemplative experience methodically deconstructs perceptions of the world, in order to expose the suffering "at the root of the meanings, structures, and social constructions that constitute daily life" (p. 32). It cultivates a radical honesty which never shies away from the reality of suffering, but which instead transforms it through contemplative action. As Lanzetta (2005) states, "True contemplation always overflows into creation—it becomes a creative act— and some of the greatest mystics have been advocates of profound social transformation. This emphasis

31

on 'being' over 'doing' is one of degree, a shift in perspective"(p. 32). This essential unity of wisdom and compassion, theory and practice is found across traditions. For example, in Sufism, union with the divine (*Nafas Rahmani*) is "the compassion of creative love, because it is at once passion and action" (Corbin, 1997, p. 134). In Christianity, mystical union between God and creation is also "a love for all human beings and for the whole creation" (Macquarrie, 2005, p. 150). And in Hua-yen Buddhism, the perception of universal interdependence and interpenetration inspires an ethic of universal compassion. As Steve Odin (2003) points out, the essential indivisibility of openness and care, *sunyata* and *karuna* "involves a radical theory of social praxis and intersubjective moral engagement" (p. 50).

The inseparability of religious revelation and responsibility toward the world debunks long-standing myths about quietism. Many contemplatives' reported experiences simply refute the popular belief that contemplation encourages disinterest in the world. Furthermore, both Christianity and Buddhism have theological traditions which refuse to separate reality's immanent and transcendent aspects, and in establishing a dynamic engagement between ultimate reality and the finite world (McGinn, 2003; Teasdale, 1999; Abe, 1985; Abe, 1990), they demand a commitment toward contemplative action. Of course, history is multifaceted and there have been countervailing traditions which emphasize "otherworldliness, inferiority, and opposition to the body" (Lanzetta, 2005, p. 29). But the fact that the history of quietism coincided with a "muffling of the tradition of mysticism and women" (p. 11) suggests that it was a reactionary social movement, rather than an essential feature of contemplation.

Contrary to quietism, many contemplative traditions have strongly contended that solitude and engagement are both necessary aspects of the same contemplative path. In all traditions, contemplatives maintain that periods of solitude are required for the development of pure intention and refined perception (Teasdale, 1999). Generally, the act of withdrawing from the world serves to bring them closer to it. As Wayne Teasdale says, "The mystic leaves the world to better understand it" (p. 82), because withdrawal frees them from the grip of desires which distort perception. In seeking solitude, contemplatives are not escaping reality. Rather, they are awakening to its inner depths, so that they may return with a better understanding of how to act in the world. Christianity's social mystic, Catherine of Siena said, "Nothing is more frightening than ignorance in action" (Macquarrie, 2005, p. 24). She "alternated her times of contemplation with sallies into the world of affairs" (p. 151) because she understood that contemplative solitude is the necessary prerequisite for contemplative action.

Similarly, in Mahayana Buddhism, the bodhisattva represents this integration between wisdom and compassion in a contemplative social praxis. In the ox-herding pictures, for example, the bodhisattva returns to the marketplace, symbolizing the "integration between ordinary action in the world and contemplative experience" (Teasdale, 1999, p. 98). According to this view, ethical action is both the foundation and culmination of a mature contemplative journey. In the Christian tradition, Meister Eckhart advances one step further and claims that "the active life is better than the contemplative," insofar as contemplative experience culminates in action, because "the one rests in the other, and perfects the other" (in McGinn, 2003, p. 67). Even outside these two traditions, Teasdale (1999) contends that spiritualities from around the world fundamentally agree that "It is simply not possible to live a spiritual or mystical life without [the ethical] dimension" (p. 110), and the persistence of scandals exposing contemplatives committing unethical acts is a reminder that the contemplative path is not complete without an ethical transformation of the will (p. 89).

Whereas on the one hand, some views highlight the essential inseparability between contemplation and action, on the other hand, some reject the distinction altogether. For instance, the Zen Buddhist master *Dōgen*'s non-dual formulation eliminates the differentiation between contemplation and action by claiming that "practice and enlightenment are not two but one" (Abe, 1985, p. 67). This non-dual perspective denotes an important shift in agency whereby one's actions become a reflection of ultimate reality, once they become "freed from aim-oriented human action" (p. 60).

Evidence of this shift also exists in Christianity. Whereas Buddhists "'vow' to save one's self and all others and 'act' to actually pursue the vow" (Abe, 1990, p. 58), Christians express this non-duality between their intentions and actions by eliminating the distinction between their self-will and God's will. Just as Buddhists express their openness to emptiness (*sunyata*) in caring for the world (Odin, 2003, p. 50), the Christian contemplative Hadewijch of Antwerp believed the contemplative path did not demand a "diminishing involvement with the cares of the world, but rather of pouring out herself as Christ poured out himself in compassion and care for the ignorant and the oppressed" (Jantzen, 1995, p. 141). In Hadewijch's view, union with God meant acting in a way "wholly united with God, who desires compassion and service to all who are in need" (p. 142).

In these cases, Christian contemplatives collapse the distinction between contemplation and action (Sells, 1994, p. 204) by abandoning all attachments and undergoing a transformation of the will (p. 195). In discussing the mysticism of Meister Eckhart, Michael Sells says Christian contemplatives fuse their work with the "one eternal work… that must be realized anew in each moment" (p. 202). Even across traditions, contemplative wisdom doesn't culminate in an extraordinary vision of reality, but rather as "a new vision of the ordinary" (p. 202) in which the meaning and agency of human action is reinterpreted without the ego-self (p. 193).

Contemplation in Action

Contrary to modern psychological accounts, mystical texts do not describe universal experiences isolated from social realities. Rather, they describe practices for the transformation of any experience whatsoever. As Mark McIntosh states, mystical texts "allow one's own categories for understanding and experiencing reality to be given over—perhaps broken—certainly to be transformed, by the reality of the other who is always beyond oneself" (McIntosh, 1998, p. 135). Lanzetta (2005) claims that contemplation liberates contemplatives from the oppression of fixed forms and institutions, because "it opens out, even within religion, beyond religion to the indescribable otherness of reality" (p. 34). Together, these views situate the contemplative in absolute negativity, where they contest all forms of knowledge and all forms of authority except the authority of experience itself (Bataille, 2014, p. 19). But since experience empties its own contents with each passing moment (p. 14), it is an authority that subverts even itself.

In general, contemplation is a constant frustration to reification and containment, because contemplative insights give birth to a creative impulse that overflows and exceeds any attempt to control them. When the Christian Saint Teresa of Avila faced intense public scrutiny, she remained stalwart in her faith, because she realized that inner wisdom "could not be controlled or co-opted by the world" (Lanzetta, 2005, p. 129). She knew that her faith in God communicated a power and creativity beyond anything. The ideas and actions of Jesus Christ, Gautama Buddha, and Mahatma Gandhi are further testament to the revolutionary power of contemplative wisdom. The long history of mystics who have been cast out of society or persecuted for challenging the status quo is also a testament to the subversive power of strong political and religious convictions born of insight.

As Lanzetta (2005) argues, contemplation is subversive because it cultivates a liberatory state of consciousness that "takes apart our understandings of reality, our time-honored structures of meaning, and our economic and social constructions" (p. 33). She even claims spiritual authority is more threatening to prevailing power politics than economic and social inequality (p. 18). As contemplative wisdom disempowers the ego-self and dismantles social constructions, it provides a birthplace for new constructions. Though poststructuralism makes clear the dangers of exclusionary social constructions, contemplation "obligates one to *construct* values reuniting *from the outside...* what was missing on the day when one contested the constructions" (Bataille, 2014, p. 16).

If, as Alfred North Whitehead (1968) wrote, philosophy rationalizes mysticism in order "to maintain an active novelty of fundamental ideas illuminating the social system" (p. 174), then contemplation in action is the necessary translation of those ideas into reality. Historically, contemplation has had a profound capacity to subvert existing institutions and power structures precisely because it opens a space for possibility beyond present-day constraints, inviting the impossible to become possible. Contemplation doesn't just destroy and rebuild the world simply by reorganizing the elements given to one's experience. Rather, in giving oneself to that which is wholly other, it allows genuine freedom and novelty to emerge. True contemplation in action is the opposite of contemplation in isolation, because every act informed by insight is world-forming. In her discussion of the Buddhist philosopher Hisamatsu, Joan Staumbaugh (1999) explains that Zen activity is world-forming and history-creating, because "religious time...is at the basis of history, creating history, but not bound by history. It is always freed from creation while constantly creating" (p. 137). In David Loy's (2015) contemporary view of the bodhisattva path, this process of deconstructing and reconstructing one's relationship to the world should fundamentally join contemplative self-transformation and social transformation (p. 40).

Naturally, every disruption is simultaneously a construction (Taylor, 2007), but contemplation's fusion of subject and object is what makes the difference. As George Bataille (2014) maintains, "experience attains the fusion of the object and the subject, being as subject nonknowledge, as object the unknown" (p. 16). Over the course of history, contemplatives have changed what society thought possible by introducing this active novelty into the world through

36

their world-forming activities, and often, the most revolutionary contemplatives have come from the fringes of society where order and disorder entangle one another at the boundaries of possibility. Rather than ignoring or transcending differences, "spiritual liberation involves an awareness of the simultaneous, interpenetrating, and dynamic interrelationship between embodiment and transcendence—finite and infinite—that constitutes the whole complex of the person" (Lanzetta, 2005, p. 29). Spirituality allows contemplatives to directly enter into differences—whether of gender, culture, race, or sex—in order to more fully experience them, while at the same time transforming the causes of suffering by recognizing their underlying unity (p. 22).

Being on the fringes, female contemplatives like Hadewijch of Antwerp and Julian of Norwich offer spiritualties of integration (Jantzen, 1995, p. 155) which were criticized by their male counterparts, but which are essential today for understanding contemplation in action. In Hadewijch, the integration of "mind, passion, and will are drawn together in unified action" (p. 143). Hadewijch's emphasis on the importance of the body in the spirituality of a whole person countered the predominant belief in mind-body dualism, which is essential for contemplation in action, "since it is the body, not a disembodied spirit, which performs the mighty works of justice" (p. 145). Similarly, Julian of Norwich does not preoccupy herself with the male prerogative to master or transcend the flesh (p. 240). Instead, she emphasizes the unity of human sensuality and divine substance in Christ (p. 150). Although ultimately, neither woman fully escaped the dualistic thinking that framed their spirituality, they provided a significant alternative to challenge the church and society of their time (p. 224). They also highlighted the intrinsic connection between contemplation and social justice.

Not only is the subversive power of contemplation reflected in external challenges to institutional authority, but in the case of the dark night, it can also liberate contemplatives from the internalization of oppression. Today, as mindfulness-based stress reduction programs prove wildly successful, people have generally forgotten that contemplation can also be stress-inducing. Since they often think of contemplation in psychological terms, they view meditation as a tool for improving health and well-being without recognizing that contemplation seeks a radical realism, one which is intended to inspire compassion for the suffering of oneself and others, rather than alleviate distress.

Both Buddhism and Christianity agree on this point. When the active aspect of contemplation is understood, Buddhist meditation achieves more than a passive realization of suffering. It motivates an active desire to reduce suffering through compassion. Similarly, Thomas Merton affirms that Christian contemplation "awakens a tragic anguish… [It is not] an escape from conflict, from anguish or from doubt" (Merton, 2007, p. 12). Rather, it is a path to understand God's love so that the contemplative works for social justice (p. 18).

Historically, the dark night experience of Teresa of Avila provides powerful testimony of how contemplation liberates contemplatives from social and political oppression by allowing them to experience suffering more deeply. By considering contemplative experiences to be universal, just as scholars and practitioners often do today, the women of her time assumed that the advice of male directors and confessors offered a path which applied equally well to men and women, even though it disregarded the need to heal "social, religious, or gender oppression" (Lanzetta, 2005, p. 124). Since contemplative communities did not acknowledge the suffering of women, Teresa realized that they could not provide her with spiritual nourishment.

In defiance and at great peril, Teresa's experience in contemplation released her attachments to the male-dominated culture and thereby affirmed the authority of her own experience in their place. As a result, Teresa denied her oppressors' power over her and destroyed "the foundation upon which women's debasement has been constructed" by "emptying out the 'content' of the term 'woman' in the same way that the mystic empties out the content of the term 'God'" (p. 133). In uncovering the ground of absolute negativity, Teresa was able to disidentify with her oppression and contest the cultural and institutional authority that generated it.

With this in mind, Lanzetta (2005) argues that incorporating the dark night experience into religious vocabulary can help clarify the pain of gender oppression which is neglected in Christian literature (p. 25). Within the context of contemplative studies, the ongoing study on Varieties of Contemplative Experience[1] can similarly unearth ethnographic information on contemplation's connection to deeper trauma and oppression, while recent engagements between contemplative studies, critical theory and pedagogy can provide additional help in understanding how the practices can more effectively address social and political realities (Berila, 2016).

Limitations in Contemplative Studies
Throughout this chapter I have contested the meaning and uses of contemplation, critiquing in particular what I view to be the narrow psychological interpretations of contemplation, abstracted from their significance to social and political contexts. As I have already mentioned, the creative insights born of contemplative experience can never be controlled or contained, much less by attempts to understand them objectively. Contemplation is essentially saturated with meaning, and it can never be completely understood, because it elicits "a depth of meaning which we can never fully exhaust" (Macquarrie, 2005, p. 2). While recognizing the absolute limits of any inquiry, it is important to continue pursuing greater understanding. To that end, I will briefly describe what I perceive to be some of the current limitations of contemplative studies, so that I may contextualize my proposal for the advancement of the field.

Although contemplative studies is a unique field that offers many avenues for generating knowledge, its promise is matched by the perils of finding meaningful synergies between seemingly irreconcilable positions. Whereas science seeks mastery and precision by manipulating nature and analyzing it into reducible components, contemplation encourages a receptivity to nature that places its components within a more holistic context (Macquarrie, 2005, p. 25). For full and rich descriptions, contemplative studies requires both the precision and clarity of the scientist, as well as the visions of the contemplative (p. 28).

As such, it is important to affirm the partnership between contemplative wisdom and science, especially after centuries of suppression and neglect (Lanzetta, 2005, p. 11), but it is also especially important to exercise caution in how scholars study contemplation, because it cannot be studied in the same manner as other phenomena. One of the key distinctions between contemplation and other subjects is that contemplation requires "participative knowing, a knowing which shares more and more in the pattern of life of the 'known' (who is now discovered to be as much the *knower* as the known)" (McIntosh, 1998, p. 132). The fusion of subject and object which is quite unique to contemplation prevents scientists and scholars from fully understanding it as an object of analysis that can be isolated from its subject. Since the subjectivity of the observer is transformed in the process of observation, a study of contemplation requires an understanding of how that transformation elicits understanding.

The study of contemplation through textual analysis requires the same appreciation for the subject's involvement. Though in this case, a material object (a text) can be found and analyzed, its contents cannot be fully understood unless the observer understands how the text's language draws the reader beyond a referential relationship to the text (McIntosh, 1998, p. 132). As McIntosh explains, contemplative texts are "linguistic performances, and it is the very patterning of their language which allows them to draw the reader into a new perceptivity" (p. 142). The meaning of contemplative texts is essentially supplied by the interaction between the reader and text, and the metaphorical language is intentionally left open and vague in order to solicit that interaction.

In light of this participatory nature, contemplative inquiries will be limited by an objectifying and reductive approach to contemplative traditions, which describe them without understanding how the subject is involved in the process of creating knowledge. The current tendency in contemplative studies to abstract contemplation from its relation to concrete particulars already distorts contemplative inquiry and limits contemplation's efficacy. When scientists and scholars strip contemplation of its cultural associations in an attempt to universalize their findings, they often remove the very aspects of contemplation that provide it value and allow it to function. In the case of psychological interpretations of contemplation, religious doctrines are often treated as irrelevant, even though "Christian mystical writers have generally found their theological understanding to be of the very essence of their mystical journey" (McIntosh, 1998, p. 139).

Contemplative Ecologies of Knowledge

Now that a few limitations have been identified, I will briefly sketch general ways to expand contemplative studies, because "deconstructive critic is not enough— it is also necessary to articulate alternative struc-tures that can inform creative cultural production and effective sociopo-litical transformation" (Taylor, 2007, p. 11). At the outset, it is important to note that I use the term contemplation in lieu of meditation, because I view contemplative studies in the broader context suggested by the for-mer term. The tendency to restrict contemplative studies to the science of meditation, which garners comparatively more attention, is counter-productive to the claims I have been making, and in fact, I focus on contemplation because, unlike meditation, it cannot be easily separated from social and political concerns. In general, I take John Macquarrie's position that "meditation has a clearly definable content…. While in contemplation, one grasps some larger truth in its wholeness…,the con-tent of contemplation is usually much more indefinite than the content of meditation" (p. 31-33). Whereas meditation can be adapted to specific contexts with well-defined goals, the depths of contemplation lack any definable content that can be easily coopted.

Let me make clear that I do not refute the science of meditation or the therapeutic potential of mindfulness-based interventions, but I do believe that contemplative studies ought to recognize the limitations of those enterprises and supplement them with a more robust understanding of contemplation. In this chapter, I have focused especially on the social and political dimensions of that critique, given the pressing need to respond to the lack of social and political awareness in current iterations of mindfulness. Going forward, I believe contemplative studies should learn from a broader engagement with other religious and spiritual traditions, and I have intentionally integrated Christian and Buddhist sources in this chapter to partially advance that aim. In particular, I have chosen these two traditions, because as many authors have noted (Whitehead, 1933; Snyder, 1969; Teasdale, 1999; Loy, 2015), the compatibility between Christianity's emphasis on liberation through action and Buddhism's emphasis on liberation through contemplation make them particularly well suited for a discussion on the social and political significance of contemplation. What I have also done in this chapter is to highlight the work of female contemplatives, because they speak from positions of marginalization which address social justice in ways that current studies often miss. As Lanzetta (2005) says, "women live between realities" at the borders of "uncharted spiritual territory." They break through "inherited cultural patterns and religious systems" which enable oppression, and in their place, they create "new revelatory landscapes that transform the whole of life" (p. 7). Together, the inclusion of diverse religious traditions and marginalized perspectives offer branch points for contemplative studies to expand.

Of course, there are many other perspectives which I have not yet discussed, so in the remainder of this chapter, I will offer a general framework to help coordinate these perspectives within a more coherent vision for contemplative studies. As I have argued elsewhere (Walsh, *A critical theory-praxis for contemplative studies*, in preparation), it should be clear by now that the formation of contemplative studies is "implicitly bound with issues of authority" and shaped by "the social context of the people who determine" what counts as contemplative knowledge (Jantzen, 1995, p. 12). Since contemplation is in part a socially contested field of knowledge, the power to create that knowledge should be distributed across a much vaster terrain. In an attempt to distribute that power and broaden the context of contemplative studies, I henceforth propose viewing the field as an ecology of knowledge. Here, I have adapted Mark C. Taylor's (2007) schemata for religion to illustrate what I mean by an ecology of knowledge in the context of contemplative studies. At a minimum, developing theories in the field should:

1. describe and/or explain the complex origin, operational logic, and multiple functions of [contemplation];

2. clarify the dynamics of the emergence, development, and transformation of different [contemplative traditions];

3. show how [contemplative traditions] relate to and interact with each other as well as the physical, biological, social, political, and economic aspects of life; and

4. include a 'principle' of 'internal' criticism that leaves the theory open to endless revision (p. 12).

Taylor's schemata provides an inclusive frame for understanding the many perspectives in contemplative studies, because the logic of complexity theory on which it is based applies equally well to a study of nature, society, and culture, which are governed by the same underlying structure and operational logic (p. 28). Although an in-depth discussion of Taylor's schemata is beyond the scope of this chapter, the benefit of using such a structure is that it allows creativity to flourish by acting as "a whole without necessarily totalizing" (p. 12). By organizing the production of knowledge around the logic of complexity, contemplative studies can avoid today's problematic tendency toward an academic division of knowledge into hyperspecialized disciplines (p. 32). The other benefit of using Taylor's schemata is that it connects cultural production to effective sociopolitical transformation, because theory and praxis "are not separate in schemata: descriptive representations provide models *of* the world that serve as models *for* activity in the world" (p. 17). Rather than being constrained by one particular organizing structure or logic, a complex view of contemplative studies would reflexively understand how discursive practices both regulate and constitute the institutions of power and the social realities in which they define contemplative phenomena (Jantzen, 1995, p. 13-14).

The democratization of creating knowledge across different perspectives would reject the foundational claim that contemplative experience is universal, and it would instead permit contemplation to be defined by a multiplicity of social locations related to gender, sex, age, race, culture, belief, and class. Under Taylor's schemata, contemplative studies also would not exclusively define contemplation according to academic interests. Instead, discursive practices would establish a fundamental pluralism. Within academia, the democratization of contemplative studies would delegitimize scientism and deny science's disproportionate influence in defining what counts as legitimate knowledge. Outside academia, it would open up new spaces for co-creating knowledge where experts and non-experts can collaborate.

Philosophically speaking, it is worth noting that the turn toward complexity also rejects both the separation and simple identification between transcendence and immanence, which historically justified the oppression of marginalized groups by enabling an uncritical fusion of religion, culture, and society (Sölle, 1990, p. 13-15, 172-177). Instead,

Taylor's (2007) schemata situates itself within a virtual space—a sort of immanent transcendence, which "keeps complex systems open and makes them subject to constant transformation yet also preserves them from disintegration and simple extinction" (p. 41). According to this view, identity and difference are neither opposed nor conflated, but engaged in "a creative play of differences" (p. 40) between members of self-organizing networks. In cases where contemplative traditions contact one another, an ecotone emerges where the boundaries between discursive practices, rituals, beliefs, narratives and histories are contested, allowing co-evolution to occur.

Practically speaking, there are already several proposals that help scholars and practitioners ground a more complex understanding of contemplative studies. For starters, Kwok Pui-lan's (2005) "postcolonial theology of religious difference" provides a starting point for religious studies to engage cultural studies (p. 203) in ways that remain equally relevant to contemplative studies, while Jeannine Hill Fletcher's (2003) view of religious pluralism can help place multiple and hybrid identities at the base of contemplative studies. As traditions come into contact with one another, Richard King's (2009) analysis of epistemic policing can help reveal the political dynamics involved in the construction of the field, so that cultural essentialism does not dictate the terms of discourse. Also, the tree of contemplative practices published by the Association for Contemplative Mind in Higher Education (Center for Contemplative Mind in Society, n.d.) provides an outline of different practices for further explorations, and finally, David Germano's (2014) keynote address at the 2014 International Symposium for Contemplative Studies[2] provides a list of relevant disciplines and contexts to consider. Together, these proposals chart a preliminary path to a more democratic and pluralistic approach to contemplative studies. As attention is called to the urgency of social and ecological justice in the 21st century, it is my hope that scholars and practitioners join in such a reimagining of the future of contemplative theory and praxis.

Endnotes

[1] See http://cheetahouse.org

[2] The author describes six disciplines and 12 contexts. The six disciplines are: (1) Hermeneutics, (2) Ethics, (3) History, (4) Phenomenology, (5) Ethnography, (6) Discourse Analysis. The 12 contexts are: (1) Dependencies, (2) Conceptual Systems, (3) Aesthetic factors, (4) Social settings, (5) Environmental factors, (6) Boundary conditions, (7) Intention, motivation, and expectations, (8) Emotional dimensions, (9) Physical embodied contexts, (10) Individual differences, (11) Cultural belief paradigms, (12) Temporal contexts.

References

Abe, M. (1985). *Zen and Western thought.* Honolulu, HI: University of Hawaii Press.

-------. (1990). "Kenotic God and Dynamic Sunyata." In *The emptying God: A Buddhist-Jewish-Christian conversation*, J. Cobb & C. Ives (Eds.), pp. 3-65. Maryknoll, NY: Orbis Books.

Bataille, G. *Inner experience.* S. Kendall (Trans). Albany, NY: State University of New York Press.

Berila, B. *Integrating mindfulness into antioppression pedagogy.* New York, NY: Routledge.

Corbin, H. (1997). *Alone with the alone: Creative imagination in the Ṣūfism of Ibn ʿArabī.* Princeton, NJ: Princeton University Press.

Fletcher, J. H. (2003). "Shifting identity: The contributions of feminist thought to theologies of religious pluralism." *Journal of Feminist Studies in Religion, 19*(2), 5-24.

Germano, D. (2014). "Contemplation in contexts: Tibetan Buddhist meditation across the boundaries of the humanities and sciences." Presentation at the International Symposium for Contemplative Studies, Boston, MA, October 30 – November 2, 2014. https://www.youtube.com/watch?v=QEciEIaAUMM&list=P-

LOafJ4rP1PHyAel4TaBVEvDW3U7d1C2zT&index=10.

James, W. (1982). *The varieties of religious experience.* London, England: Penguin.

Jantzen, G. M. (1995). *Power, gender and Christian mysticism.* Cambridge, UK: Cambridge University Press.

King, R. (2009). "Philosophy of religion as border control: Globalization and the ecolonization of the 'Love of Wisdom' (*philosophia*). In *Postcolonial Philosophy of Religion,* P. Bilimoria and A. B. Irvine (Eds.), pp. 35 53. New York, NY: Springer.

Lanzetta, B. J. (2005). *Radical wisdom: A feminist mystical theology.* Minneapolis, MN: Fortress.

Loy, D. (2105) *A new Buddhist path: Enlightenment, evolution, and ethics in the modern world.* Somerville, MA: Wisdom Publications.

-------. (2013). "Why Buddhism and the West need each other: On the interdependence of personal and social transformation." *Journal of Buddhist Ethics*, *20*, 2013. Retreived from http://blogs. dickinson.edu/buddhistethics/files/2013/09/Loy-Why-Buddhism-final.pdf

McGinn, B.. *The mystical thought of Meister Eckhart: The man from whom God hid nothing.* New York, NY: Herder and Herder.

McIntosh, M. A. (1998). *Mystical theology: The integrity of spirituality and theology.* Malden, MA: Blackwell.

Macquarrie, J. (2005). *Two worlds of ours: An introduction to Christian mysticism.* Minneapolis, MN: Fortress.Merton, T. (2007). *New seeds of contemplation.* New York, NY: New Directions.

No author. (2015). "The Tree of Contemplative Practices." *The Center for Contemplative Mind in Society.* Retrieved from http://www. contemplativemind.org/practices/tree.

Odin, S. (2003). *Process metaphysics and Hua-yen Buddhism: A critical study of cumulative penetration vs. interpenetration.* Albany, NY: State University of New York Press.

Pui-lan, K. (2005). *Postcolonial imagination and feminist theology.* Louisville, KY: Westminster John Knox Press.

Purser, R., & Ng, E. (2015). "Corporate mindfulness is bullsh*t: Zen or no Zen, you're working harder and being paid less." *Salon*, September 27, 2015. Retreived from http://www.salon.com/2015/09/27/corporate_mindfulness_is_bullsht_zen_or_no_zen_youre_working_harder_and_being_paid_less/.

Sells, M. A. (1994). *Mystical languages of unsaying.* Chicago, IL: University of Chicago Press

Snyder, G. *Earth house hold.* New York, NY: New Directions.

Sölle, D. (1990). Thinking about God: An introduction to theology. Philadelphia, PA: Trinity Press, International.

Stambaugh, J. (1999). *The formless self.* Albany, NY: State University of New York Press.

Taylor, M. C. (2007). *After God.* Chicago, IL: University of Chicago Press.

Teasdale, W. (1999). *The mystic heart: Discovering a universal spirituality in the world's religions.* Novato, CA: New World Library.

Walsh, Z. (In preparation). "A Critical Theory-Praxis for contemplative studies." *Journal of the International Association of Buddhist Universities*, Volume VII. Ayutthaya, India: Mahachulalongkornrajavidyalaya University Press.

-------. (In preparation). "Critical Theory and the contemporary discourse on mindfulness." *Journal of the International Association of Buddhist Universities*, Volume VIII. Ayutthaya, India: Mahachulalongkornrajavidyalaya University Press.

Whitehead, A. N. (1933). *Adventures of ideas.* New York, NY: Free Press.

-------. (1968). *Modes of thought.* New York, NY: Simon and Schuster.

Wylie, M. S. (2015). "How the mindfulness movement went mainstream -- and the backlash that came with it." *Alternet*, January 29, 2015. Retrieved from www.alternet.org/personal-health/

how-mindfulness-movement-went-mainstream-and-backlash-came-it.

Zack Walsh (PhD Candidate, Process Studies, Claremont School of Theology) is a research specialist and steering committee member at Toward Ecological Civilization, a scientific committee member of Wise and Smart Cities, and a research fellow at the Institute for the Postmodern Development of China and the Institute for Advanced Sustainability Studies. His research engages process studies, contemplative studies, engaged Buddhism, cultural studies, sustainability studies, post-capitalism and China. For further information, see: https://cst.academia.edu/ZackWalsh, http://ecociv.org/, http://wiseandsmartcities.eu/en/, http://postmodernchina.org/, http://www.iass-potsdam.de/en

Knowing as Being: Somatic Phenomenology as Contemplative Practice [1]

By Valerie Malhotra Bentz, PhD
School of Leadership Studies, Fielding Graduate University,
United States

"The flesh is at the heart of the world."
—Maurice Merleau-Ponty, *The Visible and the Invisible*

Abstract

The social sciences followed the path of the physical sciences, taking an objectivist view governed by positivist assumptions (see Bentz & Shapiro, 1998, pp. 177f). Phenomenology, the study of consciousness, seeks to reconnect the knower with the self and with the known, reclaiming the "things themselves" of direct experience (Husserl, 1970). Somatic psychology developed techniques of knowing from deep body awareness (Hanna,1980; Johnson, 1994). Alfred Schutz's (1970) phenomenology provides a framework for reclaiming the lifeworlds, in which all meaningful experience is shared.[2] Recent discoveries from neuroscience (Damasio, 1999) and ancient insights from yoga and Vedanta (Shankaracharya, 1946) affirm and intensify somatic phenomenology. Studies over the past decades reveal the power of somatic phenomenology as contemplative inquiry and practice. Phenomenology reveals itself as an ontological practice while maintaining its powerful epistemological stance.

Somatic Phenomenology:

Phenomenology as Contemplative Inquiry

Phenomenology and somatics are by nature contemplative inquiry and practice. Phenomenologically based research over the past 40 years has supported Edmund Husserl's (1954/1970) original understanding that phenomenology is transformative:

> Perhaps it will even become manifest that the total phe-
> nomenological attitude and the *epoch*é belonging to it
> are destined to effect, at first, a complete personal trans-
> formation, comparable at first to a religious conversion,
> which then, however, over and above this, bears within
> itself the significance of the greatest existential trans-
> formation which is assigned as a task to mankind as
> such (p. 137).

In psychology and the social sciences, when phenomenology is taught
at all, it is viewed as a research method or a kind of epistemology.
However, phenomenology reveals itself as more than either. Rather, it
is an ontology and a contemplative practice. Phenomenology unlocks
the doors of consciousness, illuminating the "whatness" of ourselves
as well as those persons, animals, and situations we are investigating.

The phenomenological inquirer is passionate about her[3] topic,
and she is able and eager to explore it through contemplation and writing. She may have enough richness in her own experience to complete
an investigation without seeking other participants (Maxwell, 2013).
She will establish what Alfred Schutz (1970) called a "we-relationship"
with participants, should she include them. She is not "collecting data"
that she can then "analyze." Rather, she engages in conversations, as
opposed to "interviews," with participants where the pair "grow older
together."

Empathizing with them, she is also able to let go of her preconceptions and desires without the assumption that the other needs "help,"
"healing," or "fixing" and without the notion that she as a researcher is
a "professional expert" who knows more about the experience than the
participant (Weinstein, 1997). This is similar to the process of caring
"detachment" in meditation. Moving into the true "whatness" of an experience reveals phenomenology as ontological. The phenomenologist

is open to changing the question or topic as she discovers the nature of the beings she is studying (ibid.).

This discovery of the "whatness" of things is the heart of phenomenology and necessitates description as the primary task. Summaries, categorizations, interpretation, and explanation are secondary. What we experience with our complex body-minds is difficult to describe. However, Husserl contended, as did Wittgenstein (1997), that "failure to describe correctly can lead to disaster" (in Mulligan, 1995, p. 169). For example, if we describe a rodent as a "pest," it may be exterminated, but as a "pet" we surmise a relationship and it will be allowed to live.[4]

A century prior to Damasio's (1999) neuroscience, which called into question Descartes' brain/body-mind/body split, phenomenology held consciousness as embodied. Husserl (1887/1900) demanded that we reflect upon our direct experiences as sources of knowledge. In his earliest and latest work, he viewed description as fundamental (Mulligan, p. 169). Such deep reflection required the *epoché*, the recognition and setting aside of prior assumptions about objects of consciousness (phenomena), which are all we can actually know anyway. Looking at experience this way frees perception and understanding from the social and political demands put upon it. Phenomenological reflection also frees one from one's own autobiographical constraints, such as trauma and indoctrinations.

Husserl's (1970) *epoché* places reflective demands upon the inquirer. First, one must "bracket" the assumptions coming from research and any concepts that affect thinking about a thing. Proceeding deeper, the researcher must then describe what is left to experience, setting aside the assumptions and concepts from her everyday lifeworld. Should several different situations of the same phenomena leave a matching footprint, one arrives at an "essential structure."[5]

The descriptions that result within the processes of the phenomenological *epoché* are written so that they can be compared and contrasted with additional experiences, and also with the experiences of others. This removal of layers of associations with and attachments to a thing is similar to meditation, an idea I take up in the second part of this chapter.

Other techniques used to distill an essence include imaginative variations, horizontalization, and horizonalization. In the choreography of a romantic couple in conflict, the tone and dynamics of the conflict became violent when the dance was speeded up, romantic when slowed down (Bentz, 1993). Similarly, inherent and variable qualities of a situation may be revealed through imagination. One may come to imagine that aspects of the experience were changed around, or taken in a different order, or equally significant (horizontalization). Or one may look at aspects of the experience which seem tangential, off in the horizon and put these in the center (horizonalization). The flakes of dandruff on the lawyer's blue sport coat may come to have deeper meaning than only a temporary scalp condition.[6]

The inherent somatic component of the phenomenological process can also clarify what is at stake in an experience. Learning to read the body's internal, glandular, muscular tensions and the releases related to an experience tells stories of their inherent meaning. The practice of the phenomenology of consciousness may be a personal revolution. One can no longer take what is presented by a parent, teacher, boss, or the media at face value. Phenomenological inquiry decolonizes psychic space. It asks the inquirer to examine the grounds of her knowing from within (Oliver, 2004).

Phenomenology is, at its best, collaborative. Sharing descriptions with other phenomenologists provides a group of colleagues who can collectively see aspects not immediately apparent to the writer. Such groups provide a safe ground to explore important experiences often pushed to the background by societal norms.[7]

Once we have clarified and distilled a phenomenon through the assumptions in the lifeworld and in the world of science, we may go deeper. Husserl calls this level the "transcendental ego," although it bears no similarity to the self-centered ego of everyday life. Instead, by bracketing the phenomenon being investigated, we are left with the pure flow of experience without content. Perhaps this is like the flow of energy vibrations underlying all that exists. This is a level of consciousness that we share with all life forms. As Corey Anton (2006) pointed out, in dreamless sleep we have no awareness, yet we share this realm with all other living beings.[8]

Husserlian phenomenology as transformative. Dudley Tower (2008) came to see his process of recovering from what had been diagnosed as terminal cancer as a liberation from the constraints of his life as a vice president in a large corporation. This realization came as part of a process of phenomenological writing about the experience as it occurred. He found that he had become a different kind of person and reached a stage of being that developmental theorists such as Kegan (1994) viewed as a "higher" level of consciousness. His interviews with other male survivors of cancer showed that some of them experienced a similar transformation.

Novokowsky (2008) discovered the nature of a true personal power that transformed his private life and his work as a management consultant. As an aftermath of trauma from an abusive father and reinforced by experiences in the military, he recaptured descriptions of himself acting abusively to those under him in the National Guard. Becoming clear to himself that this was not what he meant by true personal power, he was able to distill its nature.

Lifeworld phenomenology. Alfred Schutz, an economist, moved phenomenology into the social realm (see Wagner, 1983). He insisted that social scientists concerned with describing and understanding the social realm or the lifeworld (as opposed to the consciousness of the individual) ought not to be bracketing out the typifications, relevances, stocks of knowledge, and other awarenesses that make up a lifeworld. Instead, Schutz developed a framework for revealing aspects of shared consciousness and meaning structures that occur in all lifeworlds.

A phenomenologist who looks at the lifeworld as a living-moving-functioning conscious system also describes the "whatness" of it as experienced, but in relation to what is particular to that unique social world.[9] Schutz's work makes it clear that lifeworlds are crucial for humans and other creatures. From a practical standpoint, accurate descriptions of lifeworlds are very important for those working in and with organizations and communities. To not understand a lifeworld can lead to extreme consequences.[10]

The contemplative dimensions of lifeworld phenomenology become apparent when one realizes we are unaware of many of the lifeworlds' operating principles. Instead, we operate on our own assumptions and preconceptions. We limit our awareness to what to us at the time is "relevant" (Schutz, 1962) and thus do not perceive elements of the everyday world that are most important to it and even to our own survival.[11] For example, in this age of devices, couples on dinner dates are looking at their cell phone screens more than into each other's eyes. This disconnection leads to dismissing the importance of intimacy to well-being.

Lifeworld phenomenology goes beyond slogans from popularizers of mindfulness such as "be here now" to the challenging endeavor of perceiving and describing the components of a lifeworld. It is the task of the researcher of lifeworlds to bring to light the operating principles and to thereby increase the self-understanding of those who dwell therein.

Professionals develop and use scales and measuring devices to codify complex information. They may also help clarify problems, concerns, and useful solutions. On the other hand, scales may become fortresses against understanding actual lived experience. These are what Schutz (1970) in his lifeworld phenomenology calls "typifications."[12]

Phenomenologists practicing a Schutzian lifeworld approach will find that their own ways of being may change. Lucy Dinwiddie's

(Rehorick & Bentz, 2008) perception of the "whatness" of high-performance teams required her to discard the idealizations of these highly stressful, repressive, and ego-driven entities. The "high performance" lifeworld was loaded with physical and mental anguish covered up by false enthusiasm and ruthless competition. Dinwiddie found the same Schutzian "homunculi" or "puppets" functioning in each of the 20 teams she studied. By her calling awareness to them, the teams were enabled to step out of these roles and move toward a more humane way of working together. "Mrs. Leave-a-Legacy" could be asked to tone down her drive. "Mr. Fixit" could let loose the feeling that he should always be able to fix any situation.

Knobel (2014) used Schutz's lifeworld structures to uncover the lifeworld of Nelson Mandela as a leader. Knobel had worked with Mandela prior to the end of apartheid in South Africa. Originally she intended to interview others who had worked with Mandela using a Husserlian essential phenomenology approach. However, it appeared that what she found was mostly already packaged by the media to the point of being clichéd. She instead took a Schutzian approach to study Mandela's lifeworld as a leader (Knobel, 2014).

Knobel used Mandela's letters from prison as her primary source of data. To Schutz, a person stands behind his "fully intended meaning," not simply what he may have said at one point in time.[13] Mandela's letters from prison over many years were clearly "fully intended meaning" statements in that he was only allowed to write one letter a month of limited length. He had to say what was most important to him in these letters. Knobel entered into an imagined dialogue, with Mandela answering questions using his own words in the letters. The result is a clear and evocative understanding of Mandela's lifeworld as a leader, the challenges he faced, and how he moved through them.

Another example of change in a researcher's way of being through phenomenological practice lies in the field of "executive coaching." Jim Marlatt (2012) found his executive coaching practice moved to a deeper level when he took a phenomenological approach. He calls his work "essence-based coaching," as distinct from the popular "evidence-based coaching."[14] He now focuses upon the essence of experiences in the client's lifeworld.

Hermeneutics and transformative phenomenology. Husserlian phenomenological inquiry involves writing descriptions and working with them using aspects of the *epoché*, such as bracketing and imaginative variations. Schutzian lifeworld phenomenology also involves writing descriptions of the operating principles in a lifeworld. In the process the researcher finds numerous iterations—texts (sometimes called "protocols") about a phenomenon or lifeworld. This not only requires disciplined focus free from attachments but also the sensibilities of the artist. There is a sense of play involved, with colors, tones, and feelings, using the clay of everyday life.

There is a danger of falling back into an objectifying stance, using standardized "tools" for "processing the data." For the "qualitative" researcher, textbooks, manuals, and computer programs are available to take over. Such tools as "content analysis" and "thematic analysis" provide convenient ways to make the reader or dissertation committee member feel "safe." Nothing surprising, new, confusing, or demanding of deeper investigation is likely to emerge. The documents, sometimes in the form of narratives or stories, will be cut up like a cadaver, and may lose their life.[15]

The phenomenologist is loath to desert her participants and texts in favor of a canned analysis. Rather, she will wish to look deeply at these texts and use a powerful hermeneutic ally in the process.[16] Hans Georg Gadamer's (1989) playful hermeneutics emphasizes bridging horizons with radically different experiences and engaging with them, all the while being aware of one's own prejudices. Gadamer's three levels of hermeneutics begin with a view from a distance to get an overall picture of a phenomenon. For example, you see a wild horse in the forest and you describe its size, speed, way of moving, how it looks. At the next level you befriend the horse, perhaps stroke it and feed it, describing the world as the horse may see it, akin to a biography. Finally, you may get on the horse and ride, not sure where it will take you, or whether you will be thrown. This third level is the truly transformative level of hermeneutics (Rehorick & Bentz, 2008).

Somatic Psychology as Contemplation

Somatics was indebted to phenomenology from its beginnings in the 1970s (Johnson, 1994) and is inherently congruent with phenomenological work. It can enhance phenomenology's promise to be faithful to the things themselves—as embodied.

Somatic psychology uses the knowledge of the body to increase understanding, reduce pain, and restore function. Because of our habitual ways of moving and being or because of injuries, our joints, ligaments, and tendons rigidify into a hunched-over forward lunge. This cramps the internal organs and glands, causing pain and disease. Thomas Hanna (1980) founded an institute devoted to reversing these malfunctions that had been attributed to age. Hanna saw somatics as a necessary complement to third-person physiological sciences (p. 21).

Somatic awareness arises from within our bodies, as opposed to viewing them as objects from the perspective of another (see Varella, 1999).[17] The dysfunctions of sensory motor amnesia occur not only through the aging process but are also the result of trauma and stress in childhood. Disturbed family situations lead children to have permanently raised shoulders, sunken chests, and curved necks (Hanna, 1988, p. xiii).[18]

Hanna highlighted two common bodily dysfunctions: the Green Light reflex (constant tension to keep doing and working) and the Red Light reflex and its trauma reflexes. The Green Light reflex is a response to stress and the Red Light to danger. The Green Light is the sense of being pushed to act, head shoving forward, neck crooked, and shoulders bent; low back pain is a common reaction to unrelenting responsibility. The Red Light reflex is a tightening of the abdomen and hunching forward, the typical posture of the old. These conditions can be corrected through focus on the body and retraining it with stretching and exercise. I have experienced this myself: through a somatically based treatment, I recovered from a frozen second chakra[19] from decades-old, ignored trauma.

As Sheets-Johnstone (2011) shows, the living body is necessarily a moving body. All animals have six directions that govern movement: facing; standing; moving forward; elongating; moving sideways; and turning. This starts with the head, elongating the body. Although apes walk on two feet, they can still move with elongated spines as they hand-crawl among trees. All creatures who do not stand lengthen their spines as they fly or swim forward. Only dead bodies are "stiff." We also move laterally, side to side, and tend to be right-handed. Stress causes us to cringe inward from the stomach area, rounding our shoulders.

Demands for action stretch the neck and shoulders in a forward direction. Humans normally move forward without elongating our spines. Instead, our spines are crushed downward as we move. Yogic reverse postures seek to release this pressure on the joints and nervous system, bringing circulation to the brain and heart. We all sit as we meet, write, and talk, and we so rarely (if ever) dance. Besides the tendencies to frontal curves and distortions from stress, there are the many reactions to trauma.

Through somatic awareness, we can come to question the authority of the social codes that we initially had to adopt to become a part of the meaning-making apparatus of social order. Through the incessant questioning ("Why, why, why?") and refusals ("No! no!") of the two-year-old, a child develops an autobiographical self. This questioning comes from one's own body. As Oliver (2004) says:

> Through questioning as intimate revolt, negativity becomes a transformational force that opens up and maintains the world of idealization, sublimation and creativity without which we face the colonization, even

annihilation, of psychic space. And this questioning is an infinite process (p. 107).

Oliver also asserts that the bodies of women are reduced to animality in patriarchal culture, as either sex objects or mothers. They are "trapped within the crypt of their psyches with an abject and lifeless maternal body" (p. 107). As prematernal sex objects they are even more abject and lifeless. She ties this in with a crippling of the imagination of the feminine psyche: "We have lost the ability to imagine, including and perhaps most important, to imagine the meaning of our own lives" (p. 135).

Alternatively, both Jane Addams and Maurice Merleau-Ponty exemplify "embodied care" (Hamington, 2004). Addams—pacifist, social activist, founder of the famous Hull House settlement in Chicago, writer, professor of sociology, suffragette, and leader in the fight against child labor—is a model of what embodied care means. Merleau-Ponty (1945/2014) shows how interactions can include caring. Learning implies risk-taking, which requires a caring other, such as the guiding hands of a father helping a child learn to swim, so that our bodies can experience security. Caring requires habits of the body and mind that go beyond traditional theories of morality and justice. From embodied habits of care can come a caring imagination, which removes viewing what it would take to care for others out of our direct reach, but still in need.[20]

Somatic awareness is a way to tune in with oneself, establish intimacy with oneself, and hence be available to tune in with others. Phenomenology is a path of consistent questioning of the authority of the social order and its concepts and words, even those we have come to think in.[21] Together, these are powerful ways of inquiry and of being that are contemplative in nature (see Todres, 2007).

Through somatic phenomenological inquiry, we are able to release the personal accumulations of power distortions such as trauma, ego, money, and sensual decadence, thereby opening the space to plug in to the transcendent. As happens in the phenomenological *epoch*é, we can make space for our deeper beings to emerge.

From Brain to the Beyond: Consciousness, Neuroscience, and Vedanta Neuroscience and Somatics

Neuroscience and Vedantic philosophy provide important insights for somatic phenomenology. These areas of knowing and being strengthen and support somatic phenomenology, extending our range of understanding deep within the brain and outward to the universe and beyond. Here we will suggest some ways of moving forward to fuller appreciation of human time and being.

Damasio (1999), a neuroscientist, has shown via case studies that awareness of oneself as an "I" is essential to being human. He divides human consciousness and the human self into core consciousness and the core self, and extended consciousness and the autobiographical self.

Core Consciousness (CC): I am, therefore I think. Through his studies of brain-damaged patients, Damasio (1999) demonstrated the pre- and post-verbal nature of the core self. Without it, we could not have what we generally perceive as consciousness. Core consciousness is inner sense. It is your awareness of yourself and of the existence of others. It is selective and continuous, referring to objects other than the self.

Outside of our awareness, we perceive and act upon a myriad of information. We notice very little of what we know and do. It is dangerous to remove even a part of the brain where core consciousness exists because we would then act without awareness that we were acting. Moving images closely resemble core consciousness. The human preoccupation with movies, television, and computer games supports this insight. The silent movie speaks to us perhaps more fundamentally than Shakespeare's writing. The continuous "wordless storytelling" of all living creatures, including us, is the embodied neural basis of all knowing and being (Damasio, 1999, p. 188).

Consciousness is always accompanied by emotion, although it is often unrecognized. Patients with global aphasia can neither speak nor write words, and no conversation is possible. Yet their emotions are expressed through gestures, hand-body movements, and facial expressions, and they are richly connected to ongoing events.[22]

We cannot see this deeper luminosity; we can only apprehend it through contemplation, meditation, or divine blessing. The concept and word-laden world may drive out being and life.[23] Damasio (1999) demonstrated, through studies of those with severe language disorders caused by nerve disease, that patients' thought processes remain intact along with consciousness of their situation. Surprisingly, he finds no evidence of a contribution from language to core consciousness!

It is the core consciousness that grounds us in the present, the precious "be here now."[24] Timing too is part of core consciousness, which operates unconsciously and involuntarily (Hanna, 1993, p.121). Ideally, timing brings all of our being together into efficient, balanced functions. However, sometimes we are unbalanced and our conscious attention can come to our aid. This is somatic learning. We can thereby reduce entropy and gain energy. But growth of this nature takes courage and risk.

Extended Consciousness (EC). Damasio (1999) takes us next to the "glory" of extended consciousness (EC), which "at its peak" is uniquely human. In his words, "On any given day, if only you let it fly, extended consciousness can make you a character in an epic novel, and if only you use it well, it can open wide the doors to creation" (p. 196).

As extended consciousness emerges with language, we grow with words and stories, becoming aware of ourselves. Our "core self" becomes the "autobiographical self."[25] Through words, we are able to transcend the here and now, and to live in the past and the future.[26] Extended consciousness allows us to learn and retain records of a myriad of experiences, and to reactivate those records as self-training. The "autobiographical self" is also present in baboons and chimpanzees.

Extended consciousness is shared much more broadly than Damasio discussed. Studies of crows indicate that not only can they recognize particular human faces for a lifetime (Narzluff, 2013), but they can transmit to others what the faces of humans to avoid look like. They and those they communicate with will avoid people who have harmed or threatened one of them, and approach people they trust.

As Heidegger (1947/1993) said, "Language is the House of Being" (p. 217). Or so it is with humans. But the house can become a prison, or cluttered or decayed, filled with the static of computers, iPhones, TVs, and tweets. Kenneth Burke (1968) reminds us that language is a two-way street, a "terministic screen" that conceals as well as reveals. The autobiographical self is susceptible to colonization and repression, intensified today via the constant barrage of canned images. Our psyches are overloaded with the stories and opinions of those powerful enough to commission the programs and broadcast them.[27]

We are caught in a feedback loop as these stories, concepts, and opinions affect the molecules of our emotions, which in turn affects our cells and our brains. Poisoned in this way, we breathe in each other's toxic emotions (Brennan, 2004). Unpleasant thoughts, feelings, movies, or pictures of these things can all cause tension if not released. Such images have been compounding exponentially via video games and violent films, in addition to the barrage of actual wars and tragic events around the world, put before us via computer and television images (Hanna, 1988, pp. 151-152). Constant unresolved tensions can cause changes in body structure. This is why phenomenological somatic inquiry and practice are so important for clearing space within our beings.

Conscience. From the proto-self in core consciousness to the autobiographical self in extended consciousness, we can attain the highest levels of human achievement as we develop conscience. In conscience, we sense discords of feelings and ideas, as well as senses of truth, justice, and beauty. Because we can sense incongruities or dissonances between what we have learned and what we experience, we develop a conscience. Conscience comes from the inner "no" to what we perceive. Did not Plato teach these ideas in dialogue with dissenting others? Of interest is that romance languages have no word for "conscience" as distinguished from "conscious" or for "self" (Damasio, 1999, pp. 232-233).

With the freedom granted by extended consciousness, humans are capable of evil. Mensch (1996) makes a clear case for humans' ability to willfully harm ourselves, others, and the earth itself. Denying our nature as interdependent, we can act without conscience. Humans are capable of "radical evil," which destroys what can never be recovered (p. 214).

Vedantic Thought

Somatics and phenomenology are powerful forms of contemplative practice. In our first inward glances, and through reflective writing, at first a dim light of our own psychic space shines forward. As we continue to read our soma and write our descriptions, we reveal levels of our consciousness all the way to the transcendental level. Husserl (see Sawiki, n.d.) found that this "inner spaciousness," the transcendental consciousness, was shared by all. It connects us with something like Brahman, or bliss, god, or spirit.

As I use these words, I am aware of the irony that this level is beyond words or concepts. The worlds' religions have often misused these concepts and ideas, making them sound sour to many ears. As the great Hindu philosopher of the seventh century, Shankaracharya (1946), said, the deepest truths, "spiritual truth," must be experienced to be known. The transcendent can only be discovered by a prepared and dedicated devotee, learning from a true and loving guru.

There have been attempts to link Indian-Vedic philosophy with phenomenology (Mohanty, 1992), as well as with Buddhism and phenomenology. While philosophers have found no easy equation between them, there are fundamental affinities between phenomenology and Vedantic thought. To each of them, contemplative practice is central. I will focus here on two forms of Indian philosophy, Kundalini (Khalsa, 2001) yoga and the yogas of Vedanta as represented by Yogi Bhajan and Sri Ramakrishna and his heritage, respectively. The overall goal of all the yogas is to recognize and realize the inherent unity between one's individual Self (Atman), all others, and the universe (Brahman).

Contemplative practices ask us to be silent, sit quietly, or move mindfully. We reflect upon and gradually learn to control our mind's flow. Recognizing the challenges involved in releasing the mind from the barrage of words and images, Vedantic teachings stress repetition of the mantra, *japa* (repeating a mantra or names of god), or chanting, which will drive out the obsessive flow. A direct link to the higher transcendent Self (Atman) may be accessed through images or prayers. We can know the transcendent by replacing the images that saturate our worlds with those we choose. If we are open, these "gods" may surprise or stun us into a bliss-like state (*samahdi*).

Yogi Bhajan and his disciples, such as Dharma Singh Kalsa, M.D., have had an enormous impact on yoga as practiced in the United States.[28] The system of the seven chakras or energy centers in the body, as taught by Bhajan and Khalsa, offers a powerful and effective way of coming into greater harmony with oneself and others. There is a deep connection between the chakras and the glands and organs of the body. Using breath and posture, these centers can be activated, cleared, and reenergized. The goal is to bring the energy up the spine, releasing any stored negative energy or emotions along the way. For example, the third chakra, around the belly, tends to store anger. Here is where we have the liver and the spleen. We can release this anger using breath of fire or other techniques and feel more of a sense of personal power. Finally, the energy reaches the seventh chakra, the crown chakra at the top of the head, and one thereby feels a blissful connection with oneself, others, and the Spirit (by whatever name you wish to call this entity).

The Vedanta tradition was brought to the United States by Swami Vivekananada, a disciple of Sri Ramakrishna, who is considered by many to be a great modern day incarnation or god-realized being. Vivekananda codified the many yogas practiced in India in the late nineteenth century into four: Bhakti; Raja; Jnana; and Karma. Each of them provide a pathway to an enlightened life (Vivekananda, 1953).

Bhakti is the path of devotion. Through worship of a chosen ideal being such as Buddha, Shiva, Sarasvati, Ganesha, Durga, or Krishna, one increasingly becomes like this ideal. Worship includes prayer, meditation, japa, and chanting. Raja is the path of meditation, as taught by one's personal guru (or teacher). What is called "yoga" in many modern yoga classes is hatha yoga or some variation of it that focuses on body postures and movements for health and well-being. These exercises are important and effective but only as subsidiary to the other yogas. Bodily pain may be an obstacle to meditation.

Jnana yoga is the practice of discrimination. Through study of the Upanishads, Vedas, Gitas, and other works, one increases one's knowledge of Brahman. One can also use reason to understand that one is not one's ego, body, mind, property, relationships, or other objects. One is the light behind these, the knower, the Atman.

Finally, with Karma yoga, one attains unity by working always for the good, for god, if you will, rather than for selfish ends. One realizes that this world as we understand it is unreal and filled with illusions and bondages. The Atman/Brahman bond is the insuperable luminosity that propels the world.

From Core Consciousness to Brahman—Is This the Connection?
Damasio (1999) highlighted the importance of core consciousness to ourselves, our beings, and our relationships, despite the fact that we hardly understand it. Much of what we do and the pathways of our lives are moved from this core, of which we know little.[29] Our large brain capacities and the enormous power of human institutions control and manage our autobiographical selves from birth to death.

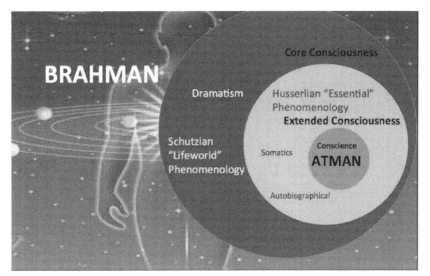

Illustration 1. From Core Consciousness to Brahman. (Design: Barton Buechner)

Words for "god," "the divine," "spiritual," and "religion" may lead us astray because they cannot adequately express the connection of beings to each other and to a Higher Power. These words and the institutions around them have often become sources of confusion, torture, wars, usury, and fraud. Despite this, we still seek the good. So I stand with Porpora (see Chapter 3 in this book) in being a "critical realist" in regard to the spiritual. Vedanta too takes a critical realist posture because it contends that a person must take as truths only what comes from her direct experience. Neuroscience has discovered brain centers that propel us to seek the spiritual dimension (d'Aquili & Newberg, 1999). Mystical experience is sourced in our brains. Perhaps this is the joke of Brahman for all of us. It holds that all gods are one and god is one and we are one. And it ends always in *Shanti, Shanti, Shanti*—peace, peace, peace.

Endnotes

[1] After writing this chapter I came across James Mensch (1996), whose book *Knowing and Being: A Postmodern Reversal,* provides philosoph-

ical insight into the issues of the primacy of being over knowing.

² In sociology, *Verstehen* sociology (Weber, 1949), symbolic interactionism (Mead, 1964), and dramatism (Burke, 1968; Duncan, 1962) remind us that we can know ourselves from within.

³ I use either feminine or masculine pronouns, depending upon the context and my intuitive sense of the context. Either one represents both genders.

⁴ Both Wittgenstein (1953) and the great Vedantic philosopher Shankara (600s A.D.) pointed out the limits of language: "That of which we cannot speak, we must needs remain silent." Philosophers and scientists seek to expand the ranges of knowing by finding new devices and pathways to see, and ways to perceive and accurately describe experiences. We will explore this later in this paper.

⁵ An "essence" or "essential structure" in this sense is not the same thing as "essentialism." It is rather a clarification about what must be a part of a thing or experience in order for it to be seen as such. A rose is a rose is a rose, but a daisy is not a rose. So please, Dear Reader, do not jump up in arms crying "Essentialism!"

⁶ Despite the similar spelling, "horizontalization" (note the "t") is a different reflective process from "horizonalization." Uniforms are a way of equalizing, "horizontalizing," different types of persons with a similar role. "Horizonalization" (no "t") is a process for such as that described by Bell Hooks in *From Feminist Theory: From Margin to Center* (2000), which makes color the focal point instead of whiteness.

⁷ Years of working with such groups either face-to-face or through sharing descriptions online gave me ample proof of the power of phenomenologists collaborating and supporting each other.

⁸ This level hovers near the idea of the oneness of Being, perhaps a shared Core Consciousness, as explained later.

[9] Habermas (1972) pointed out the fragility of lifeworlds, as they were increasingly destroyed by rational-legal entities, much as ecosystems such as rain forests are destroyed by strip mining.

[10] Ken Liberman's (1981) work with Aborigines is a clear example of deadly consequences, as the judicial authorities had no knowledge of the meaning of their testimony, which led to the conviction of innocents.

[11] Because of the many car accidents caused by drivers texting or talking on cell phones, it is illegal to use them while driving in California.

[12] Social scientists' methods and epistemologies not only discover what realities are; they also create them. For example, the *Diagnostic and Statistical Manual of Mental Disorders*, Fifth Edition (DSM-5), identifies pathologies that may not have existed prior to the diagnosis (American Psychiatric Association, 2013). In addition, the pharmaceutical industry makes billions from these diagnoses.

[13] Typically, in much qualitative research, transcripts of interviews are taken as deep descriptions. However, they may dangerously miss the mark. No matter how careful the analysis or how much high-powered software is used to analyze "themes" and "content," they will miss what is most meaningful to that lifeworld and the consciousnesses within it. Often, those interviewed may be telling stories based on the framework of something they saw on Facebook as opposed to what their actual experience is (Habermas, 1972).

[14] The relatively new field of "executive coaching" has spawned numerous certificates. One such is called "evidence-based," meaning quantitative data that supports the intervention. However, this kind of external evidence may miss the mark of what is the case in the lifeworld of the client.

[15] Ironically, some astute nurses developed a program called "Martin," reputedly to automatically apply Heideggerian analysis to interview data. Would Martin turn in his grave? Maybe, but he probably predicted

this. See also https://philosophyforchange.wordpress.com/2014/09/01/ heidegger-in-silicon-valley-social-operating-systems-technological-en-framing-and-the-hacker-way/

[16] I have used Droysen, Heidegger, Ricoeur, and Gadamer as hermeneutic allies in working with texts because various texts and phenomena have an affinity for certain hermeneutic approaches. This is much like a golfer knowing how to pick the right club to make the hole. Or, choosing the best hermeneutic is like a fisherman knowing which bait will catch the fish. *In Becoming Mature: Childhood Ghosts and Spirits in Adult Life*, I used Ricoeur to help me unlock the "world reached for by the texts" of the 53 women, most of whom were still carrying wounds from childhood (Bentz, 1989; see also Palmer, 1969, for an excellent overview).

[17] Berman (1970) pointed out the neglect of the body and spirit in Western thought and culture, from without as well as from within.

[18] Mensch (1996, p. 210) highlighted the "radical evil" that can be done to children by actions such as incest that may forever scar their future relationships.

[19] The second chakra, according to Kundalini yoga, is the center for creativity and generative energy. It includes the reproductive organs (Mukhyananda, 1986). I experienced a rape and an abortion done without anesthesia. Two years later, I experienced a traumatic birth with my legs held together during the final birth stages as a spinal was administered to dull the excruciating pain of a dry birth. Because of the extreme shock, my autonomic nervous system did not let me experience the pain at the time; instead, it froze these parts of the body as in suspended animation. The healing was stimulated by two gurus using shiatsu practice, which triggered these parts of the body through my feet (Bentz, 2003).

[20] Addams' life and work illustrate the habits of care she learned growing up with a father who encouraged her not to wear clothes that would set her apart from the less fortunate children in their small town, but

rather to see them as equals. Even thought she was from a wealthy background, she lived and worked at Hull House, directly caring for poor and impoverished immigrants in all areas needed. She wrote books about the needs of the youth and the mothers in language they could all understand. She used her caring imagination to help organize social change movements, including the Women's International League for Peace and Freedom, which confronted the world leaders involved in World War I. Hamington (2004) ties this work in with feminist theory such as Gilligan's, which suggests that caring is a richer and deeper perspective on relationships than theories of justice (Gilligan, 1982; see also Deegan, 1990).

[21] Over the past seven years, I have conducted somatics retreats where we used a variety of somatic modalities, including Kundalini yoga, sacred circle dance, somatic dance, and group reflection to begin to hear the messages from our bodies. Together we create positive energy to enhance our well-being and build connection with each other.

[22] Alphonso Lingis (1994), in *The Community of Those Who Have Nothing in Common*, tells a moving story of falling ill while on a solo journey in India. A man took care of him and nursed him to health. All the while they were not able to understand a single word of each other's language. Damasio (1999) shows that the verbal story could not live without the deeper preverbal story. This is why the cries of wolves and whales, the songs of birds and waves can thrill us. Suzanne Langer (1967) convincingly links human feeling to nature and music. Music is the human reminder of the body/brain link and our link to the earth.

[23] As Heidegger said, we must be courageous to enter the forest pathway in solitude and find a clearing. Only then may the "gods arrive."

[24] It is this consciousness that yoga recognizes as a necessary link to the higher Self. Simple presence is so elusive that popularizers from the music group the Beatles to Eckhart Tolle (1999) made fortunes from selling it. Since it is beyond the verbal, packaging it ironically drives

it away. Core consciousness is the "soma" toward which somatic psychology would pull us back (Hanna, 1980; Johnson, 1994) and that Carl Jung (1964) approaches through analyzing the archetypical imagery that appears in our dreams.

[25] At about 18 months a baby can recognize his own image in a mirror, just at the same time that language is developing. The clear demarcation of human identity comes with the child's most-used word (apart from "Mama"), the word "no." Through this "no" he asserts his difference from Mother and other. From this and the grammar of assertions, questions, declarations, answers, and delineations, come motives (Burke, 1968).

[26] Hofstadter's (2007) *I Am a Strange Loop* contends that our "self" exists as a feedback loop, as if it were a camera connected to a television capturing a picture of itself on the screen. "We" only exist at all in the world so long as we share such loops with others. Because of telephone cameras, we can now photograph ourselves in various locations and share this via the cell phone.

[27] Postmodernists, post-structuralists, and post-humanists, following Derrida's "there is nothing but the text" (Bentz & Kenny, 1997), may be willing to discard core consciousness and the body. Do they prefer a text message to holding hands? Are they looking forward to post-life existence as an eternal polyrhythm, content to be part of a Kurzweilian Singularity (Kurzweil, 2005)?[28] I have been trained as a yoga teacher for 20 years. I trained with Amrit Joy, a student of Yogi Bhajan, and received my formal certification through the Integrative Yoga Therapy Institute. I taught yoga for 10 years. In my somatics workshops and in my own practice, I integrate many of these teachings. I am also a member and initiate of the Vedanta Society of Southern California, initiated by Swami Sarvadevananda.

[29] McGinn (2016) has shown how our consciousness of color, shape, taste, and other awarenesses are inborn.

References

American Psychiatric Association. (2013). *Diagnostic and statistical manual of mental disorders* (5th ed.). New York, NY: American Psychiatric Association.

Anton, C. (2006). Dreamless sleep and the whole of human life: An ontological exposition. *Human Studies*, 181-202.

Bentz, V. M. (1989). *Becoming mature: Childhood ghosts and spirits in adult life.* New York, NY: Aldine de Gruyter.

-------. (1993). Creating visual images in dance: Works of Hanstein and Ziaks. In V. M. Bentz & P. Mayes (Eds.), *Visual images of women in the arts and mass media.* Lewiston, NY: Edwin Mellen Press.

-------. (1997). Body-as-world: Kenneth Burke's answer to postmodern charges against sociology. *Sociological Theory, 15*, 81-96.

-------. (2003). The body's memory, the body's wisdom. In M. I. Backhaus (Ed.), *Lived images: Meditations in experience, life-world, and I-hood* (pp. 158-185). Jyvaskyla, Finland: University of Jyvaskyla Press.

-------. (2013). *Flesh and mind: The time travels of Dr. Victoria Van Dietz.* New York, NY: Amazon.

Bentz, V. M., & Shapiro, J. J. (1998). *Mindful inquiry in social research.* Thousand Oaks, CA: SAGE.

Berman, M. (1990). *Coming to our senses: Body and spirit in the hidden history of the West.* New York, NY: Bantam.

Brennan, T. (2004). *The transmission of affect.* Ithaca, NY: Cornell University Press.

Burke, K. (1968a). A dramatist view of the origins of language. In K. Burke (Ed.), *Language as symbolic action* (pp. 419-479). Berkeley, CA: University of California Press.

-------. (1968b). Definition of man. In K. Burke (Ed.), *Language as symbolic action: Essays on life, literature, and method* (pp. 3-24).

Berkeley, CA: University of California Press.

-------. (1968c). Mind, body, and the unconscious. In K. Burke (Ed.), *Language as symbolic action: Essays on life, literature, and method* (pp. 63-80). Berkeley, CA: University of California Press.

-------. (1968d). Terministic screens. In K. Burke (Ed.), *Language as symbolic action: Essays on life, literature, and method* (pp. 44-62). Berkeley, CA: University of California Press.

-------. (1968e). Thinking of the body. In K. Burke (Ed.), *Language as symbolic action: Essays on life, literature, and method* (pp. 308-343). Berkeley, CA: University of California Press.

Chattopadhyaya, D. P. (1992). *Phenomenology and Indian philosophy.* Albany, NY: SUNY Press.

d'Aquili, E., & Newberg, A. (1999). *The mystical mind: Probing the biology of religious experience.* Minneapolis, MN: Fortress Press.

Damasio, A. (1999). *The feeling of what happens: Body and emotion in the making of consciousness.* New York, NY: Harcourt Brace & Co.

Deegan, M. J. (1990). *Jane Addams and the men of the Chicago School, 1892-1918.* New Brunswick, NJ: Transaction.

Dinwiddie, L. (2008). The lifeworld of high performance teams: An experiential account. In D. A. Rehorick & V. M. Bentz (Eds.), *Transformative phenomenology: Changing ourselves, lifeworlds, and professional practice* (pp. 113-128). New York, NY: Lexington Books.

Duncan, H. D. (1962). *Communication and social order.* New York, NY: Oxford University Press.

Gadamer, H. G. (1989). *Truth and method* (J. W. Marshall, Trans.). New York, NY: Seabury Press.

Gilligan, C. (1982). *In a different voice: Psychological theory and women's development.* Cambridge, MA: Harvard University Press.

Habermas, J. (1972). *Knowledge and human interests* (J. Shapiro,

Trans.). Boston, MA: Beacon Press.

Hamington, M. (2004). *Embodied care: Jane Addams, Maurice Merleau-Ponty, and feminist ethics.* University of Illinois Press.

Hanna, T. (1980). *The body of life: Creating new pathways for sensory awareness and fluid movement.* New York, NY: Alfred A. Knopf.

-------. (1988). *Somatics: Reawakening the mind's control of movement, flexibility, and health.* Cambridge, MA: Da Capo Press.

Heidegger, M. (1947/1993). Letter on humanism. In *Basic writings* (pp. 217-265). London, England: HarperPerennial.

Hofstadter, D. R. (2007). *I am a strange loop.* New York, NY: Basic Books.

Hooks, B. (2000). *Feminist Theory: From margin to center.* London, England: Pluto Press.

Husserl, E. (1970). *The crisis of European sciences and transcendental phenomenology: An introduction to phenomenological philosophy* (D. Carr, Trans.). Evanston, IL: Northwestern University Press.

Johnson, D. H. (1994). *Body, spirit, and democracy.* Berkeley, CA: North Atlantic Books.

-------. (1997). Who walks? In D. H. Johnson (Ed.), *The body in psychotherapy.* Berkeley, CA: North Atlantic Books.

Kegan, R. (1994). *In over our heads: The mental demands of modern life.* New York, NY: Norton.

Khalsa, D. S. (2002). *Meditation as medicine: Activate the power of your natural healing force.* New York, NY: Simon and Schuster.

Knobel, S. G. (2014). *A hermeneutic phenomenological study of the lifeworld of Nelson Mandela.* (Doctoral Dissertation). Retrieved from Proquest database. (Publication No. 3615745).

Kurzweil, R. (2005). *The singularity is near: When humans transcend biology.* New York, NY: Penguin Press.

Langer, S. (1967). *Mind: An essay on human feeling*, Vol. 2. New York,

NY: Oxford Press.

Liberman, K. (1981). Understanding Aborigines in Australian courts of law. *Human Organization, 40*(3), 247-255.

Lingis, A. (1994). *The community of those who have nothing in common.* Bloomington, IN: Indiana University Press.

Malhotra, V. (1975). *Toward a sociology in a new key: A discussion of dramatistic social theory.* Ann Arbor, MI: University of Michigan.

Marlatt, J. (2012). *When executive coaching connects: A phenomenological study.* (Doctoral Dissertation). Retrieved from Proquest database. (Publication No. 3518579).

Maxwell, D. S. (2013). *Classical horsemanship: A phenomenological and dramatist study.* Retrieved from Proquest database. (Publication No. 3557916).

McGinn, C. (2016). *Inborn knowledge: The mystery within.* Cambridge, MA: MIT Press.

Mead, G. H. (1964). *Selected writings* (A. Reck, Ed.). Indianapolis, IN: Bobbs-Merrill.

Mensch, J. (1996). *Knowing and being: A postmodern reversal.* University Park, PA: Pennsylvania State University Press.

Merleau-Ponty, M. (1945/2014). *Phenomenlogy of perception* (D. A. Landes, Trans.). New York, NY: Routledge.

-------. (1968). *The visible and invisible* (A. Lingis, Trans.). Evanston, IL: Northwestern University Press.

Mohanty, J. (1992). Phenomenology and Indian philosophy: The concept of rationality. In D. P. Chattopadhyaya, J. E. Lester, & J. Mohanty (Eds.), *Phenomenology and Indian philosophy* (pp. 7-18). Albany, NY: SUNY Press.

Mukhyananda, S. (1986). *Human personality and the cosmic energy cycle.* Calcutta, India: Vedanta Press.

Mulligan, K. (1995). Perception. In B. Smith & D. W. Smith (Eds.), *The Cambridge Companion to Husserl* (pp. 168-239). New York,

NY: Cambridge University Press.

Narzluff, J. A. (2013). *Gifts of the crow: How perception, emotion, and thought allow smart birds to behave like humans.* New York, NY: Atria Books.

Nikhilananda, S. (1946). Introduction to self-knowledge. In Shankara-charya (Ed.), *Self knowledge* (pp. 1-114). New York, NY: Ramakrishna-Vivekananda Center.

Novokowsky, B. (2008). Personal power: Realizing self in doing and being. In D. A. Rehorick & V. M. Bentz (Eds.), *Transformative phenomenology: Changing ourselves, lifeworld, and professional practice* (pp. 129-140). New York, NY: Lexington Books.

Oliver, K. (2004). *The colonization of psychic space: A psychoanalytic theory of oppression.* Ann Arbor, MI: University of Minnesota Press.

Palmer, R. (1969) *Hermeneutics.* Evanston, IL: Northwestern University Press.

Rehorick, D. A., & Bentz, V. M. (2008). *Transformative phenomenology: Changing ourselves, lifeworlds and professional practice.* New York, NY: Lexington Books.

-------. (2008). Transformative phenomenology: A scholarly scaffold for practitioners. In D. A. Rehorick & V. M. Bentz (Eds.), *Transformative phenomenology: Changing ourselves, lifeworlds, and professional practice* (pp. 1-32). New York, NY: Lexington Books.

Sawiki, M. (n.d.). Edmund Husserl (1859-1938). *Internet Encyclopedia of Philosophy.* Retrieved from http://www.iep.utm.edu/husserl/.

Schutz, A. (1962). *The Problem of Social Reality: Collected Papers,* Vol. 1 (M. Natanson, Ed.). The Hague, Netherlands: Martinus Nijhoff.

-------. (1970). *Alfred Schutz: On phenomenology and social relations*

(H. Wagner, Ed.). Chicago, IL: University of Chicago Press.

Shankaracharya. (1946). *Self-knowledge* (S. Nikhilananda, Trans.). New York, NY: Ramakrishna-Vivekananda Center.

Sheets-Johnstone, M. (2011). *The primacy of movement.* Philadelphia, PA: John Benjamins.

Todres, L. (2007). *Embodied inquiry: Phenomenological touchstones for research, psychotherapy and spirituality.* New York, NY: Pelgrave Macmillan.

Tolle, E. (1999). *The power of now.* Vancouver, B.C., Canada: Nameste Publishing.

Tower, D. O. (2008). Trial by fire: The transformational journey of an adult male cancer survivor. In D. A. Rehorick & V. M. Bentz (Eds.), *Transformative phenomenology: Changing ourselves, lifeworlds, and professional practice* (pp. 67-82). New York, NY: Lexington Books.

Varela, F., & Shear, J. (1999). First-person methodologies: What, Why, How? In F. Varela (Ed.), *The view from within: First person approaches to the study of consciousness.* Bowling Green, OH: Imprint Academe Philosophy Documentation Center.

Vivekananda, S. (1953). *Vivekananda: The yogas and other works* (S. Nikhilananda, Ed.). New York, NY: Ramakrishna-Vivekananda Center.

Wagner, H. (1983). *Phenomenology of consciousness and sociology of the Life-world: An introductory study.* Edmonton, Alberta, Canada: University of Alberta Press.

Weber, M. (1946). *From Max Weber: Essays in sociology* (G. A. Mills, Ed.). New York, NY: Oxford University Press.

-------. (1949). *Max Weber on the methodology of the social sciences* (S. A. Finch, Ed.). New York, NY: Free Press.

Weinstein, M. (1997, October 15). Phenomenological research practice. *Presented at the Fielding Institute Research Session.* Milwaukee, WI.

Valerie Malhotra Bentz, PhD, is a professor at Fielding Graduate University, where she has also served as associate dean for research and co-founder of the Creative Longevity and Wisdom concentration. She is currently director of the Somatics, Phenomenology, and Communicative Leadership (SPCL) concentration. She previously taught at Texas Woman's University, was editor of *Phenomenology and the Human Sciences* (1994-1998), and served as president, board member, and co-chair of several professional associations. Her practice includes psychotherapy, yoga teaching, somatic learning and therapy, and social and environmental activism. Her current interests include sociological theory, consciousness development, Vedantic and Buddhist theories of knowledge, and social somatics.

Critical Realism and Spirituality

By Douglas V. Porpora, PhD
Department of Anthropology, Drexel University, United States

Abstract

Critical realism (CR) is a philosophy of science that is more hospitable to spiritual matters than either positivism or social constructionism. Positivism has led to a naturalist orientation in social science that excludes the spiritual. According to social constructionism, spiritual realities are social constructions. CR is more open to the spiritual or transcendental domain as an independent reality. This chapter will introduce the basic features of critical realism and illustrate how it supports a more spiritual approach to the social sciences.

Introduction

Critical realism (CR), strictly speaking, is not an epistemology. Maybe better said, it is not *only* an epistemology. It is more properly a philosophy of science and, as such, encompasses ontology as well as epistemology (Porpora, 2015). In fact, one of the tenets of CR is that in most social science theorizing, epistemology has completely swallowed ontology, constituting what CR terms the *epistemic fallacy* (Bhaskar, 2009).

The epistemic fallacy involves a disregard for ontology, either by evading ontological questions altogether or, more commonly, by reducing questions of ontology to questions of epistemology. Epistemology concerns how we know what we know, if indeed we can be said to know anything at all. It is on epistemological grounds that we formulate our various research methodologies, upon which the social sciences place so much stress. We fall into the epistemic fallacy, however, when we confuse or conflate our knowledge of something with the thing our knowledge is about.

Let us take the above point more slowly. Knowledge is what

philosophers, following Franz Brentano (1973), call an *intentional* state. It has the quality peculiar to mentality of being *about* something. Knowledge is always knowledge of something, something that is there to be known. Ontology is about what there is to be known. Ontology thus concerns what there is in totality or at least what there is in a particular domain such as the social domain. Ontology concerns such matters as what objects there are, what relations there are among them, what kinds of causes exist, and even the nature of causality itself.

Is *care* something real? If so, what is care and what are its properties? How does care interact with other features of the world? These are all ontological questions. They are not questions about how we know anything about caring or how we should study it. Such questions would be epistemological. But to ask what caring is is to ask what the properties are of the object of knowledge.

Perhaps it will help to distinguish among the *subject* of knowledge, the *content* of knowledge, and the *object* of knowledge. For the purposes of this discussion, we ourselves are the subjects of knowledge, the knowers who know something. The content of knowledge is what we know or think we know. CR refers to this content as the *transitive dimension* of knowledge (Bhaskar, 2008; Hartwig, 2007).

The transitive dimension of knowledge is always a subjective state; it is the possession of distinct knowers situated in distinct socio-historical contexts. Thus, it is always subject to two kinds of difference. First, there will be difference over time as thinking changes, which is one reason the content of knowledge is called the *transitive* dimension. At one time, for example, it was believed—or believed known—that the sun revolved around the earth. Now we believe—or think we know—the opposite.

There is a second difference to which the content of knowledge is subject: The purported content of knowledge differs across cultures and standpoints. The classic example of such difference is the contrast between Zande magic and Western science. Such cultural difference in purported knowledge is part of what gave rise to talk of "knowledges" within postmodern and social constructionist paradigms.

Who is to say which knowledge—Zande magic or Western science—is correct? Is either? Is there any such thing as correct knowledge? These questions in turn lead us to ask the more general questions of whether there is any such thing as knowledge and, if so, what it is.

The above questions are no longer epistemological but ontological because we are asking not how we know what we know about knowledge but what knowledge *is*. Ontology asserts itself against epistemology by forcing us to ask what knowledge is. In this case, knowledge is the object of knowledge, at least the object of our discussion about knowledge. Such object of knowledge is what CR calls the *intransitive dimension* (Bhaskar, 2008; Hartwig, 2007).

According to CR, there is a crucial difference between the transitive and intransitive dimensions of knowledge. Our transitive thoughts about something may change over time or differ by culture, but those differences do not alter the intransitive object of knowledge. Presumably, the actual earth and sun did not change position when our understanding of them changed. The intransitive objects and their relations stayed the same even as our thoughts about them reversed (Pickering, 2012).

The same would apply to knowledge as an object of knowledge. Whatever we come to consider knowledge to be, what it is presumably does not change. If we come to understand knowledge as something plural, then presumably what knowledge is always was so—or at least potentially so—and did not come into being at the moment when we came to so regard it.

From the CR perspective, it is a mistake to confuse or conflate the transitive and intransitive dimensions of knowledge. That mistake is common both to positivism and to postmodern post-positivism, including post-structuralism and social constructionism. Both tendencies seek to distance themselves from any reality independent of what we humans think of it.

In effect, by denying access to any ultimate reality beyond our ken, both tendencies dismiss what CR calls the intransitive dimension of knowledge, leaving only the transitive dimension. With only the transitive dimension to work with, both tendencies end up only with epistemology. Ontology seemingly disappears.

The apparent disappearance of ontology is part of what CR means by the epistemic fallacy. One reason it is a fallacy is that the ontology seems to disappear but the attempted distancing of ontology from epistemology is untenable. Ontology and epistemology are dialectically related. Our ontological claims about what exists depend on some epistemic warrant for those claims. Conversely, our epistemological understanding of warrant always depends on one or another set of ontological claims. Thus, even if we deny access to the world independent of human thought, that denial itself is an ontological claim. As noted above, so is defining what knowledge is under such conditions.

Ontology is thus inescapable. So is epistemology. CR does not deny the importance of the latter or its dialectical tie to the former. But as other perspectives continue to try to do without ontology, CR is distinctive in its stand against epistemological reductionism.

So one way in which ontology asserts itself against epistemology is by the inescapable need for ontological posits in any theory of epistemology. But there is also another way. According to popular understanding, one difference between knowledge and mere belief is that knowledge constitutes belief that is *true*. According to this distinction, if in fact the sun does not revolve around the earth, then earlier, opposite viewpoints were never knowledge; they were always only mere belief, and mistaken belief at that. Similarly, if there are in fact no witches, then what the Zandes believe is not actually knowledge. On the contrary, you cannot *know* something that is not true. You only truly know something if what you believe to know is true. Truth brings us back to ontology because determining whether a belief or claim is true involves ontology.

CR, at least, would so argue.

The 20th Century ended with a crisis of truth, and we are still in it. Witness the continued popularity of Jean Baudrillard. There is even an *International Journal of Baudrillard Studies*. According to Baudrillard, the possibility of truth has vanished in our era. Baudrillard's argument is essentially a poststructuralist one: The very words we would use to speak of reality merely conjure other words, the whole a self-referential system that fails to make contact with wordless reality as it is in itself. As Jacques Derrida (1983) put it, *"Il n'y a pas hors-texte"* or "There is no outside-text" (p. 36).

Unfortunately for Baudrillard and poststructuralism in general, truth, like ontology, is inescapable. Thus, Baudrillard's very claim about the disappearance of truth falls into what is called a *performative contradiction*. Baudrillard's claim is an assertion. As speech acts, assertions ineluctably carry with them their own validity claims, among them that what is asserted is true. Severed from that validity claim, any putative assertion becomes unintelligible. If we are to make any sense of Baudrillard's assertion, we must take him to be asserting it true that, in our era, access to reality has passed. But then does not Baudrillard's own assertion imply contact with at least one reality, the possibility of which the assertion denies? To avoid the contradiction, Marc Poster (2001) understands Baudrillard from a more defensible perspective:

> Baudrillard is not disputing the trivial issue that reason remains operative in some actions, that if I want to arrive at the next block, for example, I can assume a Newtonian universe (common sense), plan a course of action (to walk straight for X meters, carry out the action, and finally fulfill my goal by arriving at the point in question). What is in doubt is that this sort of thinking enables a historically informed grasp of the present in general. According to Baudrillard, it does not. The

concurrent spread of the hyperreal through the media and the collapse of liberal and Marxist politics as the master narratives, deprives the rational subject of its privileged access to truth. In an important sense individuals are no longer citizens, eager to maximize their civil rights, nor proletarians, anticipating the onset of communism. They are rather consumers, and hence the prey of objects as defined by the code (p. 7).

This clarification helps. Baudrillard is saying something quite interesting about what used to be called ideology. Still, however, Baudrillard contradicts himself. According to Poster, Baudrillard denies only the "possibility of an historically informed grasp of the present" (Porpora, 2015, p. 67). Yet is not "an historically informed grasp of the present" precisely what Baudrillard himself is offering by denying that contemporary possibility? Is not the reality of global warming yet another instance of "an historically informed grasp of the present" (ibid.)?

As I have said, the point here is that truth, like ontology, is inescapable. Truth is a validity claim built into assertion by its very nature as a speech act (Apel, 2003; Habermas, 1999). Assertions cannot be made without entailing a claim to truth.

What is truth? What do we mean by it? If truth is as inescapable as ontology, CR would argue that it is because the two are related. It is this claimed relation that makes CR a form of realism, for the claim is that truth is the link between our beliefs and assertions on the one hand, and objective reality on the other.

When we talk about care and caring, do we not want to arrive by whatever methods at something true about them? Do we not want to assert that care and caring and their properties are real and consequential? As a philosophy of science, CR secures these aspirations. In addition, we also mean experiencing truth and communicating about it. Contemplative knowledge invites us to share our experience with others and ask ourselves if we recognize the existence of suffering. The truth is about this individual recognition: an experiential empirically proven event. It is not a matter of logical assertions along the line of analytic philosophy.

Still, we need to ask what truth is, and that returns us to the epistemic fallacy which, from the CR perspective, characterizes much of social science. From the CR perspective, positivism and postmodern poststructuralism are like evil twins. Both share an *epistemic* as opposed to an *alethic* conception of truth.

The distinction has to do with what philosophers call the *truth-maker* (Alston, 1997). What is it that makes a statement or belief true? According to the epistemic account, the truth-maker is an epistemic protocol or methodology that produces the epistemic state of certainty. This approach to knowledge is called *foundationalism*. The idea is that by building on firm methodological foundations, we arrive, almost algorithmically, at certainty. The content of the certain knowledge attained is truth. Stated otherwise, truth is knowledge content that is certain. As its name implies, for the epistemic account, truth is equated with ways of knowing. Thus, truth-makers are epistemic.

I say that both positivists and constructionists accept this epistemic account of truth. The positivists accept it and, believing certainty possible, likewise believe in truth. In contrast, constructionists, also accepting the epistemic account of truth but rejecting foundationalism, do not believe certainty is possible; hence, they reject the possibility of truth. This perspective holds that absolute certainty may not be possible but relative certainty is. Contemplative knowledge, at least in the Buddhist traditions, does not provide foundations of any kind, especially in terms of cognitive knowledge. Instead, contemplative knowledge is an invitation to a sort of embodied awareness grounded on the observation of one's daily life from within.

In contrast with constructionism, the epistemic conception of truth shared by positivism, CR upholds an *alethic* conception of truth.

Again, the distinction between an epistemic and an alethic conception of truth concerns the truth-maker—that is, what makes a belief or claim true or not. As we saw, for the epistemic view, what makes a belief or claim true is an epistemic property, namely the certainty achieved via some foundational protocol. The epistemic view more or less equates truth with certain knowledge.

In contrast, the *alethic* view detaches truth from both certainty and from methodological algorithms. For the alethic view, reality (or ontology) itself is the truth-maker. If reality actually is as a belief or claim holds it to be, then the belief or claim is true—however certain or uncertain about that belief or claim we might be. I may be uncertain that I left the keys in the car, but if the car is where the keys are, then, from the alethic point of view, my suspicions, however uncertain, were nonetheless true (Porpora, 2015).

Likewise, the alethic view detaches truth from methodology. For the alethic point of view, it does not matter how one arrived at a belief or claim. Even if we are only speaking of an unproven hypothesis, if reality is as expressed, the hypothesis is nonetheless true. Precisely because the alethic view detaches truth from both certainty and methodology, it is said to offer a non-epistemic account of truth. The alethic account is not an epistemic account of truth but ontological, insofar as it is reality or ontology itself that is the truth-maker rather than our belief states or methodological protocols.

Is the alethic view not simply the traditional correspondence theory of truth, the idea that a belief or claim is true if it corresponds to the way the world is? Yes, actually, it is. Has not the correspondence theory been proven untenable? No. In fact, among philosophers, the correspondence theory remains the most frequently held theory of truth. Of course, it has competitors and, like most ideas, critics. Here, I confine myself to dismissing the most frequent reason cited in the social sciences for dismissing the correspondence theory. The reason is a Kantian one. The putative problem with the correspondence theory is that we have no access to the world independent of our own conceptions against which to match our claims or beliefs.

This putative problem might indeed threaten correspondence theory if correspondence theory were meant primarily as the criterion of truth, or the way we determine the truth. It is meant, however, less as the criterion of truth than as the meaning of truth. Per correspondence theory, a claim or belief is true if it matches the world. That correspondence, according to the theory, is what it means for a claim or belief to be true. It is not, however, how we necessarily determine the truth.

How then, according to the correspondence theory, do we determine what is true? The correspondence theory itself does not say because, for the alethic view, that question is a separate matter. How we determine what matches the world is the separate question of epistemology. Correspondence theory analytically separates the meaning and determination of truth.

Having said that, at one quotidian level, correspondence theory does indeed suggest how to determine truth: simple inspection. As prosaic as the point may be, it is nonetheless fundamentally important. In our daily routine, we most directly determine the truth of things by looking. I say I left the keys in the ignition; you say I didn't. How do we determine the truth? By looking. In this case we can not only look, we can look together in a public way that can in principle also include the observation of neutral third parties with no skin in the game. "Yes," they can concur. "There are the keys. *Les voilà!*" (Porpora, 2015).

As banal as the point may be, it is fundamentally important. At the end of the day, much comes down to simple inspection. What persuades us that what some social researcher says about society is true? What persuades even the researcher himself? His data. And how do we know what the data say? We look. We look at it in a way that is in principle public. Ultimately, without inspection, we have nothing. Not even our data.

For most of what we do in life, simple inspection is how we determine truth. Of course, most of what we do in life takes place within a common, shared scientific paradigm or cultural conceptual scheme. We may not agree on where I left the keys, but we agree that there are such things that we call keys, cars, and ignitions. We likewise generally agree on the existence of statistical correlations.

Things get interesting when correspondence with reality cannot so directly be determined. That happens when we are between paradigms or conceptual schemes—for example, when we are trying to decide not where I left the keys but whether there are such things as keys, or when we are between entire frameworks such as Western science and Zande magic. That is where epistemological questions loom to the fore.

In contrast with postmodernist tendencies such as radical social constructionism, CR affirms what it calls *judgmental rationality* (Bhaskar, 2009). Judgmental rationality means that, despite differences in construction that vary across cultures or social structural positions, there are always ways to judge between them. It is always possible to decide whether one viewpoint rests on better grounds or is better argued than the others.

As an example, consider the position of women in society. Is it only from a particular viewpoint that women are still unfairly subordinated in a whole range of ways within society? To say so suggests that it would be equally valid from a different standpoint to deny that such is the case. If the two viewpoints are equally valid, why should men heed the women's complaint? Why should not men continue to defend what, from the women's standpoint, is male privilege?

We begin to see that moral and political charges rest on implicit claims to truth, without which the charges lose their bite. The only reason for the men to heed the women is because they themselves conclude that the women are right, that what shows up from the women's standpoint is actually truer than what the men perceive from their standpoint. As Donna Haraway (1991) concedes, politics and morality cannot only rest with different standpoints, each considered to be equally valid. Perhaps we never start with a view from nowhere, but vindicated moral and political claims must end there. In this case, if the men are to change, then the men must overcome their original perception from their own standpoint to arrive at the final view from nowhere that vindicates the claims of the women.

This raises two questions: Who is it that decides on this view from nowhere, and how is to be done? Postmodernism simply assumed that these questions are unanswerable, but they are not. To begin with the second question first, postmodernism assumed that without foundational methods capable of generating certainty, there can be no truth and thus no rational decision between rival points of view. All was decided simply by power. Such a theoretical position is self-refuting. Is it itself only an exertion of power to assert that all theoretical conclusions represent exertions of power? Are we not instead to consider this claim a reasoned conclusion arrived at through evidence? If so, then some conclusions can be arrived at through reasoning and evidence, in which case it cannot all be reduced to power.

One mistake here is to equate truth with certainty; CR denies that equation. From the CR perspective, we can arrive at truth with epistemic stances short of absolute certainty. First, as in a criminal trial, instead of absolute certainty, the truth can be attained by certainty beyond a reasonable doubt. In tort cases, jurors are not even asked to judge with certainty. They are asked rather to judge which of rival claims enjoys the preponderance of evidence. And of course, it might be the case that, at any given moment in time, neither claim does (Porpora, 2015).

Let us jump for the moment to the second question on the table: Who is to make these judgments? Who decides what the truth is? Well, who decides in the court cases considered above? We might say the jury as a whole, but the decision of the jury as a whole reflects the judgments of each individual juror. And so it is more generally: Individually, each of us must judge what the truth of any matter before us is. We do not thereby make the truth; we simply arrive at a judgment as to what it is.

If there is often no certainty, will not those truth judgments frequently be wrong? Yes. According to CR, our truth judgments are fallible. Although what it means to believe something is to regard it as true, many of our beliefs are mistaken. We simply cannot know in advance which of our beliefs are the false ones. That is why, although CR believes in truth, it counsels humility about truth. While there always is a truth, we ourselves may not be in possession of it. If we know that some of what we hold true is not, we must ever be open to correction. Correction from whom? From those who hold different points of view.

On what basis do we decide which view is correct? Some would say on the basis of best argument. If we are open-minded and oriented toward truth, we can see in the course of discussion that at times it is not we who hold the best argument. In addition, the criteria for what makes a best argument change with perspective. If we are oriented toward truth, we will not cling to our original views as if they were sacred objects, but rather will modify our beliefs, perhaps even abandoning some of them altogether. In fact, contemplative science focuses on "points of existence" or situational moments. "Simple inspection" and "best argument" cannot fit for human living beings in search of a meaning for their lives. We must allow other ways of knowing and judging truth. There must be humility in good research, no matter the basis.

If, as certain postmodernist perspectives contend, there is no truth, then no one, including we, can ever be wrong. There is instead only the exercise of power. Of course, if no one can ever be wrong, no one can ever be right. As we saw above, moral and political claims require a basis in truth. For that reason, an orientation toward truth is always a spiritual orientation. Orientation toward truth underlies an orientation toward the good and the right.

To be oriented toward truth, we must place ourselves within a space of critical arguments and monitor which of them is most compelling, open always to the possibility that even in our own considered judgment, our own views may be dethroned (Porpora, 2001). An orientation toward truth is spiritual because it requires us to transcend ourselves and our own interests.

To be oriented toward truth in this way is itself an attitude of care. Care is not simply a micro-matter of the private sphere. It extends into the public sphere as well. To the extent that we are social animals, we have an obligation to orient ourselves toward a common good, a good that transcends our own individual good. We must care about that common good. And to the extent that we care about the common good, we must also care about what the common good in truth is. It is care about the truth in general and the truth about our collective good in particular that should keep us involved in public affairs, public dialogue and, ultimately, public decision-making.

Care for the truth and common good is not the only spiritual value that CR upholds. Against both positivism and postmodernist post-positivisms, CR is distinctive in providing the metaphysical or philosophical framework for securing other spiritual values as well. Some of that framework is epistemological but much of it rests on an ontology different from what is proposed by either positivism or postmodernist post-positivism. In particular, CR has a different view of causality. Although it is an ontological position, it results in a methodological pluralism beyond simple statistical analysis that is epistemological in nature. Along with a rejection of the positivist equation of causality with deterministic laws, CR denies physicalist reduction and even what is called the causal closure of physics, the view that all causality must unfold ultimately in physical ways. Instead, CR upholds an emergentist perspective, according to which non-physical and what might be considered spiritual causes have a role to play. Above all, CR defends a humanist conception of an ontologically unified self that can be the object of care and without which there is, arguably, nothing to care about.

Let us in closing unpack these various points. Positivism understands causality in terms of the laws of the if-then form. If one thing—or set of things—occurs, then something else follows. For deterministic laws, what follows follows necessarily. For statistical laws, what follows does so with some definite probability.

If causality involves general laws, then causal explanation requires us to know what the laws are. If the laws are general, then we researchers must claim that the putative causal relations we observe are in fact general. In this way we arrive at extensive research methods that privilege statistics over qualitative, intensive methods such as ethnography or in-depth interviews.

It is doubtful, however, that many general laws exist, even laws of a statistical nature. Those doubts apply even more to the social domain. Against positivism, CR rejects an understanding of causality in terms of laws. Instead, it understands causality in terms of conjunctures of mechanisms. Because the same conjuncture of mechanisms may occur only once, CR justifies causal attributions even in historical narratives of unique events. Understanding causality in terms of mechanisms rather than general laws, CR is equally comfortable with ethnography, in-depth interviews, and other intensive research methodologies. When it comes to care, CR would justify concern not only with comparative statistical accounts about what kind of care or caring occurs where, but also descriptive elaborations of how care is realized in any particular case.

Positivism believes not only in general causal laws. For positivism, all causal laws are physical. With such a premise—called the causal closure of the physical—positivism is ultimately reductive in nature, reducing what we might consider spiritual to what is mechanical. CR, however, is anti-reductive. Positivism regards the physical as a complete closed system of causal laws that does not subscribe to laws at all. CR, on the other hand, regards the physical, or any level of it, always as an open system of mechanisms to which other mechanisms (even non-physical or what we might call spiritual mechanisms) contribute effects. Whereas positivism is reductive, CR is emergentist. With that emergentism, CR is open to the spiritual. In fact, critical realists have written specifically on spiritual matters (for example, see Archer, Bhaskar, Collier, Lawson, & Norrie, 1998).

Post-structuralists too have lately addressed themselves to causality and have come up with vitalism (Coole & Frost, 2010). While, from the CR perspective, vitalism is better than positivism's law-like approach to causality, it confuses causal agency in general with the more specific, intentional agency of human persons. Post-structuralism does not generally invoke the category of person and, in fact, declaims the existence of unitary or coherent selves.

From the CR perspective, such denial of human selfhood is anti-spiritual. It certainly undermines any concern with care. In the first place, care, like knowledge, is an intentional state. As such, it requires an object. One cannot care without caring about something. If we are speaking of care for humans, there must be a self there to care about, somebody who is at home in that body. We do not, after all, care about zombies devoid of inner life. In the human sphere, care is rooted in the I-Thou relation. For that relation to occur, there must be a Thou to care about (Buber, 1970).

For that matter, there must be an I as well. In the same way that the I-Thou relation requires a self to care about, it likewise requires an I to do the caring. The existence of a self is again not an epistemological point but one that is ontological. Further, it is an ontological point that poststructuralism rejects. Poststructuralism celebrates all deconstruction, including deconstruction of essential selfhood. As an early Judith Butler (2006) put it, "There is no doer behind the deed" (p. 34). CR disagrees. If a deed has been done, then there must be a doer. Deeds do not simply happen uncaused. If deeds are "performed," then there must be a performer.

In relation to the self, CR stands not only against poststructuralism but against positivism as well. The positivist view, most stubbornly upheld in the philosophy of mind, is that all reality, including mental and putatively spiritual morality, is reducible not only to physical causes but ultimately to physics. That premise too is ontological rather than epistemological; it vitiates any special regard for human beings. Human choices are not in a metaphysical sense freely chosen and, although philosophers of mind would deny it, human beings are not, therefore, morally responsible.

Against positivist reductionism, CR affirms an emergentist ontology, according to which reality is stratified: Elementary particles combine to form atoms, atoms combine to form molecules, organic molecules combine to form life, and so on. At each level, new properties come into being that make for new, irreducible behavior.

Finally, CR differs from positivism in its understanding of causality. Positivism understands causality in terms of law-like regularities among events. It is according to this view that physics represents a closed system of laws that cannot be disrupted. Because CR breaks completely with this positivist view of causality, it does not share the commitment to physical causal closure (Bhaskar, 2008; Porpora, 2015). CR does not at all understand causality in terms of laws but rather in terms of operative mechanisms, which combine and interfere with each other.

If there are causal laws, those laws must be general; indeed, they must be universal. Thus, the search for laws privileges statistical methodology, and ethnographic and other intensive methods get dismissed as unscientific. Because CR, on the contrary breaks, with an understanding of causality in terms of laws, how a mechanism generally operates becomes a question separate from what the mechanism is. Whereas statistics remain useful to determine how generally operative a mechanism is, in order to determine what the mechanism is in the first place, ethnography and other intensive methods remain of scientific importance. CR, unlike positivism, supports a plurality of scientific methods.

References

Alston, W. (1997). *A realist conception of truth.* Ithaca, NY: Cornell University Press.

Apel, K. O. (2003). The response of discourse ethics to the moral challenge of the human situation as such and especially today. Wilsele, Belgium: Peeters.

Archer, M., Bhaskar, R., Collier, A., Lawson, T., & Norrie, A. (Eds.). (1998). *Critical realism: Essential readings.* New York, NY: Routledge.

Bhaskar, R. (2008). *A realist theory of science.* London, England: Verso.

-------. (2009). *Scientific realism and human emancipation.* New York, NY: Routledge.

Brentano, F. (1973). *Psychology from an empirical standpoint.* (A. C. Rancurello, D. B. Terrell, and L. McAlister, Trans.). London, England: Routledge.

Buber, M. (1970). *I-Thou.* (W. Kaufmann, Trans.). New York, NY: Charles Scribner's Sons.

Butler, J. (2006). Gender trouble: Feminism and the subversion of identity. New York, NY: Routledge.

Coole, D., & Frost, S. (Eds.). (2010). *New materialisms: Ontology, agency, and politics.* Durham, NC: Duke University Press.

Derrida, J. (1988). *Of grammatology.* (G. C. Spivak, Trans.). Evanston, IL: Northwestern University Press.

Habermas, J. (1999). *Moral consciousness and communicative action.* Cambridge, MA: The MIT Press.

Haraway, D. (1991). Simians, cyborgs, and women: The reinvention of nature. New York, NY: Routledge.

Hartwig, M. (2007). *Dictionary of critical realism.* New York, NY: Routledge.

Pickering, A. (2012). The world since Kuhn. *Social Studies of Science, 42*(3), 467-473.

Poster, M. (2001). Introduction. In Marc Poster (Ed.), *Baudrillard: Selected writings.* Stanford, CA: Stanford University Press.

Porpora, D. V. (2001). Landscapes of the soul: The loss of moral meaning in American life. New York, NY: Oxford University Press.

-------. (2015). *Reconstructing sociology: The critical realist approach.* New York, NY: Cambridge University Press.

Douglas V. Porpora, PhD, is a professor of sociology at Drexel University in Philadelphia, PA. He is also a professor of sociology in the Department of Culture and Communication. He has written widely on social theory and philosophy of science. His most recent book, *Reconstructing Sociology: The Critical Realist Approach*, will be released in October 2016. His empirical work concerns the social creation of moral indifference and the failure of American public moral discourse. He is co-editor of *The Journal for the Theory of Social Behaviour*.

Inside-Out: The Mindfulness-Based Interventions as a Model for Community Development

By Donald McCown, PhD
West Chester University of Pennsylvania, United States

Abstract

Even though mindfulness-based interventions (MBIs) were developed as contemporary applications of contemplative practice, they reflect the same psychologically reductionist individualism that ultimately maintains the oppressions of neoliberal power in our society. However, by recognizing that the MBIs are *group-based* and *relational*, we become aware of new and powerful possibilities. An MBI group, then, is seen as a potential site of resistance to modern trends toward isolation and subjectification; such a group can even become a model for building just and caring communities. Forgoing a conclusion, this chapter opens another inquiry, looking more closely at what makes an MBI class work as a transformative community. No resolution is proposed; rather, there is an open-ended contemplation of the utility and power of the *sublime*.

Introduction

Despite the aura of innovation that characterizes the contemporary application of contemplative practices in medical and mental healthcare treatment, mindfulness-based interventions (MBIs) ultimately serve to maintain the oppressions of neoliberal power because they are framed within psychologically reductionistic individualism. Within psychological science, pathologies are viewed as located "inside" the individual, to be solved by "inner" changes that are actuated and controlled by professional expertise. This view is all but unchallenged in the scientific evidence base that has supported the dramatic growth of MBIs.

However, when we remember the often overlooked fact that MBIs are group-based and relational—that is, when we turn the MBIs *inside out*—we become aware of new and powerful possibilities that extend far beyond individual wellness and recovery, and that in turn can open considerations of deepened community. From this reversed perspective, an MBI group may be seen as a site of resistance to the isolation and subjectification that is the experience of people with diagnoses of mental and physical disorders, and of anyone who is embedded in what Kenneth Gergen (1994) refers to as a "culture of deficit." MBI curricula and the atmosphere created in the unfolding actions of such groups might be analyzed at a different level, as vehicles or catalysts for a larger undertaking of building just and caring communities.

This chapter pursues the possibilities of understanding groups, using the framework of the MBI curricula, as gatherings within which participants experience being together in ways that undermine the discourses of individualism and deficit. These groups would instead reflect the concept of *friendship*, as it is variously conceived within the contemplative traditions. Such groups may be seen as unintentional intentional communities of the moment. They are limited in their time of existence, being together only long enough for participants to take on new potentials for being together. Percival Goodman and Paul Goodman (1960) offer a timeless reminder:

> Yet perhaps the very transitoriness of such intensely motivated intentional communities is part of their perfection. Disintegrating, they irradiate society with people who have been profoundly touched by the excitement of community life, who do not forget the advantages but try to realize them in new ways..Perhaps these communities are like those "little magazines" and "little theaters" that do not outlive their first few performances, yet from them comes all the vitality of the next generation of everybody's literature (p. 109).

We will begin with a description of the relational dimensions of MBIs, in which the *pedagogy* rather than the meditation practice is presented as the work of the group. This work generates an atmosphere and ethos that is named an *ethical space* (McCown, 2013, 2016). A model is presented in which the ethical space is formed as participants attend to and care for their bodies, observe the contingency of their singular and shared experiences, and allow an unhindered emergence of meaning. In addition, the space is formed by absences—of the diagnostic deficit discourse, of hierarchical power relationships, and of prescriptive instrumental uses of contemplative practice. The model is entirely pervaded by the characteristic of friendship, in which the participants *steep* again and again.

Second, we will explore the process and outcome of this steeping. It juxtaposes a variety of insights: From neurophysiology, we consider Stephen Porges's (2011) *polyvagal theory*; from social psychology, Kenneth Gergen's (1994) idea of *relational being*; and from anthropology, Tim Ingold's (2013) concept of *enskillment*. The object of this bricolage is to brighten our understanding of how the intense experience of an eight-week MBI course can infuse participants with new potentials for being together in "community." It also infuses them with how they may then irradiate the other communities they inhabit, as well as the larger society.

Third, we begin to think about practical approaches to community development. We will take hold of the two ends of Western thinking, from Aristotle's vision of friendship as a key to the flourishing of the *polis* to the aporetic attempts of contemporary philosophers to attain such a goal. While this chapter makes no attempt at prescription or resolution, its integration of the relational and the contemplative dimensions may point toward novel pathways for practice.

Finally, this chapter will forego a conclusion, instead opening another inquiry about attempting to look more closely at what makes an

MBI class work as a community. The intensity of the atmosphere may be what is transformative, and it may be better described in aesthetic terms than educational or clinical ones. Instead of conclusions, we will engage in an open-ended contemplation on the utility and power of the *sublime*.

The Relational Dimension of the MBIs

The realm of the relational in MBIs is relatively unexplored and certainly under-researched. This is unsurprising, given the nearly four decades of focused efforts aspiring to or modeled on medicine's gold standard of the randomized controlled trial (RCT). This work is now coming to its cultural fruition, resulting not only in scientific legitimation and adoption within medicine and mental health care, but also in popular acceptance and promotion in a wide range of applications within scientific cultures, both East and West.

Misdirection

The success of the legitimation of positivism within the social sciences required large-scale adoption of prevailing diagnostic systems, acceptance of the reductionist individualism that underpins the medical model, and submission of participants to treatment and surveillance by professionals. Much has been gained, particularly in the enormous expansion of the MBIs to help relieve suffering in medical and mental health care settings. At the same time, much has been lost. Such an understanding has limited the potential of these forms of practice, which might offer greater freedom to individual participants. It has also limited the possibilities of understanding the role that learning contemplative practices might play in the transformation of small groups and larger communities.

Consider that a single quantitative study (Imel, Baldwin, Bonus, & MacCoon, 2008) remains the principal indicator for MBI group effects. The study is of scientific significance, with a sample size of nearly 60 MBSR groups and more than 600 participants, and statistical controls for pretreatment symptom severity and teacher effects. The effect of the group on its participants accounted for seven percent of the variability in outcome. For perspective, consider that the highly vaunted therapeutic alliance in psychotherapy, closely associated with positive outcomes, accounts for about five percent of variability (Horvath & Bedi, 2002). In a model of curative factors (Miller, Hubble, & Duncan, 1999), the therapeutic alliance is about 30%; replacing that with this group effect would put it at 40% of curative factors, a powerful influence. Imel, Baldwin, Bonus, and MacCoon (2008) note:

> MBSR does not appear to simply be an individual intervention delivered in a group setting, but rather its methods and effects occur at the individual and group levels. Thus, group variables are not merely a statistical nuisance to be controlled in the hopes of detecting the direct effects of meditation techniques, but important treatment variables worthy of clinical attention and empirical investigation (p. 742).

However, such is the hold of the individualist orientation among MBI researchers that pursuit of these insights has not become a priority.

The relatively few qualitative studies of MBI classroom experiences also perpetuate the individualist perspective. In a review of 17 studies, Dulcie Cormack (2012) found that group experience provides individual participants with a supportive and normalizing environment, motivates and supports meditation practice, provides a sense of belonging and community, and supports the learning of mindfulness. However, the effect on the group itself has not been a specific subject of inquiry.

Even MBI teachers, who live deeply within the relationships of the group, are often misdirected by the reductionist individualism of clinical thinking. A qualitative study of the teacher's role (van Aalderen,

Breukers, Reuzel, & Speckens, 2012) suggests that teachers fail to recognize how highly participants value the group's support. Participants
do not simply value encouragement from their peers; they also grow
in relationships to find themselves less dependent on the teacher. This
irony is not lost on the authors, who note, "Although some teachers
are aware of the importance of the group, the importance might be an
underestimated factor in the MBCT training and might need more attention in training teachers" (p. 171).

Misdefinition

The MBI community has struggled from the start to operationalize a
definition of mindfulness for its research. Scientists as well as philosophers and religion scholars have been dancing around definitions rooted in the twin assumptions that the meditation practice is the key to
MBI efficacy, and that the individualist view of contemporary clinical
practice is correct and unassailable. We can add to this, of course, the
debates of the interpreters of Buddhist concepts of mindfulness, calling
on philological studies of Pali and Sanskrit terms such as *sati* and *sm-
rti*. We can also compare practices and uses of mindfulness across and
between Buddhist traditions widely separated in time and geographic
location. This has generated far more heat than light, even expanding to
fill a special issue of the journal *Contemporary Buddhism* (Williams &
Kabat-Zinn, 2011).

　　The misdirection of such efforts is obvious when we turn to the
relational view. Wittgenstein's (1953) concept of a "language game"
comes to bear. He suggests that a word comes into its meaning through
its use within a form of life, a community. The most important community in this case is decidedly not the community of researchers and
scholars in the MBIs. Rather, it is each MBI classroom with its participants and teacher. The meaning of "mindfulness" that matters there is
not—indeed, cannot be—imposed from outside or above and remain
fixed. Instead, it is *co-created* within the actions and relationships in

each class. Therefore, mindfulness is not most usefully thought of as a skill or mind state that each participant comes to own. It is better considered as identical with its pedagogy, which is a relational process, a growing into a different way of being with others. This is the view through which we can begin to understand the possibilities of its use in community development.

Co-creation

The pedagogical activities in the MBI classroom are participatory explorations prompted by the structure of the curriculum. A full analysis of this structure may be found in my work with colleagues, *Teaching Mindfulness: A Practical Guide for Clinicians and Educators* (McCown, Reibel, & Micozzi, 2010). A distillation useful for the purpose here would include the co-creation of a definition of mindfulness, an approach to dialogue, and an attitude toward experience. The ongoing elaboration of these three activities across the weeks of the course is the essence of the curriculum, if it is possible to say that.

The definition of mindfulness is a co-creation that is very often seeded by Jon Kabat-Zinn's (1994) highly influential "paying attention in a particular way: on purpose, in the present moment, and nonjudgmentally" (p. 4). This incorporates the duration of the program, then, negotiated by the group through evolving understandings of this, shared aloud by participants in dialogue and inquiry with the teacher about experiences, and shared as well in participants' "unfinished dialogues," which is a relational way of speaking about thinking. From first class to last, the definition of mindfulness is in constant flux as experiences unfold.

The approach to dialogue is often framed by Kabat-Zinn's (1990) line, "from our point of view, as long as you are breathing, there is more right with you than there is wrong..." (p. 2). The guideline that arises is that no one is broken, so no one needs fixing. The actions of the participants toward each other in classroom dialogues (and unfinished dialogues) rest on the co-created sense of this respite from pathologizing and surveillance.

The attitude is the key move of the pedagogy, which Kabat-Zinn (1990) has expressed as "putting out the welcome mat" (p. 295) and Saki Santorelli (1999) names "hospitality" in the profound sense of the religious traditions. "Mindfulness is an act of hospitality," he notes (p. 74). The key move is to be open to whatever comes through experience, to take the chance that it may be enemy or angel, as in the Bible story of Abraham extending lavish hospitality to three men who turn out to be angels bringing blessing (Genesis 18:1-5). We could say that this attitude is to choose to be with and in the experience of the moment.

Of course, none of the texts quoted from Kabat-Zinn and Santorelli are meant to be memorized or held as authoritative in the classroom. Rather, the true texts of the MBIs are the experiences of the participants reported in dialogue with the teacher and class (or held in unfinished dialogue). The knowledge of the group is co-created and made available in this way, in a distributed fashion.

The Ethical Space of Mindfulness

From the work of co-creation in the classroom comes a potential way of being together that may be referred to as the *ethical space* of mindfulness (McCown, 2013). This ethical space can become the basis for thinking through contemplative contributions to community development. It can be outlined in three dimensions: a dimension of three pedagogical actions; another of refraining from three actions; and a third that gives character to the others.

The "Doing" Dimension. Actions of the pedagogy are actions of all participants. The teacher, as one who tends the curriculum, is a catalyst, while the co-creation of the class includes all. How this may be so will become clear as we move beyond definitions of what the space comprises to analyze how it works.

The active contributions to the qualities of the ethical space can be listed as three Cs: corporeality; contingency; and cosmopolitanism.

Corporeality is the quality that foregrounds the experience of the body. The corporeal focus in mindfulness practice is quickly recognized as different from typical modes of investigation in mental health interventions. Mindfulness meditation is founded on sensation, particularly of the breath moving in the body. The senses of proprioception and interception generated through this focus help to bring participants into intimate contact with their present moment experience in new ways. It helps make aesthetic and affective experiences available for exploration and dialogue. The most common inquiry about an experience—whether thought, emotion, or sensation—is "What is that like, in your body? How does it feel?" As participants become more proficient with this way of exploring, they find many opportunities for unfinished dialogues.

Contingency is the quality that deconstructs these corporeal experiences, as the class tracks the arising and subsiding of sensations, emotions, and thoughts. The curriculum is designed around opportunities for participants to undergo such changes. They observe how sensations continually change and pass away. They come to recognize the association of distressing (or desired) emotion to the arising and passing away of sensations. Further, they begin to notice the evanescent quality of thoughts, from which insight and meaning may arise.

Cosmopolitanism is the quality that allows the meaning created by participants in the group to be met without commentary, correction, or critique from some privileged outside position. This quality is particularly important because participants often open up to the spiritual dimensions of their lives, with specific religious commitments and interpretations, or an ever-shifting but profound curiosity.

The "Non-Doing" Dimension. There is a significant difference between the MBIs (particularly MBSR) and more typical therapeutic group interventions. Three qualities outline that difference: non-pathologizing; non-hierarchical; and non-instrumental.

Non-pathologizing refers to the defining perspective of Ka-bat-Zinn's (1990) statement, "If you are breathing, there is more right with you than there is wrong" (p. 2). There is freedom in the encounters of the group—from diagnostic labeling, from expectations of a particular role, and from self-surveillance. Opportunities are available for participants to discover on their own, and with caring others, how to work with and around their singular suffering to live the fullest life possible.

Non-hierarchical refers to the fact that each participant is the expert of his or her own experience. The term describes the group's relationship in dialogue, in which no one is expert on the unfolding experience of the present moment. No meaning can be imposed from without. To phrase it in American vernacular speech, the teacher is as clueless as anyone else and is simply interested in facilitating explorations.

Non-instrumental is perhaps the most important of the three qualities, and it may be the most difficult to grasp. It signals that the class does not practice the pedagogy of mindfulness in order to be changed or transformed in a particular way. Mindfulness practice is not "because" or "in order to"; it is instead an exploration of the unknown of the present moment. Transformation, however, is in the nature of the practice—watching all contingent structures of sensation, affect, and thought deconstruct themselves as they unfold within the space and its associated qualities: always changing; eluding ultimate meaning; guided only by the relationships of the moment.

The third dimension. Friendship is not actually an additional dimension; rather, it is the total character of the confluence of the MBIs. It is not "held" by the teacher in some way. There is no choice to be friendly; instead, friendship is a "possibility of being" in which participants in MBIs steep. The friendship of the ethical space is a living relationship that need not be spoken, and often is not. Ralph Waldo Emerson (1841/2000) captures this feeling in the opening paragraph of his essay "Friendship":

We have a great deal more kindness than is ever spoken. Maugre all the selfishness that chills like east winds the world, the whole human family is bathed with an element of love like a fine ether. How many persons we meet in houses, whom we scarcely speak to, whom yet we honor, and who honor us! How many we see on the street, or sit with in church, whom, though silently, we warmly rejoice to be with! Read the language of these wandering eyebeams. The heart knoweth (p. 201).

Space, Objects, and Atmosphere

What must be made clear here is that the ethical space in which participants steep is not a cognitive or metaphorical space; it is the real architectural volume in which the group is gathered. The participants, furnishings, and objects of the room, as well as how all of that is organized and contained, contribute to the atmosphere that makes it possible for participants to welcome whatever comes. This is the key move of the pedagogy. This atmosphere is experienced by participants objectively and subjectively, from both without *and* within, through an undivided relationship between self and other (Böhme, 1993, 2011; Bollnow, 2011; Ingold, 2015). Participants can engage in dialogue about, and even agree on, the answer to the question, "What is it like in the room right now?"

Sites of Steeping and Infusion

We move now to some descriptions of how an experience of "undivided relationship between self and other" may come about. This is difficult to speak about in most Western languages because individualist notions are so well supported by vocabulary and grammar. Languages of collective cultures can contribute helpful and valuable terms if they are adopted.[1] The descriptions thus far have referred to participants in groups or classes, typically understood as aggregates of discrete individuals. As we move into the second part of this chapter, the intent is to shift that typical understanding, to make it sensible to read the words "participant" or "group" as placeholders for something without separation.

The descriptions below are from different discourses—religion, social psychology, neurophysiology, and anthropology—that capture many facets of this holistic subject and yet are challenging to integrate. They are presented, therefore, in the spirit of bricolage, trusting that the result of their juxtapositions is more than the sum of the parts, while aware that there can be no settled whole. The ultimate hope is for more clarity and more mystery, simultaneously.

A Spiritual Model

Within a religious community, there can be the experience of "undivided relationship between self and other." In the Society of Friends (Quakers), for example, the meeting for worship is framed as a silent waiting for the moving of the Spirit. This "waiting" is meant in the older sense of attending to a royal personage. The practice involves being still and silent yet ready to respond fully and sensitively to whatever is required in the moment. In this practice of waiting as a community, special times come:

> A blanket of divine covering comes over the room, and a quickening Presence pervades us, breaking down some part of the special privacy and isolation of our individual lives and bonding our spirits within a super-individual Life and Power—an objective, dynamic Presence which enfolds us all, nourishes our souls, speaks glad, unutterable comfort within us, and quickens in us depths that had before been slumbering. The Burning Bush has been kindled in our midst, and we stand together on holy ground (Kelly, 1947).

This vignette is the example we will consider, although there are many other routes we could take. In fact, the MBI group as a site of transformation echoes other historical and contemporary paradigms. We could add many more pieces to our bricolage, including Vittorio Gallese's (2003) "we centric" space, Edward Tronick's (2007) dyadic states of consciousness, Yvonne Agazarian's (1997) living human systems, Len Vygotsky's (1978) Zone of Proximal Development, John Shotter's (2008) spontaneous joint action, Martin Buber's (1947) possibility of silent dialogue, Arnold van Gennep and Monica B. Visedon's (1909) rites of passage, and Victor Turner's (1969) liminality and communitas (1969).

Confluence

Gergen's (2009) discourse on *relational being* outlines a view of life with others that helps turn the MBIs inside out. He describes the reductionist, individualist view as *bounded being*, in which autonomous selves set their own intentions and take voluntary actions in a world characterized by causality. This is the world of Western clinical practice, in which we explain how people are broken on the inside; research then finds ways of fixing people by putting something else inside—a virtue, a belief, a pill, even a meditation practice. It is a world of pathology, expertise, and instrumental intervention. On the other hand, what Gergen calls relational being is *unbounded*. There is no preexisting inner "me" that can be broken and then fixed. That which can be labeled as me is co-created within relationships moment by moment. If I am in distress, I am not broken inside and in need of a fix; instead, an adjustment in the relationship may change how I feel.

As noted, the language we have inherited is within the bounded discourse, so new terms must come into play. Gergen uses the idea of *confluence*, in which a group of "participants" (who are not discrete individuals) mutually define each other within the activity of the moment. For example, in an MBI class, a session of formal meditation mutually defines meditators who are sitting still and quiet, and a teacher who is speaking words of "guidance." Then, when that meditation confluence ends, the meditators become dyad partners in the new confluence that forms as they speak aloud to one another.

In the confluence, there is no causality. Nothing forces the participants or teacher to do what they do; it is in the relationship. Likewise, there is no agency. No force inside compels any particular actions. Whatever happens next in the class issues from the confluence of relationships in which, say, a plenary dialogue of teacher and participants makes sense.

A confluence and the mutually defining relationships that it comprises imbue participants with what Gergen (2009) refers to as *potentials* for being and acting in particular ways. A vast store of such specialized ways of being is developed—a *multi-being*, as it were—throughout life in many and varied confluences. In another situation, another relationship, any and all of these potentials are then available as required. As Gergen puts it, "In sum, all meaning/full relationships leave us with another's way of being, a self that we become through the relationship, and a choreography of co-action. From these three sources, we emerge with enormous possibilities for being" (p. 137).

Neurophysiology

Key to a scientific description of the ethical space is the action of the mirror neurons in the brain's motor cortex. These help to sense, represent, and track another's actions and intentions (Gallese, 2003). Through this mechanism, we can coordinate our movements with, and understand the emotional and physical condition of, another person.

When we witness another's pain or joy, we feel it in our bodies. What we see activates the brain's "resonance circuit," as Daniel Siegel (2007) calls it. This circuit carries our perception of the other's movement or expression to the mirror neuron system (where we "try it on"), to the superior temporal cortex (where we learn how it feels in the body), then through the insula to the limbic system (to grasp emotional content), and back through the insula to the prefrontal cortex, where we can think about how the other feels (Carr, Iacoboni, Dubeau, Mazziotta, & Lenzi, 2003).

Siegel (2007) suggests that this interpersonal resonance circuit also works *intra*personally for the person practicing meditation. The prefrontal cortex is active, so it downregulates the limbic system, particularly the amygdalae, thus reducing negative effects such as anxiety and fear (Creswell, Way, Eisenberger, & Lieberman, 2007; Lieberman, Eisenberger, Crockett, Tom, Pfeifer, & Way, 2007). In an MBI class, then, we can consider that many participants are resonating intrapersonally and feeling some equanimity. Their faces and body postures reflect this. They look relaxed or perhaps even happy.

Now we need to add one more neuroscientific concept: Stephen Porges's (2011) "polyvagal theory" of autonomic nervous system (ANS) regulation. This theory is based on the evolution of the ANS, particularly the vagus nerves. Mammals have three subsystems, from three phylogenetic stages. These are linked to three behavioral strategies for adapting to (1) catastrophic and life-threatening situations, (2) challenging or dangerous ones, and (3) situations of safety and caring. In order, the strategies are *freeze*, *fight*, or *flight*, and Porges's contribution of *social engagement*. This fourth and surprising response is associated with the latest phylogenetic stage's subsystem. When we sense safety in the environment, the heart rate slows, the fight or flight reaction is inhibited, and we are prepared to be together with others in a caring and productive way. In fact, the muscles of the face and head gain tone for optimal expressiveness and reception of communication. Our eyes open wider to see others better, our ears are tuned to the range of the human voice (and away from sounds of predators or alarm), the face and neck muscles are toned to make subtle expressions and gestures, and the voice becomes richer and more variable. Best of all, there is a release of oxytocin, the "love" hormone of birthing, nursing, and pair bonding.

The togetherness of the group is a feeling, not a thought or idea.

Arriving in the MBI group, participants, some of whom may be in an anxious state, begin to discover familiar or friendly faces, voices, gestures, and postures. After a session of meditation practice, when many are relaxed and emotionally regulated, this is even more likely. In such a human environment, the sense of calm and safety may tip the group into the social engagement response, which is self-reinforcing as it travels through the mirror neurons and resonance systems around the group. As a result, participants may find it easier, or at least possible, to make the key move of the pedagogy—to turn toward and be with/in whatever experience is arising in the present moment. The welcome mat begins to roll out. By steeping in this atmosphere again and again, participants are infused with a potential to help co-create it, so that they can feel it in other situations as well. This affect may be a permanent change in how the participants engage and connect. We will return to this shortly.

Enskillment

Anthropologist Tim Ingold (2008) brings another view of steeping and infusing. He offers the example of a child learning to make an omelet. Because every egg is different, there is not one right way to crack any given one. The would-be cook must learn the feel of it, again and again, from skilled hands—not just watching, but having those hands guide hers. This process is specific to the actions, certainly, but also specific to the particular kitchen, its bowls and pans, utensils, and stove. Thus the "knowledge" of the process is located outside, not "inside," the child: "You only get an omelet from a cook-in-the-kitchen," Ingold says (p. 116). MBI course participants go through this process of finding how to make the key move of the pedagogy—rolling out the welcome mat—and to be together with others in the ethical space. An MBI teacher may begin the process as a catalyst, yet the entire group contributes to the co-creation of this potential. Participants sense into it in a specific place, with specific others, and get the feel for it, growing *into* knowledge, as Ingold (2013) puts it.

(Un)intentional Communities

Now we reach the crux of these considerations: Is it possible that the potentials infused in participants of MBI programs can be useful, even transformative, in the constitution of other groups, organizations, and the larger society? Recall Goodman and Goodman's (1960) insight about intentional communities: "Disintegrating, they irradiate society with people who have been profoundly touched by the excitement of community life, who do not forget the advantages but try to realize them in new ways" (p. 109). Every eight weeks or so, an MBI class that has steeped in its atmosphere and practices disintegrates. These classes are decidedly not intentional communities; community is a side effect, as it were, of the intervention, which is targeted at individual outcomes. The classes are, then, naïve to the building of community as it happens. They are *un*intentional communities that nonetheless release the potential for transformation.

In our exploration, it may be helpful to think along with some of those who have shared the same concerns—from Aristotle, strongly invested in the flourishing of the *polis*, to current philosophers such as Jean-Luc Nancy (1991), Maurice Blanchot and Pierre Joris (1988), and Giorgio Agamben and Michael Hardt (1993). There is a common struggle to conceive of the very possibility of a community that neither demands conformity nor excludes the other.

Aristotle's Excellent Friendship

Aristotle's discussion of friendship, possibly the most important discussion of virtue in the *Nichomachean Ethics*, is significantly longer than any other; it is fully 20% of the work. It concerns him deeply because he is searching for ways of being that will lead to the flourishing of the *polis*. In opening his discussion, he makes links between friendship, enmity, justice, and something beyond.

In a translation of 1155a21-29 presented by Claudia Baracchi (2008), Aristotle says, "In travels, too, one may observe how close and dear every human being is to every other human being" (p. 261). This statement offers an image of how travelers—on a sea voyage, in ancient times, perhaps—respond to their shared vulnerability to storm and accident and other vicissitudes of nature and the journey. (This is a little like an MBI class, yes?) He suggests that the solidarity, sympathy, and like-mindedness that arise are like the excellent form of friendship (*teleia philia*). The next lines push further, stating that:

> ...friendship seems to hold a *polis* together, too, and lawgivers seem to pay more attention to friendship than to justice; for concord seems to be somewhat akin to friendship, and this they aim at most of all and try their utmost to drive out faction, which is enmity (p. 261).

Here Aristotle implies the tendency of likeminded communities to create outsiders and insiders, to amplify differences and engender conflict, and to require rule of law. This concern links him to thinkers today, as we will see. At last, he notes, "And when human beings are friends, they have no need of justice at all, but when they are just, they still need friendship; and that which is most just is thought to be done in a friendly way" (p. 261). So, friendship in its excellent form exceeds justice. It is not simply just; it comprises a superfluity of benevolence.

This excellent form of friendship is analogous, if not identical, to the character of friendship in the ethical space of mindfulness. It is relational in a particular manner. Aristotle notes in 1156b7-10 that the friends involved are not oriented toward each other, looking to gain something that the other owns; instead, they share a common orientation toward excellence, toward the good:

Perfect friendship is between human beings who are good and similar with respect to virtue; for, insofar as they are good, it is in a similar manner that they wish each other the good, and such human beings are good in themselves (Baracchi, 2008, p. 268).

In the case of the MBI class, the good that participants are oriented toward is the key move of the pedagogy, the turning toward and being with/in the experience of the present moment. Each participant is steeping in the possibility of this orientation. The class, then, is a gathering of friends facing their own lives together, creating something barely acknowledged among them.

Interlude: First-Order Moralities

As we have seen, the structure of the ethical space takes care of itself. When the class is practicing the pedagogy, participants have a particular know-how about being both with themselves and being together. Gergen (2009) calls this a first-order morality; the confluence, as he would put it, has defined its own goods, and those in the confluence will act in accordance with those goods. A first-order morality is not written out or encoded; it is inherent in the co-creation of the confluence. For Aristotle, perhaps, this would be why there is "no need for justice at all" within perfect friendship.

The difficulty with first-order moralities is that the multi-beings of participants contain potentials from other first-order moralities. For example, if for some reason a participant cannot stay with the key move of the pedagogy, even with the help of the teacher, that participant may "step out" of the ethical space and disturb the confluence by enacting other potentials from other first-order moralities. The teacher may "step out" of the ethical space of mindfulness and align instead with the ethical code of her particular profession—psychologist, social worker, nurse, or physician—and that code comes into play, structuring relationships in terms of rules, rather than friendship.

As they steep in the confluence of the ethical space, participants are infused with potentials. They develop a greater capacity to turn toward and be with/in what is arising in the moment. The more they steep, the less likely it is that they will "step out" and interrupt that steeping, and the more likely the confluence will continue reinforcing the potential of friendship.

A Postmodern Aporia

The know-how that MBI participants come to have about being with themselves and being with others is not explicit. Participants are enacting a potential with which they have been imbued by steeping in the group. There are no rules, no procedures, there is simply (or not so simply) a way of being in the moment. In the practice of the pedagogy, this potential goes very nearly unremarked, so we are considering not only an unintentional community but also an unremarkable one.

This undefined sort of community has connections to the thinking of a number of contemporary philosophers on this central concern. Blanchot (1988), in *The Unavowable Community*, describes the aporia clearly:

> If the relation of man with man ceases to be that of Same with Same, but rather introduces the other as irreducible and—given the equality between them—always in a situation of dissymmetry in relation to the one looking at that Other, then a completely different relationship imposes itself and imposes another form of society which one would hardly dare call a "community" (p. 3).

The defining of a community leads to fusion of its members and the loss of each member's individuality. It seems we cannot be in the community and also be an irreducible singularity. Choosing one locks the other out. At the same time, singularity does not exclude interaction and transformation. That is, in fact, an important point to remember. Singularity does not necessarily coincide with atomism. Openness might be seen as a process, life being a flux of experiences from openness to closeness in the next now because situations change and people develop.

It does not even seem possible to imagine a community in which all are included. Blanchot (1988) suggests that such a community would be an absence of community, that we could all belong to the absence. Certainly this has powerful resonance in an abstract consideration, but could it be practicable? The study of the gathering that is an MBI class belongs in a different discourse than the attempt to reconcile this aporia. However, it is possible to identify partial connections—such as resonances, perhaps—in the thought process and direction that may better reveal the value of an unintentional contemplative community.

The ethical space of the MBIs allows for the singularity of each participant to be expressed in the class, while a sense of belonging (though often unremarked) is present as well. The non-doing dimension does the work. The non-pathologizing quality prevents limiting identities from being imposed, from within or without. Participants are free from expectations of fixing or being fixed, and from surveillance and self-surveillance. The nonhierarchical quality emphasizes the expertise of each participant in his own situation, reinforcing his autonomy while acting as a shared characteristic. Finally, the noninstrumental quality undermines any sense of comparison or competition with fellow participants because there is no goal to strive for, no change or transformation to make one better (than oneself or another).

The balance of singularity and community is clearly expressed in a formulation of the group for use by the teacher in observing what is happening within it. The formulation was drawn directly from practice, identifying the need to balance *freedom* (to live from one's singularity of being) with *belonging* (which acknowledges the acceptance of one's singularity in the group) and *resonance* (which is the affective tone of the experience for the participants), and is shared (McCown et al., 2010). The model describes a circular relation: The group operates at an optimum level when these three forces are balanced, each contributing to the other, but collapses should even one of them weaken. This seems to be a resolution to the aporia that concerns us. It is, however, constrained in its possible applications by the limits of the MBI class—small size, short duration, and the very specific context of medical and mental health care. However, it may also be possible that these limits are valuable in practice.

The *doing dimension* of the ethical space also makes very concrete contributions to the solution of the aporia; through steeping, the capacities are imbued. The emphasis on corporeality sensitizes participants to affective experiences, bringing them more into their singular self-understanding. It also promotes the aesthetic response, with its possibilities for shared experience. Contingency opens new vistas of the temporal, with self and context constantly in flux. Cosmopolitanism supports hospitality, insisting on openness and courage in holding the meanings that emerge both within the group and within the individual. The welcome mat rolls out for all.

An important side note here is that the pedagogical skills in use in the MBIs contribute to the generation of the ethical space, reducing the resistance of participants, giving them their freedom, but also the chance of belonging and resonance in the group. All elements of the context influence the experience: whether it is a secular course in a hospital or a spiritual course in a Zen center; whether the course is free or participants pay a fee; whether the teacher is secular or a guru. Other factors include the culture that hosts the course, who the participants are, and the verbal and nonverbal language symbols used.

While there are many considerations of technique in guidance that colleagues and I have parsed (Moss, Reibel, & McCown, 2016), a simplified discussion of them uses the skillfulness of diplomats as an epitome. As Richard Sennett notes (2013), this ancient craft applies three modes of practice. First, one does not insist on one's own ideas but takes on another's view of the situation. Our question is, from whose position are we guiding? The teacher, the participant, the confluence? Second, one deploys the *subjunctive mood* in language as much as possible, using "what if..." and "perhaps..." constructions to open up possibilities for dialogue. Third is *sprezzatura,* or a lightness of touch, a nonchalance that makes it difficult for others to find offense in what one says. This was recommended by Baldassare Castiglione (1523/1976), a 16th-century Italian diplomat, in his *Book of the Courtier.* Lives are difficult, and in the MBI classroom lightness and humor are a powerful salve. Steeping in these diplomatic skills, participants are infused with them, and may find that in other situations they have ways to bring others together readily available.

An Ambiguity of Presence

For the contemporary philosophers with whom we are thinking, one example of an event of community, a moment when "there is no need of justice at all," would be the political moment in France in 1968. Blanchot (1988) describes that moment as:

> ...an incomparable form of society that remained elusive, that was not meant to survive, to set itself up, not even via the multiple "committees" simulating a disordered-order, an imprecise specialization. Contrary to "traditional revolutions," it was not a question of taking power to replace it with some other power. . . . It was not even a question of overthrowing an old world; what mattered was to let a possibility manifest itself, the possibility—beyond any utilitarian gain—of a *being-together* that gave back to all the right to equality and fraternity through a freedom of speech that elated

everyone...Poetry was an everyday affair (pp. 29-30).

Here is a grander analog to the ethical space of the MBI classroom, with its (potential) overthrow of the medical model and the possibility for each participant to experience the present moment as a singularity in a being-together that contributes to but does not detract from the experience. There is a presence in the present that is ineffable though not inexpressible—poetry is an everyday affair in the MBIs. We may turn back to Blanchot's (1988) description: "That was, and still is, the ambiguity of presence—understood as instantly realized utopia—and therefore without future, therefore without present: in suspension as if to open time to a beyond of its usual determinations" (p. 31).

The ethical space is created spontaneously, without directives, in the event of the co-creation of the pedagogy of the MBIs. Unintentional communities come into being, week after week, steeping in the play of their own skills and insights. The participants (multi-beings) that comprise them are imbued with new capacities to recreate the way of being together, again and again. Those capacities may ultimately carry far beyond the dissolution of the MBI class community (finally acknowledged in its last moments) and irradiate through presence the possibility of poetry in everyday interactions in a world that is always poised on the brink of community.

A Conclusion That Begins in Death

There is a power hidden somewhere in the group that makes the ethical space, that makes unintentional community present itself. Blanchot (1988) suggests that community is founded on the death of another person:

> To remain present in the proximity of another who by
> dying removes himself definitively, to take upon my-
> self another's death as the only death that concerns me,
> this is what puts me beside myself, this is the only sep-

aration that can open me, in its very impossibility to the
Openness of a community (p. 9).

In the existential intensity of an MBI class, in which participants directly encounter their own suffering (and the possibility of death) with and
through the others' situations at the limit, strong affective charges arise,
and the participants co-create a way of being with such a situation.

Clearly, something is at work in the MBI group when it is
co-creating mindfulness with and around its most vulnerable participants. We might look at this as an experience akin to (if not exactly) the
aesthetic response of the *sublime*. Sublime as a term has a long history
and many uses and interpretations. To choose a useful one, the 18th-cen-
tury Irish philosopher Edmund Burke (1759/1999) makes the experience of "terror" a central idea in his definition. The terror to which he
refers is found in viewing overwhelming natural phenomena, such as
storms at sea or ascents of mountains, in which death can be seen as immanent even though, as a spectator, one is not in immediate danger. One
cannot express such experiences, and so is carried beyond the rational
dimension, and ultimately beyond the limited self. The sense of "I" is
reduced and one becomes more open to the experience.

In an MBI group, then, the moments when participants confront
more of the fullness and contingency of human existence—the possibilities of death and madness, to name two extremes—may be considered
sublime. As Burke and other theorists note, *the terror of the sublime*
may include a paradoxical sense of pleasure which, Burke suggests,
becomes possible when there is space for observation. One may watch
a frightening storm at sea from the safety of land. Likewise, in an MBI
classroom, one may witness a courageous grappling with anxiety or
grief while seated in a chair across the room. One may even view one's
own frightening situation with the clarity of mindfulness practice and
the support of a silent, caring, resonant group.

The experience of the sublime arises in observing in a clear and spacious way the things that may deeply frighten or move us. It is made possible in the group by the co-creation of mindfulness, turning towards and being with/in the experience of the moment. And so, the sublime is a possible measure for the "working" of the MBI group. When the atmosphere in the classroom has been sublime for moments at a time, we may assume that participants are steeping in those possibilities, being endowed with potentials for living in more profound and authentic ways.

As contrast to the sublime, however, Burke (1759/1999) proposes the beautiful:

> Where the sublime "dwells on large objects, and terrible," and is linked to the intense sensations of terror, pain, and awe, the focus of the beautiful, by contrast, is on "small ones, and pleasing" and appeals mainly to the domestic affections, to love, tenderness, and pity. Crucially, with the sublime "we submit to what we admire," whereas with the beautiful "we love what submits to us" (p. 79).

Beauty brings people closer together as they agree on the pleasure of an experience. The sublime also connects people, but through terror, through facing a fearful prospect, together. The distinction is useful in thinking about the power of a group experience to imbue potentials of community building. When a group steeps solely in the beautiful, without opportunities to experience the sublime, the power of the co-creation of mindfulness is not clearly revealed and participants cannot steep in it.

Clinical situations are rich in possibilities for sublime moments. Fear, madness, and death may not actually appear, but they hover nearby, affecting the atmosphere of the group. This is rarely the case for applications of mindfulness in business and education. Unfortunately, rather than seeking the existential situation of their participants, such classes often turn to evocations of beauty, of a "cheap" mindfulness, not bought at the expense of terror. Participants all feel good with "let me read you this quote," or a practice of "loving kindness." The intensity of the steeping, however, is lower, and we might presume that the infusing of potentials is less. A new question opens, then: How do we find power in groups not formed around clinical need? How do we found a group on death, to bring it to life?

Endnote

[1] For example, in a dialogue with the Korean MBSR teacher and scholar of education Heyoung Ahn (McCown & Ahn, 2015), we began to incorporate Korean terms into the discussion of the pedagogy. We noted:

> It is exciting for MBSR pedagogical theory (in English) to become acquainted with the Korean vocabulary, with such terms as *Ahwoollim* and *Shinmyong*, and the different structure and syntax, which support the insights that humans are relational beings. *Ahwoollim* suggests that when more than two different persons or things meet—wherever they are from, however different they are—they may come to deeply resonate with each other, losing their ordinary self-boundaries. *Shinmyong* captures the affective tone of the gathering, suggesting a powerful emotional experience, an ecstatic state of aliveness and mutual sense of becoming one another. Both terms are a contribution to MBSR thought, taking us beyond the atomistic, individualistic discourse enforced by the dominant academic and medical research paradigm. With expanded resources of language, it may be possible to build a mode of expression within MBSR that can capture the experience of the pedagogy in its most profound moments" (p. 43).

References

Agamben, G., & Hardt, M. (1993). *The coming community.* Minneapolis, MN: University of Minnesota Press.

Agazarian, Y. M. (1997). *Systems centered therapy for groups.* New York, NY: Guilford.

Baracchi, C. (2008). *Aristotle's ethics as first philosophy.* Cambridge, England: Cambridge University Press.

Blanchot, M., & Joris, P. (1988). *The unavowable community.* Barrytown, NY: Station Hill.

Böhme, G. (1993). Atmosphere as the fundamental concept of a new aesthetics. *Thesis Eleven, 36,* 113-126.

-------. (2013, February 10). The art of the stage set as a paradigm for an aesthetics of atmospheres. *Ambiances* [Web log post]. Retrieved from http://ambiances.revues.org/315.

Bollnow, O. F. (2011). *Human space.* London, England: Hyphen Press.

Burke, E. (1759/1999). *A philosophical enquiry into the origins of the sublime and beautiful: And other pre-revolutionary writings.* London, England: Penguin.

Buber, M. (1947). *Between man and man.* New York, NY: Macmillan.

Carr, L., Iacoboni, M., Dubeau, M-C., Mazziotta, J., & Lenzi, G. (2003). Neural mechanisms of empathy in humans: A relay from neural systems for imitation to limbic areas. *Proceedings of the National Academy of Sciences, 100,* 5497-5502.

Castiglione, B. (1523/1976). *Book of the courtier.* (G. Bull, Trans.). New York, NY: Penguin Classics.

Cormack, D. (2012). The role of group in mindfulness-based interventions. (Doctoral Dissertation). Retrieved from http://create.canterbury.ac.uk/11134/.

Creswell, J. D., Way, B. M., Eisenberger, N. I., & Lieberman, M. D. (2007). Neural correlates of dispositional mindfulness during affect labeling. *Psychosomatic Medicine, 69,* 560-565.

Emerson, R. W. (1841/2000). *Essential writings of Ralph Waldo Emer-*

son. B. Atkinson (Ed.). New York, NY: Modern Library Classics.

Gallese, V. (2003). The manifold nature of interpersonal relations: The quest for a common mechanism. *Philosophical Transactions of the Royal Society of London, Series B: Biological Sciences*, *358*, 517-528.

Gergen, K. J. (1994). *Realities and relationships: Soundings in social construction*. Cambridge, MA: Harvard University Press.

Goodman, P., & Goodman, P. (1960). *Communitas: Ways of livelihood and means of life*. New York, NY: Columbia University Press.

Horvath, A., & Bedi, R. (2002). The alliance. In J. Norcross (Ed.), *Psychotherapy relationships that work: Therapist contributions and responsiveness to patients* (pp. 37-70). New York, NY: Oxford University Press.

Imel, Z., Baldwin, S., Bonus, K., & MacCoon, D. (2008). Beyond the individual: Groups effects in mindfulness-based stress reduction. *Psychotherapy Research*, *18*(6), 735-742. doi:10.1080/10503300802326038.

Ingold, T. (2013). *Making: Anthropology, archeology, art, and architecture*. New York, NY: Routledge.

-------. (2008). The social child. In A. B. Fogel, B. J. King, & S. G. Shanker (Eds.), *Human development in the twenty-first century: Visionary ideas from systems scientists* (pp. 112-118). Cambridge, MA: Cambridge University Press.

Kabat-Zinn, J. (1994). *Wherever you go, there you are*. New York, NY: Hyperion.

-------. (1990). *Full catastrophe living*. New York, NY: Delacorte.

Kelly, T. R. (1947). *The gathered meeting*. Philadelphia, PA: Tract Association of Friends.

Lieberman, M. D., Eisenberger, N. I., Crockett, M. J., Tom, S. M., Pfeifer, J. H., & Way, B. M. (2007). Putting feelings into words: Affect labeling disrupts amygdala activity in response to affective stimuli. *Psychological Science, 18*(5), 421-427.

McCown, D. (2013). *The ethical space of mindfulness in clinical practice.* London, England: Jessica Kingsley.

McCown, D., & Ahn, H. (2015). Dialogical and Eastern perspectives on the self in practice: Teaching mindfulness-based stress reduction in Philadelphia and Seoul. *International Journal of Dialogical Science, 9*, 39-80.

McCown, D., Reibel, D., & Micozzi, M. (2010). *Teaching mindfulness: A practical guide for clinicians and educators.* New York, NY: Springer.

Miller, S., Hubble, M., & Duncan, B. (1999). *Escape from Babel: Toward a unifying language for psychotherapy practice.* New York, NY: Norton.

Moss, A., Reibel, D., & McCown, D. (2016). Guidance: Refining the details. In D. McCown, D. Reibel, & M. Micozzi (Eds.), *Resources for teaching mindfulness: An international handbook.* New York, NY: Springer.

Nancy, J-L. (1991). *The inoperative community.* Minneapolis, MN: University of Minnesota Press.

Porges, S. (2011). *The polyvagal theory.* New York, NY: Norton.

Santorelli, S. (1999). Heal thyself: Lessons on mindfulness in medicine. New York, NY: Random House/Bell Tower.

Sennett, R. (2013). *Together: The rituals, pleasures, and politics of cooperation.* New Haven, CT: Yale.

Siegel, D. J. (2007). *The mindful brain: Reflection and attunement in the cultivation of well-being.* New York, NY: Norton.

Shotter, J. (2008). *Conversational realities revisited: Life, language, body, and world.* Chagrin Falls, OH: Taos Institute Publications.

Tronick, E. (2007). *The neurobehavioral and social-emotional development of infants and children.* New York, NY: W. W. Norton.

Turner, V. L. (1969). *The ritual process.* Chicago, IL: Aldine.

van Aalderen, J. R., Breukers, W. J., Reuzel, R.P.B., & Speckens,

A.E.M. (2012). The role of the teacher in mindfulness-based approaches: A qualitative study. *Mindfulness*. doi:10.1007/s12671-012-0162-x.

van Gennep, A., & Vizedon, M. B. (1960/1909). *The rites of passage*. London, England: Routledge & Keegan Paul.

Vygotsky, L. (1978). *Mind in society: The development of higher psychological processes*. Cambridge, MA: Harvard University Press.

Williams, M., & Kabat-Zinn, J. (2011). Mindfulness: Diverse perspectives on its meaning, origins, and multiple applications at the intersection of science and dharma. *Contemporary Buddhism*, *12*(1), 1-18.

Wittgenstein, L. (1953). *Philosophical investigations*. Oxford, England: Blackwell.

Donald McCown, PhD, is Associate Professor of Health, Co-Director of the Center for Contemplative Studies, and Director of the Minor in Contemplative studies at West Chester University in Pennsylvania. He trained as an MBSR teacher through the Center for Mindfulness at the University of Massachusetts and at Thomas Jefferson University. His primary research interests include the pedagogy of mindfulness in clinical applications and higher education, applications of complementary and integrative medicine in the community, and the contemplative dimensions of the health humanities. He is author of *The Ethical Space of Mindfulness in Clinical Practice* (2013) and other books.

Contemplative Science and the Contemplative Foundation of Science: A Proposal of Definitions, Branches, and Tools

By Xabier Renteria-Uriarte, PhD
Professor of World Economy and Management,
University of Basque Country, Spain

Abstract

Contemplative knowledge is the deliberate and intentional practice of being aware of one's own nature and, through this practiced focus, becoming aware of the interconnected nature of all beings and processes. It is, arguably, the oldest and most present knowledge system in the different cultures of our world, but its potentials for modern science are yet to be fully developed, even in that which is called "contemplative science." Until now, modern science has focused more on the analytic side (as meditation research) and the enactive dimension (with social innovation proposals), mostly leaving aside the heuristic possibilities (as a point of view from which to understand any object of study). In this chapter we will differentiate these three sides: We interpret the analytic dimension from the worldview of contemplation and wisdom traditions; we propose to foster the heuristic potentials with suitable research tools; and we describe some enactive implications. We will also consider a new *contemplative economics*. The need for both a contemplative foundation for modern science and a consistent practice of contemplative science is argued.

Introduction

Contemplative science originates as a group of proposals related to those deep states of mind that so far psychology and cognitive sciences have not been able or have not endeavored to analyze (Casacuberta, 2013). The term "contemplative science" was popularized by B. Alan Wallace (2007), in the sense of "a trans-disciplinary project aimed at understanding the effects of various kinds of mental and physical training

129

on the body, brain, and mind" (Roeser & Zelazo, 2012, p. 143). Today the field is mature enough to take on different contributions and to offer advanced reviews (Garland & Gaylord, 2009; Karna, 2013; Laumakis, 2011). Other areas of specific focus are consistent with more recent scientific trends, such as contemplative neuroscience (Esch, 2014; Lutz, Dunne, & Davidson, 2008; Stimson, 2012).

Contemplative knowledge searches for the meaning of existence. The primary assumption is that all beings are connected and that this interconnectedness is a determining factor for being. Contemplative knowledge relies on *meditation* or *contemplation*—one's introspection or "looking inside"—as the way to test and confirm what we know (Renteria-Uriarte & Giorgino, in press). Contemplative knowledge is the deliberate awareness of our own nature and, through this, of the nature of all other beings and processes. This contemplative perspective forms the methodological core of the so-called "wisdom traditions" and their ontologies.

Wisdom traditions are "institutionalized and not institutionalized systems of knowledge whose main concern is the exploration of the human condition and the search for the meaning of human life," which have been "developed over thousands of years, from the religious, spiritual, and other cultural sources" (Giorgino, 2015, p. 463). The essence of wisdom traditions is known as *perennial philosophy* (Huxley, 1945). The great cultures of the planet are grounded on the idea of interconnectedness, of some underlying unity in the nature of beings, and of contemplation as the best way to know the nature of reality. In this sense, wisdom traditions are different expressions of contemplative knowledge.

Modern wisdom literature seeks to understand the character and virtues of wise persons and, thus, to codify the concept of wisdom. Its most scholarly side has a marked pragmatic element, and it is often known as *practical wisdom literature*. Overall, there are three sources of the proposals. The "person-based" literature began with contemporary persons or witnesses, with the beliefs of people about wisdom or with sayings and attitudes of exemplars of wise people (Clayton & Birren, 1980). The "tradition-based" literature updates ancient wisdom traditions (Blomme & Hoof, 2014; Walsh, 2011) and even offers fresh perspectives on historical religious figures (e.g., Manz, 2011, regarding Jesus). Finally, "philosopher-based" literature shows the essence of wisdom in the opinion of a particular philosopher (Ryan, 1999, 2014; Whitcomb, 2010).

More recent variations on contemplative knowledge have been developed. One example is the *holographic paradigm* introduced by Ken Wilber (1982) as AQAL, from which he developed *Integral Studies* (Esbjörn-Hargens, 2010b). *Neurophenomenology* is another example. It is a field with more attention to heuristic and methodological issues among the modern scientific reflections of wisdom traditions (Rudrauf, Lutz, Cosmelli, Lachaux, & Le Van Quyen, 2003; Varela, 1996). Contemplative research models applicable in different fields are of high importance. Wilber's AQAL model (in short in 2007) may be the best known, but there are alternatives. Nature's Realms' Holographic Structure (NAREHS) (Renteria-Uriarte, 2013b) and the *Autopoietic System* (Bich & Etxeberria, 2013; Luisi, 2003; Maturana & Varela, 1972) are only two.

It is clear that important inconsistencies remain between the current sense of contemplative science as a field of modern science and contemplative knowledge as an epistemic methodology, especially in the sense of wisdom traditions. We face not only a gap between the various scopes, but also a different understanding of what contemplation implies. We first need a consistent foundation for contemplative science, an argument for its validity as knowledge on the grounds of its own ontology and empiria. With this objective in mind, I will propose new definitions, branches, and tools for modern contemplative science.

Secondly, we will notice how the foundational implications of contemplative knowledge may go beyond modern science. A contemplative foundation for *any* scientific field could provide a consistent interpretation and also function as an open practical approach. I will articulate what it has done in the framework of traditional contemplative ontology from both wisdom and practical wisdom literature, and from alternative scientific methodologies such as the holographic paradigm and neurophenomenology.

In Section 1, we reiterate contemplative science's usual object of study, and we argue that this analytic side is not grounded consistently. In Section 2, we recall that contemplation responds to an ontological view that can be transformed into a suggestive research image and, thus, have heuristic potential. Furthermore, we propose that this ontology implies a consistent foundation of modern science. Accordingly, we propose specifically designed tools to research from this point of view. In Section 3, we discuss socio-epistemic enactive implications. Throughout each section, the main branches of contemplative science are defined and characterized.

Contemplative Consciousness: Focus of Contemplative Analytic Science, Contemplation as "Techniques" or "Other Mind States"

Meditation, in the conventional sense, is a "family of techniques which have in common a conscious attempt to focus attention in a non-analytic way, and an attempt not to dwell on discursive, ruminating thought" (Shapiro, 1982, p. 267). Another definition frequently found in the literature is "the awareness that emerges through paying attention on purpose, in the present moment, and non-judgmentally to the unfolding of experience moment by moment" (Kabat-Zinn, 2003, p. 145).

Whatever the technique used, the "receptive attention to and awareness of present events and experience" (Brown, Ryan, & Creswell, 2007, p. 212) lead the mind to "dispassionate, non-evaluative and sustained moment-to-moment awareness of perceptible mental states and processes [which] include continuous, immediate awareness of physical sensations, perceptions, affective states, thoughts, and imagery" (Grossman, Niemann, Schmidt, & Walach, 2004, p. 36). Thus, at least if practiced seriously, different techniques share a "focused attention" and "open monitoring" (Lutz, Dunne, & Davidson, 2008) that lead to an "automatic self-transcending" (Travis & Shear, 2010).

This is the usual meaning of contemplative science or sciences; it refers to "meditation research." Currently, the field has a striking activity and dynamism. Unfortunately, it is quite challenging to conduct a serious review that includes the different scopes (Renteria-Uriarte & Casacuberta, 2015). In general, meditation is the essential or inner performance of different contemplative practices that have been summarized in "mindfulness" and "compassion training" (Roeser & Eccles, 2015). However, these are better understood as a more complex "structured tree of different practices" (Duerr, 2015).

A survey shows us that a few practices are most present in the scholarly psychological literature. *Transcendental meditation* is based on mantras, from the Maharishian Vedic tradition, and is prominent in the research in the 1970s and 1980s (Murphy, Donovan, & Taylor, 1997). *Mindfulness* practices from the Vipassana tradition that are based on dispassionate awareness and insight are the most researched practices today (Kabat-Zinn, 1994; Kabat-Zinn & Hanh, 2009). Finally, *Zen* methods from the Soto tradition, also based on dispassionate awareness and insight, are gaining importance in contemporary research (Alda et al., 2016; Chiesa & Serretti, 2010; Pagnoni, Cekic, & Guo, 2008).

Contemplation as "Inner Mind and Nature of Reality"

After a cursory look at the definitions of modern contemplative sciences, we might conclude that meditation is a group of "techniques" leading to something like "other (rare) consciousness" or a special status or condition of mind. To this end, the often-used phrase "altered states of consciousness," for example, has not helped to overcome some misconceptions. Meditative introspection, as in the core wisdom traditions and perennial philosophy since Aldous Huxley (1945), is not satisfactorily reflected.

As some Eastern advocates remind us, *true* meditation is best understood as the real nature of consciousness and reality, not as a technique or process, or even as "*some type of awareness*," as is customary in Western semantics (Krishnamurti, 1989; Osho, 1977). The interconnection between different beings is their most determinant feature and even their nature; contemplation is the way by which humans can realize this nature. Thus, contemplation or meditation can be redefined, in the ancient wisdom sense, as the internalization into the nature of our mind and reality. Contemplative knowledge can be understood as the deliberate awareness of our own nature and, through this, of the nature of all other beings and processes (Kelsang-Gyatso, 2000).

In fact, when contemplation techniques are implemented constantly and with discipline, the practitioner would "note", "sense", "verify," or "be aware" that this dimension is not a "parallel" stage of our ordinary or daily consciousness, but a profound stage or level that is a source of our ordinary consciousness. In other words, it operates as a nondependent or at least less-dependent inner reality, and it lies in the depth of our daily perceived exterior reality and ordinary mind. This is reflected in the narrowing of the gap between the techniques and this inner consciousness when the contemplative path progresses. It is seen, sensed, or perceived that the technique is in fact like a mode of consciousness and can be progressively indistinguishable from the consciousness as a separate focus. The technique (to realize a reality) and the reality (realized by the technique) become the same.

In the Zen technique of *shikan taza* or "just sitting": "practice and realization are one and the same" (Dogen, 1231, 2009, p. 7). The ancient master Eihei Dogen described this as *shushô-itto*. In the *gnanayoga* of India, it is understood that deep consciousness is "pure presencing," and therefore the technique/action of *antarmurkhi* (Sanskrit, "the looking inside") is in fact one of its core forms (Balsekar, 1992; Nisargadatta, 1981). It is the same in the *Vajrayana* of Tibet, in

134

the attempts to directly realize the inner reality, such as the so-called "meditation of the vacuity" (Kelsang-Gyatso, 2000; Tabké, 1983). Other traditions, such as the *bhakti yoga* of India or the *Taochiao* of China, describe this in similar ways. The phenomenon suggests a number of contemplative metaphors that can be translated into English as "the way itself is the end of the way", "the travel itself is the aim of the travel," and so on (Kolm, 2014).

This methodological core of perennial philosophy is usually systematized as Asian, Oriental, or Eastern philosophy. Briefly stated, the nature of reality is something that cannot be conceptualized, and that can only be approached as deep or perfect consciousness, in unity, compassion, love, wisdom, and happiness. A more elaborate description is that (a) we are interconnected or united with, not separated from, other existences, and the nature we share with them is our deep consciousness; (b) testing this within our mind with compassion and love is the path to realize it; and (c) to act in accordance with all of existence results in happiness, in an unspeakable bliss of connection.

In contemporary Western culture there are some well-known approaches. These are *Satcitānanda*, *Nirvana*, and *Tao*. All three traditions agree that the actual nature of this experience, this "something," is unfathomable and, accordingly, cannot be described or even named. The first approach, the Hindu concept of *Satcitānanda*, may be the most understandable of the three because it appeals to common emotions and concepts. Essentially, *Sat* ("the nature of reality") is *Cit* ("consciousness directly realizable") by *Ananda* ("perfect bliss"). Shaivism explains it this way: *Sat* ("the pure nature of reality") is known as *Svarupa*. *Sat* is *Cit* ("the changeless principle of all changes") and known as *Siva*. *Sat* is *Cit* and also *Ananda Svatantrya* ("the absolute bliss"), which is known as *Sakti* (Singh, 1979, pp. XIX-XXI).

Second, *Nirvana*, or "when the last flame of desire goes extinct," was Gautama Buddha's word for this phenomenon. In the same vein, he resisted requests to explain the nature of reality, but in *Patha-*

manibbanapatisamyutta, in Udāna 8.1, he tried to describe it this way:

> [It is] where there is no earth, no water, no fire, no air; no base consisting of the infinity of space, no base consisting of the infinity of consciousness, no base consisting of nothingness, no base consisting of neither-perception-nor-non-perception; neither this world nor another world nor both; neither sun nor moon. Here ...there is no coming, no going, no staying, no deceasing, no uprising. Not fixed, not movable, it has no support. Just this is the end of suffering (Buddha, 5-1 c. B.C./1990, n.p.).

The third approach is the Chinese *Taoism*, which points directly to this innermost nature of reality. This approach has become well known even in Western popular culture. It is expressed in the aphorism "the *Tao* that can be expressed is not the enduring and unchanging *Tao*" (*Tao Te King*, n.d., n.p.).[1] This stresses that the source of the existence is not conceptually understandable, and that it is better to devote the efforts to its direct experience: no mind, then only Tao.

These approaches have Oriental expressions, but any earnest reader of different wisdom traditions can grasp the common essence of any of them. The Eastern "*neti*" ("neither this, nor that; do not try to describe it") is the parallel of the Western "*apophatic or negative theology*," with defenders such as Pseudo-Dionysius the Areopagite or Johannes Scotus Eriugena (Huxley, 1945).

Contemplative Sciences in a Wider Sense, and the Contemplative Foundation of Science

The view of meditation as merely techniques or "some special awareness" can lead us to a dismissive reduction of what contemplative knowledges, in distinct cultures of the world, have held for millennia as fundamentals. In terms of science, however, a striking implication arises: The current semantics of "contemplative sciences" seems to have a very unsatisfying foundation. There is no consistency between how meditation or contemplation are defined and researched, and how they are accordingly understood by the contemplative knowledge derived from the perceptions and realizations of a deep practice.

In other words, the objects of study in most meditation research (Renteria-Uriarte & Casacuberta, 2015) and practical wisdom literature (Renteria-Uriarte & Casacuberta, in press) are contemplation's "symptoms" (superficial manifestations) or "effects" (surface causalities) rather than meditation or wisdom themselves. Their inner nature has certainly not been a focus of research. Moreover, in this sense, the usual mechanical reasonings explain very little of the essence of the issue (Renteria-Uriarte, 2016).

This assessment does not imply a disparagement of the current literature, but is rather a call for more ambitious assessment. From contemplative wisdom traditions, modern contemplative science can be defined not only as meditation research, but also and more extensively as the study of the deep nature of reality and consciousness through an analysis of the various types of mental and physical training that involve a nonanalytic focus of attention on effects in the body and mind. Contemplative (analytic) science is not only meditation research, but also the study of the interconnection and deep nature of beings (Renteria-Uriarte, 2016).

Not only is a better foundation of modern contemplative sciences desirable, but we have a chance to interpret all of the aspects of modern science according to a special ontology—contemplative ontology. We shall now explore this possibility.

Contemplative Ontology and Worldview, Tool for the Contemplative Heuristic Science

There are several reasons that might lead a person to the practice of contemplation. The two most common are probably the existential quest (the search for the meaning of the universe and life), and overcoming suffering (with its different forms of pains, malaises, and afflictions). All reasons involve a certain hope, however: that ordinary reality hides some "sense", "logic," or "meaning." There is a sense that some mystery or some sort of secret can be deciphered, and that it may be the solution to our discomforts. Consequently, those motivations assume that we are able to unravel the nature and sense of our complex and heterogeneous world, and act accordingly.

This goes beyond a deep contemplative consciousness that can be found, "tasted," or realized by disciplined meditation techniques, and described in metaphors and myths by wisdom traditions. A meditative mind is not merely some type of consciousness; it is also what explains existence and its beings. Contemplative consciousness implies an ontology, which is an explanation of the nature of things, and a consequent worldview or *Weltanschauung*, which are key statements about what the world is, how to know it, and how to act in it.

Contemplative Ontology

The realms of reality, or nature's realms, are a way of naming an ontological structure, a structure of reality according to a certain view. The contemplative realms of reality, "the structure of reality according to contemplative evidence," is the way to show this process of emergences and returns. There are a number of taxonomies whose essence is generally similar. Basically, in contemporary Western ontology, the realms or levels of reality are usually limited to matter (physical objects), life (living beings), and mind (rational humans). But in perennial philosophy, especially as formulated in the Eastern ontologies, things are much more complex. One of the most simplistic Eastern taxonomies includes a physical level, life level, mind level, creative level, and various unitive levels like the Atmanic, Brahmanic, and Nirvanic.

This structure of reality's realms synthesizes the essence of varied sources, such as the Hindu *Taittiriya Upanishad* (6-5th c. B.C., 1998,

2008) with its "sheaths" or *koshas*. These are the physical or *annamya kosha*, the vital or *pranamaya kosha*, the mental or *manomaya kosha*, the intellectual or *vijnyanamaya kosha*, and the causal or *anandamaya kosha*. The Buddhist *Satipaṭṭhāna Sutta* (5-1 c. B.C./1967) has five aggregates or *khandhas*: *rūpa*; *vedanā*; *saññā*; *saṁkhāra*; and *viññāṇa*. There is also the analogy of gross and subtle "bodies" or *kayas*, which are matter or body (*kāyā*); sensations or feelings (*vedanā*); mind or consciousness (*cittā*); and mental contents as essences (*dhammā*). The two layers of *saguṇic* and *nirvanic*, or *buddhakāyā* and *dhammakāyā*, are unitive dimensions (Sangharákshita, 1996).[2]

Heuristic Research Images: The Hologram and Its Models
In the philosophy of science, "heuristics studies the patterns of thinking" that foster scientific discovery (Kiss, 2006, p. 315). However, more attention is devoted to simpler procedures as being heuristic (e.g., Polya, 2014; Schnickore, 2014) than to suggestive research structures and metaphors that take advantage of analogical reasoning and perform the same function (regarding scientific analogies, see Bartha, 2010; Mc-Mullin, 1993; regarding their metaphoric form, see Lakoff & Johnson, 1980; for examples, see Morgan, 1986). In this vein, the history of science reveals a succession of some research images or metaphors, the most important being the clock and the computer in mechanics, the auto-regulated organism and the ecosystem in vitalism, the structured system in mentalism, and the hologram in integralism (Renteria-Uriarte, 2013b).

Analysis, therefore, becomes heuristic when it can provide valid research tools to establish inroads to scientific practice. Of the scientific images that act as such, the heuristic metaphor that reflects contemplative knowledge is the optical hologram, because "dividing it into two produces not two halves of the whole but two wholes" (Zinkin, 1987, p. 1).

Thus, holography offers us a good physical metaphor for the

ancient wisdom ontology that sees how all beings are interconnected, and that the very nature of Nature is within all of us. The holographic principle has been applied in the research of physical phenomena (Bohm, 1981; Bohm & Hiley, 2006), live processes (Sheldrake, 1981, 1988), brain research (Di Biase, 2009; Pribram, 1971, 1976), deep experiences of consciousness or transpersonal psychology (Anderson, 1977; Caplan, Hartelius, & Rardin, 2003; Daniels, 2005; Friedman, 2002; Grof, 2008; Hartelius, Caplan, & Rardin, 2007; Scotton, Chinen, & Battista, 1996; Sutich, 1968; Walsh & Vaughan, 1980), anthropology (Futterknecht, 2012; Laughlin, 1998, 2012), sociology (Navarro, 1994; Schwartz, 2013), economics (Arnsperger, 2010; Bowman, 2010, 2011), and overall as integral philosophy (Banerji, 2012; Hartelius & Ferrer, 2013; Sen, 2015; Shirazi, 2015).

As previously stated, the most well-known cross-disciplinary model is Wilber's AQAL (Esbjörn-Hargens, 2010a; Helfrich, 2007; Wilber, 1995, 2005, 2007). AQAL places human experience and knowledge, including academic disciplines, along two *axes*, interior-exterior and individual-collective. These axes form four *quadrants*: "I"; "It"; "We"; and "Its." Wilber also includes *levels* of development within the quadrants, from pre-personal through personal to trans-personal. He draws *lines* of development across those levels, describes *states* of consciousness according to levels and lines, and *types* or other topics. At the top of the model is the *formless awareness* or "the simple feeling of being" that transcends the phenomenal world, or the existences we perceive and know through this human experience.

NAREHS (Renteria-Uriarte, 2013b) proposes that all beings and processes, as forms and manifestations of the nature of existence, incorporate as information or structure its levels of material, life, mind, creativity, and deepness. Each existence and its actions is differentiated by the degree to which they make physical separability the highest unfolding of the shared deepness, the vital connectivity between separations, the mental stability of connections, the creativeness of all of these

140

phenomena, and the absolute awareness of the shared deepness of their existence. Within this holographic structure, each *being* experiences processes or makes choices in a unity-separation dialectic, and takes a certain position in the holographic emergence or folding and unfolding of the shared deepness among beings. The operative method to research objects of study is a holographic transdisciplinarity by which the common logics of different disciplines are encountered. Empirical testing is a meditation or contemplation by which one can approach how shared deepness among beings explains their structure and processes.

An autopoietic system is another heuristic image widely applied in the understanding of objects of study outside the field where the image originated. An autopoietic system is "a network of processes . . . of components . . . through their interactions and transformations . . . [and] as a concrete unity" (Varela, 1979, p. 13) by which "self-production [is] the key to understand both the diversity and the uniqueness of the living" (Varela, 1981, p. 14). This image has been applied, for example, in sociology (Luhmann, 1982, 1990; Ulrich & Probst, 2012), politics and law (Jessop, 1990; Teubner & Febbrajo, 1992), management (Biggiero, 2012; Breite & Koskinen, 2014; Koskinen, 2013), and education (Herrmann, 2013; Lenartowicz, 2015). This also reflects the principle of interconnection and creativity seen in perennial philosophies.

These research images and metaphors are important because they reflect a contemplative worldview and, furthermore, they have a heuristic power—that is, they can be translated to different fields, and they have a thought-provoking creative power.

Modern Science and Contemplative Sciences from Contemplative Ontology and Heuristics

What we usually refer to as "modern science" is a systematized way of knowing, mainly developed from Nicolaus Copernicus's *De revolutionibus orbium coelestium* (1543/1995) and Isaac Newton's *Philosophiæ Naturalis Principia Mathematica* (1687/2013) as mechanistic methodology. This was relativized and broadened by Romanticism (around 1800-1880 A.D.) as anti-reductionism, connection to nature, and encouraging of self-understanding and creativity. Finally, it was shaped by several renewals that are still being developed and tested: quantum mechanics; relativity theory; systems thinking; or constructivism (Bynum, Browne, & Porter, 2014; Hellemans & Bunch, 1991). All of these share a materialistic ontology, in either "hard" or "soft" versions, by which "world" or "reality" has an existence independent of the observer, even when its perceptions or concepts are socially constructed (Armstrong, 1995; Sellers, McGill, & Farber, 1949; Vitzthum, 1995). Contemplative ontology, on the contrary, posits that the assumed outer world, perceived by the researcher, and the ordinary mind, from which it is observed, are nothing but two distinct manifestations of the same inner and deep consciousness that can be realized by meditation or contemplation techniques.

In this sense, from a contemplative perspective, modern science is not only the study of how the natural world works but also of how different beings, systems, and processes act as manifestations of their shared common nature. A contemplative researcher, thus, will not focus as intensely on the boundaries between existences and their identity as they are, as in the atomism or mechanicism of classic Western science (Dijksterhuis & Dikshoorn, 1986; Gregory, 2002). She will instead focus on the interconnections and common logics between them. Research images such as AQAL and NAREHS, or an autopoietic system, help systemize how different fields may be understood in a contemplative ontology by placing them as the source of the model. Therefore, contemplative reflection and coherence are gained through applying those structures to the understanding of the objects of study.

However, without intrasubjective testing of the underlying ontology by the researcher, the application of holographic or neurophenomenologic research structures will remain a conceptual reflection. This may sound nonsensical to noncontemplative researchers or those who do not accept the arguments of the contemplative worldview, but this is only the case if we presuppose that science is an absolutely objective and physical practice without any influence or help from the researcher. This is not a necessary presupposition. Sir Richard Timothy Hunt (2007b) was awarded the Nobel Prize for his discovery of cyclins, proteins that regulate the CDK function in cells. He presents a principle he calls the "we have to get into the mind of cells" principle:

> With cells a very rare thing happens, they "know" when the next cell is hurt and needs healing; therefore, the biologist who wants to understand the functioning of cells must empathize with them and think and act with their mind (n.p.).

Another example is the transposable elements of a genome that control others (Bousios et al., 2016). These are described as "shepherds" by the scientist who presented this finding to the press (Conchi Muñoz, in Martin, 2016). The issue is not whether this is literally so or not; it is a metaphor that explains and also may foster scientific discovery. The question is: What onto-epistemic hypothesis performs better in this process of discovery?

From a modern Western worldview, a casual similarity present in two universes of discourse—the human and the genomic—provides the metaphor. From an Eastern contemplative worldview, the same mental reorganization—consciously in human shepherds and unconsciously in those genomic elements—is present in two worlds. This is because the mental level is present, as all the logic of the universe, in all of its beings and universes of discourse.

The heuristic power of the latter ontology seems to be more powerful. Accordingly, the contemplative scientist uses her introspection to better know the objects of study, be they of human, vital, or even physical position in a holographic existence. Meditation may sound like a strange way to better know external objects of study (an intrasubjective methodology rather than an extra-subjective one), but it is absolutely consistent from the contemplative perspective. This is the most direct way to find the real nature and source of being that only appear to be "external" and, consequently, encounter and foster science as a way to increase human happiness and alleviate social and personal sufferings. A contemplative researcher puts more attention on connections and emergences than in classic mechanical science or alternative or non-holographic sciences. This self-understanding and empathy may encourage research, and it can help us understand the success of some operational practices. Aaron Godlaski (2016) describes how this transforms science into a practice "from within the heart of the researcher." The practices of contemplative science and of any science are one-legged without the practice of contemplation.

Contemplative Socio-Epistemic Implications, the Contemplative Enactive Science

Praxis, and Enaction in Knowledge

Knowing the world and acting in it are closely related. A worldview or *Weltanschauung* specifies this with cognitive-linguistic prototypes involving an active knowledge and a normative praxeology, a series of deductions on how to act in life (Renteria-Uriarte, 2013a). In the case of wisdom traditions, contemporary literature has extensively developed the issue under the label *practical wisdom* (Kessler & Bailey, 2007; Küpers & Pauleen, 2013; Pauleen, Rooney, & Holden, 2010; Trowbridge, 2006). In addition, "enactivism" is a new concept that has renewed interest in modern scientific reflections of ancient wisdom, recovering the heritage of the pragmatism of Charles S. Peirce, William James, and John Dewey. The term "enactive" refers to the idea that agents cannot be understood as isolated existences, but must be understood as context-dependent and context-building: their existence; agency; and features only appear when they survive in a particular environment, contributing to the construction of that environment (Rosch, Thompson, & Varela, 1992). It is, obviously, a concept closely related to autopoietic systems.

We can postulate an enactive side for a scientific proposal on three conditions: if it is a part of a socio-epistemic structure; if it acts as a proactive agent in it; and if this co-relational agency affects its nature. This is especially true in contemplative science. As it is framed in the socio-epistemic heritage of wisdom traditions, it is a knowledge agent for their understanding, fostering, and renewal. This co-relationship necessarily affects its nature and conclusions.

Enactivism in Contemplative Science

In this sense, *contemplative enactive science* refers to the potential of its analytic and heuristic sides as processing agents for epistemic and social environments. The enactive virtues of its analytic side have been extensively shown (Biloslavo, 2013; Borker, 2013; Didonna, 2009; Eberth & Sedlmeier, 2012; Glomb, Duffy, Bono, & Yang, 2011; Lynn, 2010; Roeser & Zelazo, 2012). In addition, its heuristic qualities, as seen in the social-scientific co-agency of institutions such as the Mind and Life Institute or the MetaIntegral Foundation have also been demonstrated. As enactive researchers who are socially and collectively committed agents, contemplative scientists aim to contribute to the happiness and the diminishment of suffering of individuals, and to propound inspiring social improvements. Several wisdom traditions provide inspiration, but the contributions of engaged Buddhism and Buddhist economics have proven to be particularly useful (Renteria-Uriarte & Casacuberta, 2015). Laszlo Zsolnai (1993, 2011) and Serge-Christophe Kolm and Jean Mercier Ythier (1986, 2006) have significantly contributed to the writing in this area.

Conclusions, With an Example of Contemplative Economics

The contemplative ontology of ancient wisdom traditions tells us that contemplative science is a transdisciplinary approach, a cluster of different views aimed at a better understanding of "deeper" and "inner" states of consciousness obtained through meditation. It proposes levels of consciousness criteria to better understand other physical, vital, or mental research subjects. In this framework, contemplative science describes the perceptions, experiences, and realizations of deep consciousness. It studies the effects of the trainings used to access it on the body, brain, or ordinary mind; this is the analytic dimension of this field. Furthermore, contemplative science proposes deep consciousness as an alternative to understanding, and to provide scientific explanations with appropriate laws, models, and theories; this is the heuristic side. Finally, contemplative science aims to be a transformative agent for the overall improvement of contemporary society; this is its enactive dimension.

Thus, contemplative science is more (or should be more) than what is currently understood; it is not merely a descriptive analysis of meditation research. Its aim is more consistently understood as the study of the interconnection and the deep nature of beings. Contemplation as a technique or other state of mind is usually seen as the object of study of contemplative science; in contrast, the inner mind and the nature of reality are its analytic focus according to the ontology of contemplation. Otherwise, this is literature on the effects of meditation, not on meditation itself. This would neutralize the gap between the current semantics of contemplative sciences and the wider scope of contemplative knowledge.

This broadening of scope invites the consideration of contemplative science in more scientific areas. The holographic paradigm, integral studies, and neurophenomenology can also be named in this way because they propose research models, practices, and methodologies that reflect this perspective. Similarly, the practical wisdom literature reflects wise character and actions that derive from the contemplative level of existence, according to wisdom traditions. All of these proposals may help us better understand the core of contemplation. In any case, they translate its logic into modern Western terms.

When we understand the actual object of study of contemplative sciences, other branches of the field are opened. A research area is often limited to its role as a field of study, but in some cases its likely merits go beyond that field and it can have either a heuristic and enactive or transformative potential. However, in order to be completely consistent with its ontology, some emphases might be intensified.

In its analytic form, meditation research might give more attention to subjective accounts of meditation in the style of neurophenomenology, and connect them with the experience of contemplation not only as a technique or kind of special awareness, but as an internalization of the nature of mind and reality. We would benefit from more accounts of how meditators penetrate a dimension where an extended interconnection between beings is perceived and embodied, and how our ordinary minds emerges from this inner awareness.

Consequently, in empirical work, we have three sources. The first is the followers and practitioners who continue to realize and transmit the knowledge chain of ancient wisdom traditions, as is the convention in meditation research. The second is persons commonly accepted as "wise," as is the convention in practical wisdom literature. Finally, there are existential seekers of the resolution of "existential absurdity"; this quest for the contemplative nature of existence is their central yet resolvable conflict. We would benefit from researchers who would focus on more specific areas, researchers who are mostly absent in current empirical psychology. The question should be the same for all: How do they perceive and experience this inner reality? What about this hidden meaning or sense of the world that they surmise in daily or ordinary life and its arising phenomena? How is the meaning of reality and the immersion in it experienced in their intrasubjective research?

In its heuristic form, the ontological foundation of contemplative science acts as an alternative heuristic foundation for other scientific practices and fields. This is based on the assumption of the shared nature of different beings as the explanation for their behavior and processes. This also allows someone who is interested to make use of research images such as the holographics of AQAL and NAREHS. In other words, a contemplative foundation and methodology of science are also available for other scientists, whether contemplation is their object of study or not.

Contemplative knowledge offers a specific foundation for overall science practice and methodology in which modern science's objects of study, research, and methodologies are framed by the heuristics of contemplative knowledge. This happens via research images. In this sense, we have a very special, but entirely consistent contemplative foundation of science: a description and interpretation of what science does; and a proposal for how science might improve what it does.

We have to differentiate all of the foundations and sides: contemplative consciousness as the nature of mind and reality according to contemplative evidence; contemplative ontology as the rest of realities according to contemplative evidence; and contemplative (heuristic) science as a viewpoint and method from which any object of study can be understood according to contemplative evidence. With this perspective, contemplative research reaches its broadest coherence: the entire path of analytic; heuristic; and enactive sides.

Finally, we will consider an example. What are the implications of contemplative knowledge when it comes to economics? The economy is self-realization through work and constructive human relationships and supported by simplified consumption. It is, as any existence or process, a manifestation of deep consciousness. The economy can be structured as a hologram that instils the structure of Nature's Realms. This is a view of the economy from the heart of people, as full agents of existence. We can locate forms close to a contemplative economic consciousness, such as the optimal experience or flow of work activities.

Choices can be contemplative or not, but all actions are contemplatively understood. Agents can act with ignorance as *homo economicus*, which implies a separation from our underlying shared essence. They can act with more awareness as *homo socioeconomicus* and *eticoeconomicus*, which brings rapprochement to this connectedness. And they can act with full realization as *homo deepeconomicus*, such as the *appamada* as a reflection of our shared awareness. To choose among these platforms is the significant economic choice. Accordingly, the economy is actually a scenery of abundance; only materialistic ignorance creates the illusion of scarcity. Contemplative economics may be grounded on these proposals, an enactive tool for improving science and society.[3]

The inner ontology of contemplation may seem an extemporaneous abstraction; it is available for empirical testing with varied techniques by anyone interested. It is also through the potential of the regularity and confluence of the human mind that distinct research may be more consistently understood in a contemplative sense. This knowledge will not be fully consistent until the researcher delves into intrasubjective empiricism so as to better understand the object of study. Contemplative insight gives the researcher the possibility to test herself with the heart of its ontology. To date, it involves the most coherent and effective way to research with this wisdom, its practical effects, and its transformative potential for modern societies.

Endnotes

[1] We chose, for this summit of world thought, a mixture of different English translations: "The Tao that can be expressed is not the Everlasting Tao, the Name that can be named is not the Everlasting Name" (Mears, 1922); and "The Tao that can be trodden is not the enduring and unchanging Tao" (Legge Tao, 1891). Other versions that show the understanding that we try to emphasize here are: "The Tao that can be spoken of is not the constant Tao" (Hohne Tao, 2009); "The Tao that can be discussed is not the eternal Tao" (Erkes, 1950); "The Way that can

be experienced is not true; the world that can be constructed is not true" (Merel, 1995); or "The Way that can be told of is not the eternal Way" (quoted in Wilber, 1982, p. 57). For additional translations, see http://www.bopsecrets.org/gateway/passages/tao-te-ching.htm.

[2] Each tradition has its own semantic nuances. See *Developing Attention and Decreasing Affective Bias: Toward a Cross-Cultural Cognitive Science of Mindfulness* by Jake H. Davis & Evan Thompson (2013).

[3] For more information see "Contemplative economy and contemplative economics: Definitions, branches, and methodologies," Volume II of the series.

References

Alda, M., Pueblo-Guedea, M., Rodero, B., Demarzo, M., Montero-Marin, J., Roca, M., & Garcia-Campayo, J. (2016). Zen meditation, length of telomeres, and the role of experiential avoidance and compassion. *Mindfulness, 7*(3), 1-9.

Anderson, R. (1977). A holographic model of transpersonal consciousness. *Journal of Transpersonal Psychology, 9*(2), 119-128.

Armstrong, D. M. (1995). *Naturalism, materialism and first philosophy*. In P. K. Moser & J. D. Trout (Eds.), *Contemporary materialism: A reader* (pp. 35-47). London, England: Routledge.

Arnsperger, C. (2010). *Full-spectrum economics: Toward an inclusive and emancipatory social science*. London, England: Routledge.

Balsekar, R. S. (1992). *Consciousness speaks: Conversations with Ramesh S. Balsekar*. Redondo Beach, CA: Advaita Press.

Banerji, D. (2012). Structure and process: Integral philosophy and triple transformation. *Integral Review, 8*(1). Retrieved from http://integral-review.org/structure-and-process-integral-philosophy-and-the-triple-transformation/.

Bartha, P. (2010). *By parallel reasoning: The construction and evalua-*

tion of analogical arguments. New York, NY: Oxford University Press.

Bich, L., & Etxeberria, A. (2013). Systems, autopoietic. *Encyclopedia of systems biology* (pp. 2110-2114). New York, NY: Springer.

Biggiero, L. (2012). Are firms autopoietic systems? In G. Zouwen & F. Van Der Geyer (Eds.), *Sociocybernetics: Complexity, autopoiesis, and observation of social systems* (pp. 125-140). Westport, CT: Greenwood.

Biloslavo, R.B.R. (2013). Mindfulness, wisdom, and leadership. *Purushartha: A Journal of Management Ethics and Spirituality, 6*(1), 43-57.

Blomme, R., & Hoof, B. V. (2014). *Another state of mind: Perspectives from wisdom traditions on management and business*. New York, NY: Palgrave.

Bohm, D. (1981). *Wholeness and the implicate order*. London, England: Routledge & Kegan Paul.

Bohm, D., & Hiley, B. J. (2006). *The undivided universe: An ontological interpretation of quantum theory*. London, England: Routledge.

Borker, D. R. (2013). Mindfulness practices and learning economics. *American Journal of Business Education, 6*(5), 495-504.

Bousios, A., Diez, C. M., Takuno, S., Bystry, V., Darzentas, N., & Gaut, B. S. (2016). A role for palindromic structures in the cis-region of maize sirevirus LTRs in transposable element evolution and host epigenetic response. *Genome Research, 26*(2), 226-237. doi:10.1101/gr.193763.115.

Bowman, K. (2010). Integral political economy. *Journal of Integral Theory and Practice, 5*(3), 1-27.

-------. (2011). Holarchically embedding integral political economy. *Journal of Integral Theory and Practice, 6*(2), 1-29.

Breite, R., & Koskinen, K. U. (2014). Supply chain as an autopoietic learning system. *Supply Chain Management: An International Journal, 19*(1), 10-16.

Brown, K. W., Ryan, R. M., & Creswell, J. D. (2007). Mindfulness: Theoretical foundations and evidence for its salutary effects. *Psychological Inquiry*, *18*(4), 211-237.

Buddha, G. (1967). *Satipatthāna sutta or the way of mindfulness* (B. Soma, Trans.). Kandy, Sri Lanka: Buddhist Publication Society.

-------. (1990). In John D. Ireland (Ed.), *The udāna: Inspired utterances of the Buddha* (J. D. Ireland, Trans.). Kandy, Sri Lanka: Buddhist Publication Society.

Bynum, W. F., Browne, E. J., & Porter, R. (2014). *Dictionary of the history of science*. Princeton, NJ: Princeton University Press.

Caplan, M., Hartelius, G., & Rardin, M. A. (2003). Contemporary viewpoints on transpersonal psychology. *Journal of Transpersonal Psychology*, *35*(2), 143-162.

Casacuberta, D. (2013). The quest for artificial wisdom. *AI & Society*, *28*(2), 199-207.

Chiesa, A., & Serretti, A. (2010). A systematic review of neurobiological and clinical features of mindfulness meditations. *Psychological Medicine*, *40*(8), 1239-1252.

Clayton, V. P., & Birren, J. E. (1980). The development of wisdom across the life span: A reexamination of an ancient topic. In P. B. Baltes & O.G.J. Brim (Eds.), *Life-span development and behavior* (pp. 103-135). New York, NY: Academic Press.

Copernicus, N. (1543/1995). *De revolutionibus orbium coelestium*. Amherst, NY: Prometheus Books.

Daniels, M. (2005). *Shadow, self, spirit: Essays in transpersonal psychology*. Exeter, England: Imprint Academic.

Di Biase, F. (2009). Quantum-holographic informational consciousness. *NeuroQuantology*, *7*(4), 657-664.

Didonna, F. (2009). *Clinical handbook of mindfulness*. New York, NY: Springer.

Dijksterhuis, E. J., & Dikshoorn, C. (1986). *The mechanization of the world picture: Pythagoras to Newton*. Princeton, NJ: Princeton

University Press.

Dogen, E.D.Z. (1231/2009). *Bendowa: A talk on exerting the way*. Ottawa, Canada: Great Matter.

Duerr, M. (2015). The tree of contemplative practices. Retrieved from http://www.contemplativemind.org/practices/tree.

Eberth, J., & Sedlmeier, P. (2012). The effects of mindfulness meditation: A meta-analysis. *Mindfulness*, *3*(3), 174-189.

Esbjörn-Hargens, S. (2010a). *Integral theory in action: Applied, theoretical, and constructive perspectives on the AQAL model*. New York, NY: SUNY.

-------. (2010b). An overview of integral theory. In S. Esbjörn-Hargens (Ed.), *Integral theory in action: Applied, theoretical, and constructive perspectives on the AQAL Model* (pp. 33-63). New York, NY: SUNY.

Esch, T. (2014). The neurobiology of meditation and mindfulness. In S. Schmidt & H. Walach (Eds.), *Meditation: Neuroscientific approaches and philosophical implications* (pp. 153-173). New York, NY: Springer.

Friedman, H. (2002). Transpersonal psychology as a scientific field. *International Journal of Transpersonal Studies*, *21*, 175-187.

Futterknecht, V. (2012). *A quest for transpersonal ways of knowing in the anthropology of religion and consciousness*. Vienna, Austria: University of Vienna.

Garland, E., & Gaylord, S. (2009). Envisioning a future contemplative science of mindfulness: Fruitful methods and new content for the next wave of research. *Complementary Health Practice Review*, *14*(1), 3-9.

Giorgino, V.M.B. (2015). Contemplative methods meet social sciences: Back to human experience as it is. *Journal for the Theory of Social Behaviour*, *45*(4), 461-483.

Glomb, T. M., Duffy, M. K., Bono, J. E., & Yang, T. (2011). Mindfulness at work. *Research in Personnel and Human Resources*

Management, 30, 115-157.

Godlaski, A. (2016). *The science of contemplative practice and the practice of contemplative science.* [ACMHE webinar]. Northampton, MA: The Association for Contemplative Mind in Higher Education.

Gregory, J. C. (2002). *A short history of atomism: From Democritus to Bohr.* London, England: A. & C. Black.

Grof, S. (2008). A brief history of transpersonal psychology. *International Journal of Transpersonal Studies, 27*, 46-54.

Grossman, P., Niemann, L., Schmidt, S., & Walach, H. (2004). Mindfulness-based stress reduction and health benefits: A meta-analysis. *Journal of Psychosomatic Research, 57*(1), 35-43.

Hartelius, G., Caplan, M., & Rardin, M. A. (2007). Transpersonal psychology: Defining the past, divining the future. *The Humanistic Psychologist, 35*(2), 135-160.

Hartelius, G., & Ferrer, J. N. (2013). Transpersonal philosophy: The participatory turn. In H. Friedman & G. Hartelius (Eds.), *The Wiley-Blackwell Handbook of Transpersonal Psychology* (pp. 187-202). West Sussex, England: Wiley Blackwell.

Helfrich, P. M. *Ken Wilber's model of human development: An overview.* Unpublished manuscript.

Hellemans, A., & Bunch, B. H. (1991). *The timetables of science: A chronology of the most important people and events in the history of science.* New York, NY: Simon & Schuster.

Herrmann, T. (2013). Learning and teaching in socio-technical environments. In T.J.V. Weert, & R. K. Munro (Eds.), *Informatics and the digital society: Social, ethical, and cognitive issues* (pp. 59-72). Boston, MA: Kluwer.

Hunt, R. T. (2007a). Entendiendo el funcionamiento celular. *Deia,* pp. 35-35.

-------. (2007b). En la mente de las células cancerígenas. *Eroski Consumer, 113*, 17-21.

Huxley, A. (1945). *The perennial philosophy*. London, England: Harper and Brothers.

Jessop, B. (1990). *State theory*. Cambridge, MA: Polity Press.

Kabat-Zinn, J. (1994). *Wherever you go, there you are: Mindfulness meditation in everyday life*. New York, NY: Hyperion.

-------. (2003). Mindfulness-based interventions in context: Past, present, and future. *Clinical Psychology: Science and Practice*, *10*(2), 144-156.

Kabat-Zinn, J., & Hanh, T. N. (2009). *Full catastrophe living: Using the wisdom of your body and mind to face stress, pain, and illness*. New York, NY: Random House.

Karna, B. (2013). *Contemplative studies in context*. (Master's Thesis). Retrieved from http://scholarworks.gsu.edu/cgi/viewcontent. cgi?article=1040& context=rs_theses.

Kelsang-Gyatso, G. (2000). *Heart of wisdom: The essential wisdom teachings of Buddha*. Delhi, India: Motilal Banarsidass.

Kessler, E. H., & Bailey, J. R. (2007). *Handbook of organizational and managerial wisdom*. Thousand Oaks, CA: SAGE.

Kiss, O. (2006). Heuristic, methodology, or logic of discovery? Lakatos on patterns of thinking. *Perspectives on Science*, *14*(3), 302-317.

Kolm, S. (1986). *L'homme pluridimensionnel: Bouddisme, marxisme, psychanalyse, pour une économie de l'esprit*. Paris, France: Alvin Michel.

-------. (2014). Happiness-freedom, who suffers? From dukkha to samadhi. In V. Giorgino (Ed.), *The pursuit of happiness and the traditions of wisdom* (pp. 23-31). Berlin, Germany: Springer.

Kolm, S., & Ythier, J. M. (2006). *Handbook of the economics of giving, altruism, and reciprocity*. Amsterdam, The Netherlands: North-Holland.

Koskinen, K. U. (2013). *Knowledge production in organizations*. New York, NY: Springer.

Krishnamurti, J. (1989). *El último diario*. Barcelona, Spain: Edhasa.

Küpers, W. M., & Pauleen, D. (2013). *A handbook of practical wisdom*. London, England: Gower.

Lakoff, G., & Johnson, M. (1980). *Metaphors we live by*. Chicago, IL: University of Chicago Press.

Laughlin, C. D. (1998). Transpersonal anthropology: Some method-ological issues. *Western Canadian Anthropologist*, *5*, 29-60.

-------. (2012). Transpersonal anthropology: What is it, and what are the problems we face in doing it? In B. A. Cox, J. M. Chevalier, & V. Blundell (Eds.), *A different drummer: Readings in anthro-pology with a Canadian perspective* (pp. 17-26). Ottawa, Can-ada: Carletton University.

Laumakis, S. J. (2011). Eastern and Western contributions to contempla-tive science. *Enrahonar: Quaderns De Filosofia*, *47*, 93-104.

Lenartowicz, M. (2015). The nature of the university. *Higher Educa-tion*, *69*(6), 947-961.

Luhmann, N. (1982). *The world society as a social system*. Abingdon, England: Taylor & Francis.

-------. (1990). *Essays on self-reference*. New York, NY: Columbia Uni-versity Press.

Luisi, P. L. (2003). Autopoiesis: A review and a reappraisal. *Naturwis-senschaften*, *90*(2), 49-59.

Lutz, A., Dunne, J. D., & Davidson, R. J. (2008). Meditation and the neuroscience of consciousness. In M. Moscovitch, P. Zelazo, & E. Thompson (Eds.), *Cambridge handbook of consciousness* (pp. 499-555). New York, NY: Cambridge University Press.

Lynn, R. (2010). Mindfulness in social work education. *Social Work Education*, *29*(3), 289-304.

Manz, C. C. (2011). *The leadership wisdom of Jesus: Practical lessons for today*. San Francisco, CA: Berrett-Koehler.

Maturana, H. R., & Varela, F. J. (1972). *Autopoiesis and cognition: The realization of the living*. Dordrecht, The Netherlands: D. Reidel.

McMullin, E. (1993). Rationality and paradigm change in science. In P. Horwich (Ed.), *World changes: Thomas Kuhn and the nature of science* (pp. 55-78). Cambridge, MA: The MIT Press.

Morgan, G. (1986). *Images of organization*. London, England: SAGE.

Murphy, M., Donovan, S., & Taylor, E. (1997). *The physical and psychological effects of meditation: A review of contemporary research*. Pentaluma, CA: Institute of Noetic Sciences.

Navarro, P. (1994). *El holograma social*. Madrid, Spain: Siglo XXI.

Newton, I. (1687/2013). *The principia: Mathematical principles of natural philosophy* [*Philosophiæ Naturalis Principia Mathematica*]. Printed by CreateSpace.

Nisargadatta, M. (1981). In Frydman M., Dikshit S. S. (Eds.), *I am that: Talks with Sri Nisargadatta Maharaj* (pp. 82). Durham, NC: Acorn Press.

Osho. (1977). *Ancient music in the pines: Talks on Zen stories*. Poona, India: Rajneesh Foundation.

Pagnoni, G., Cekic, M., & Guo, Y. (2008). Thinking about not-thinking: Neural correlates of conceptual processing during Zen meditation. *PLOS One*, *3*(9), e3083. doi:10.1371/journal.pone.0003083.

Pauleen, D. J., Rooney, D., & Holden, N. J. (2010). Practical wisdom and the development of cross-cultural knowledge management: A global leadership perspective. *European Journal of International Management*, *4*(4), 382-395.

Polya, G. (2014). *How to solve it: A new aspect of mathematical method*. Princeton, NJ: Princeton University Press.

Pribram, K. (1971). *Consciousness and the brain*. Upper Saddle River, NJ: Prentice Hall.

-------. (1976). *Languages of the brain: Experimental paradoxes and principles in neuropsychology*. Upper Saddle River, NJ: Prentice Hall.

Renteria-Uriarte, X. (2013a). Euskal mundu ikuskera: Mitologia eta euskara aurreindoeuroparrak. Paper presented at the *Euskararen Jatorriaren 8. Biltzarra,* 2013.05.25 Lazkao. Retrieved from http://www.euskararenjatorria.eu/3-Xabier_Renteria.pdf.

-------. (2013b). *Hacia una Economía Holográfica: una revisión de la ciencia económica desde la ontoepistemología oriental.* Greater Bilbao, Basque Autonomous Community: University of the Basque Country.

-------. *Scientific reflections of ancient wisdoms: Is their mechanicism ontologically consistent?* Unpublished manuscript.

Renteria-Uriarte, X., & Casacuberta, D. (2015). Should economists meditate (to be more efficient in their work)? Western and Eastern answers. *3rd VIS Conference, International Day of Happiness: Economies of Becoming.* March 30, 2015.

Renteria-Uriarte, X., & Giorgino, V. (in press). Is practical wisdom and learning literature actually wise on its "right to speak"? In W. M. Küpers & C. O. Gunnlaugson (Eds.), *Wisdom learning: Perspectives on "wising-up" management education.* London, England: Routledge.

Roeser, R. W., & Eccles, J. S. (2015). Mindfulness and compassion in human development: Introduction to the special section. *Developmental Psychology, 51*(1), 1.

Roeser, R. W., & Zelazo, P. D. (2012). Contemplative science, education and child development: Introduction to the special section. *Child Development Perspectives, 6*(2), 143-145.

Rosch, E., Thompson, E., & Varela, F. J. (1992). *The embodied mind: Cognitive science and human experience.* Cambridge, MA: The MIT Press.

Rudrauf, D., Lutz, A., Cosmelli, D., Lachaux, J., & Le Van Quyen, M. (2003). From autopoiesis to neurophenomenology: Francisco Varela's exploration of the biophysics of being. *Biological Research, 36*(1), 27-65.

Ryan, S. (1999). What is wisdom? *Philosophical Studies, 93*(2), 119-

139.

-------. (2014). Wisdom. In E. N. Zalta (Ed.). *The Stanford Encyclopedia of Philosophy*, retrieved from http://plato.stanford.edu/entried/wisdom.

Sangharákshita. (1996). *El budismo: La ensañanza y su práctica*. Valencia, Spain: Tres Joyas.

Schnickore, J. (2014). Scientific discovery. In E. N. Zalta (Ed.), *The Stanford Encyclopedia of Philosophy*. Retrieved from http://stanford.library.usyd.edu.au/entries/scientific-discovery/.

Schwartz, M. (2013). On social holons, ideologies of integral, and the kosmopolitan call of politics. *Integral Theory and Practice*, *8*(3&4), 163-174.

Scotton, B. W., Chinen, A. B., & Battista, J. R. (1996). *Textbook of transpersonal psychiatry and psychology*. New York, NY: Basic Books.

Sellers, R., McGill, V. J., & Farber, M. (Eds.). (1949). *Philosophy for the future: The quest for modern materialism*. New York, NY: Macmillan.

Sen, K. (2015). The restoration of wholeness. *Integral Review*, *11*(1), 55-64.

Shapiro, D. H. (1982). Overview: Clinical and physiological comparison of meditation with other self-control strategies. *American Journal of Psychiatry*, *139*(3), 267.

Sheldrake, R. (1981). A new science of life: The hypothesis of formative causation. London, England: Blond and Briggs.

-------. (1988). *The presence of the past: Morphic resonance and the habits of nature*. New York, NY: Random House.

Shirazi, B. A. (2015). Integrative research: Integral epistemology and integrative methodology. *Integral Review*, *11*(1), 17-27.

Singh, J. (1979). Introduction: The main sources of the non-dualistic saiva system of philosophy and yoga. In Vasugupta (Ed.), *Śiva sūtras: The yoga of supreme identity*. Delhi, India: Motilal Banarsidass.

Stimson, D. A. (2012). Contemplative neuroscience: An integrative approach for investigating consciousness. *Berkeley Undergraduate Journal*, *25*(3). Retrieved from: http://escholarship.org/uc/item/553217g6.

Sutich, A. J. (1968). Transpersonal psychology: An emerging force. *Journal of Humanistic Psychology*, *8*(1), 77-78.

Tabké, S. (1983). *Meditación progresiva sobre la vacuidad*. Madrid, Spain: Casa del Libro.

Taittiriya Upanishad. (1998). In S. Chinmayananda (Ed. & Trans.), *Discourses on Taittiriya Upanishad: Original upanisad text in devanāgarī with transliteration in Roman letters, word-for-word meaning in text order*. Mumbai, India: Central Chinmaya Mission Trust.

-------. (2008). In T. S. Raghavendran (Ed. & Trans.), *Taittirīyopanisat*. Tiruchanur, Andhra Pradesh: Onnāhinī Sabhā.

Teubner, G., & Febbrajo, A. (1992). *State, law, and economy as autopoietic systems: Regulation and autonomy in a new perspective*, D. A. Giuffre (Ed.). Milano, Italy: Giuffrè.

Travis, F., & Shear, J. (2010). Focused attention, open monitoring, and automatic self-transcending: Categories to organize meditations from Vedic, Buddhist, and Chinese traditions. *Consciousness and Cognition*, *19*(4), 1110-1118.

Trowbridge, R. H. (2006). *The scientific approach of wisdom*. Cincinnati, OH: Union Institute & University.

Ulrich, H., & Probst, G. (Eds.). (2012). *Self-organization and management of social systems: Insights, promises, doubts, and questions*. Berlin, Germany: Springer.

Varela, F. J. (1979). *Principles of biological autonomy*. New York, NY: Elsevier.

-------. (1981). Autonomy and autopoiesis. In G. Roth & H. Schwegler (Eds.), *Self-organizing systems: An interdisciplinary approach* (pp. 14-24). New York, NY: New York Campus Press.

-------. (1996). Neurophenomenology: A methodological remedy for the hard problem. *Journal of Consciousness Studies*, *3*(4), 330-349.

Vitzthum, R. C. (1995). Materialism: An affirmative history and definition. New York, NY: Prometheus.

Wallace, A. B. (2007). *Contemplative science: Where Buddhism and neuroscience converge*. New York, NY: Columbia University Press.

Walsh, R. (2011). The varieties of wisdom: Contemplative, cross-cultural, and integral contributions. *Research in Human Development*, *8*(2), 109-127.

Walsh, R. N., & Vaughan, F. E. (1980). *Beyond ego: Transpersonal dimensions in psychology*. Los Angeles, CA: JP Tarcher.

Whitcomb, D. (2010). *Wisdom: Oxford bibliographies online research guide*. Oxford, England: Oxford University Press.

Wilber, K. (1982). *The holographic paradigm and other paradoxes: Exploring the leading edge of science*. Boulder, CO: Shambhala.

-------. (1995). *Sex, ecology, spirituality: The spirit of evolution*. Boston, MA: Shambhala.

-------. (2005). Introduction to integral theory and practice. *Aqual*, *1*(1), 1-38.

-------. (2007). *The integral vision: A very short introduction to the revolutionary integral approach to life, god, the universe, and everything*. Boston, MA: Shambhala.

Zinkin, L. (1987). The hologram as a model for analytical psychology. *Journal of Analytical Psychology*, *32*(1), 1-21.

Zsolnai, L. (1993). A framework of alternative economics. *International Journal of Social Economics, 20*(2), 65-75. Doi:10.1108/03068299310025561.

-------. (2011). The contributions of Buddhist economics. In L. Zsolnai (Ed.), *Ethical principles and economic transformation: A Buddhist approach* (pp. 1830-196). New York, NY: Springer.

Xabier Renteria-Uriarte, PhD, is Professor of World Economy and Management at the University of the Basque Country (UPV/EHU). He was Deputy Director of the School of Business Studies of Bilbao (1998-2009) and then Director (2009-2012). His interest is in translating the legacy of mainly Eastern wisdom traditions—under the guidance of the principles of meditation, happiness, and love, in the research agenda established in *Hacia una Economía Holográfica* (2013)—to Western science, economics, and social science. Some preliminary applications are in economic love, socioeconomic development, rock music, and the ancient worldview of Basques.

VINCENZO M. B. GIORGINO

Contemplative Knowledge and Social Sciences: Close Encounters of the Enactive Kind

By Vincenzo M. B. Giorgino, Ph.D.
Department of Economics and Social Sciences,
Mathematics and Statistics, University of Turin, Italy

Abstract

The enactive approach in neuroscience was proposed by Francisco Varela in 1999. It was an initial step toward the encounter between social sciences and contemplative knowledge. It was later developed by others in different fields—for example, Eugene Gendlin in psychology. These fields have converged in the recognition of first-person methods of research. The social sciences are now able to review the concept of self from radically different perspectives: an enactive approach implies an embodied, interdependent self in a world without foundation. It is a perspective inspired by "groundlessness," and this facilitates intellectual work by helping the researcher to detach from his biases. An enactive approach decreases the researcher's identification of himself as unbiased and separated from his research. It helps limit the expectations of future findings that might bias those findings. It provides a way for the researcher to see alternative worldviews. It highlights the reality that life consists of interactive cycles of purifying upheavals and rebirths. Finally, as an iterative process, it leads to a profound reorganization of the dominant conception of social transformation in society.

Introduction

Addressing the dialogue between contemplative knowledge and the social sciences calls for clarification because they belong to two different realms of knowledge. They are also dissimilar in purpose. The former's aim is to answer to the human quest for meaning about life itself. In other words, its main scope is to deal with existential suffering. Intellectual elaboration and theoretical constructions are only secondary tools

163

whose main function is to contribute to that primary aim. The primary aim of the social sciences is, on the other hand, to paraphrase Max Weber (Weber & Gerth, 1958), to causally explain and meaningfully interpret human social interaction. Those who wish to contribute to the construction of a bridge between the two realms must be accomplished in both.

A definition helps us arrive at a better understanding. We can say that *contemplative practices* are those social practices:

> ...undertaken with the intention to quiet the mind and to cultivate a personal capacity for deep concentration, presence, and awareness. Ideally, the insights that arise from the mind, body, and heart in this contemplative state can be applied to one's everyday life...These practices have the potential to bring different aspects of oneself into focus, to help develop personal goodness and compassion, and to awaken an awareness of the interconnectedness of all life (Duerr, 2004, p. 14).

Contemplative knowledge is the discourse on these practices and refers to the human traditions of wisdom, be they religious or philosophical.

At the conceptual level, social sciences have contributed to the recognition of an existential turn in human affairs, as has been noted for decades (Bauman, 2008; Beck, Giddens, & Lash, 1994; Bourdieu et al., 1999; Gergen 2009; Giddens 1990, 1991).[1] Much sociological discourse remains remote from the actual experiences of persons in everyday life (Beck, 2005; Latour, 2005). The main goal of this chapter is to show how contemplative knowledge offers a way out of this impasse. Human existence can seem to be disembodied by research in the social sciences, and contemplative knowledge reintroduces us to an intelligent and compassionate body, a body with which humans can live fully in a conscious way.

An Unexpected Process of Secularization

The emerging field of *contemplative studies* attempts to understand the many ways in which human beings have developed ways to concentrate, and to broaden and deepen their conscious awareness throughout history and in every culture. Contemplative studies integrate perspectives from all disciplines. Attempting to experience and understand consciousness is both a religious and nonreligious practice. Nonreligious practices may include music, dance, acting, writing poetry or prose, painting, or sculpting, to name only a few possibilities.

Harold Roth (2008) indicates four main tasks pertaining to contemplative study:

1. Identify the varieties of contemplative experiences of which human beings are capable
2. Find meaningful scientific explanations for them
3. Cultivate first-person knowledge of them; and
4. Critically assess their nature and significance

The sister term *contemplative science* was probably introduced for the first time by Alan Wallace (2000). He followed a systematic examination of subjectivity in the West in light of Buddhism. Wallace explores the possible convergence of contemporary science and Buddhism, with the aim of laying the foundations of a new contemplative science. His efforts are confined to psychology and neuroscience, but he opened the question of its applicability to the social sciences in general.

Our current historical period might be witnessing the opening of an area of inquiry in which the secular contemplative approach can finally occupy its own space within the academy. We might regard this current phase as the second stage of the secularization process.[2] Instead, I limit my considerations to the process of secularization in the West that enjoyed a spread in the effervescent counterculture of the 1960s, a time when it spread beyond the circles of a restricted cultural elite that had characterized the previous era. A provisional chronology might help provide an overview of this modern development.

Table 1

The Westernization of Eastern Contemplative Practices

1820-1960	1960-1980	1980-2010	From 2010
▪ "Discovery" of Eastern (religious) practices ▪ Restriction to cultural elites in the West	▪ Spread within the counterculture of the 1960s ▪ First attempts of secular practices in the West Examples: ▪ Transcendental meditation ▪ H. Benson's *Relaxation Response* method ▪ S. N. Goenka's *Vipassana* (secular teaching)	▪ Setting up of secular contemplative practices, ▪ First phase: Diffusion of mindfulness practices (*MBSR*) and establishment of a new research sub-field within a psychological and/or clinical framework ▪ Enactivism as an emergent paradigm ▪	▪ Setting up of secular contemplative practices ▪ Second phase: Beyond individualistic reductionism in lay contemplative practices and opening to social transformation

In broad terms the first phase of the secular life of contemplative methods started in the 1960s and ended around 2010, with a major turning point occurring in the late 70s. I refer to the birth of the movement of mindfulness[4] after the experiences of Jon Kabat-Zinn at the University of Massachusetts. This was later followed in 1989 by the publication of his inspiring and influential book, *Full Catastrophe Living*.

The exponential increase of publications under the topic of mindfulness dates from the 1990s (see Figure 1 below; also see Kabat-Zinn, 2011; Williams & Kabat-Zinn, 2011). Mindfulness originally showed up in clinical and medical settings. Then, mindfulness-based stress reduction (MBSR) programs developed outside the clinical setting—in education, business, and leadership. 2010 was a turning point, an indicator of when this cultural movement—after a life at the margins both within academia and outside of it—turned into an established niche of science. This is witnessed by the publication of the scientific journal *Mindfulness*, the first of its kind (see http://www.springer.com/

psychology/cognitive+psychology/journal/12671).

An additional indicator of growing interest in mindfulness research is the rate of increase of related scientific publications, as shown in the figure below.

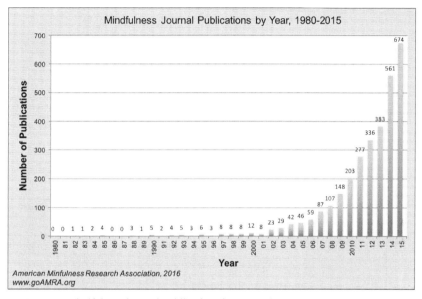

Figure 1. Mindfulness journal publications by year, 1980-2015. Source: American Mindfulness Research Association at https://goamra.org/resources/

The social evolution of a secular mindfulness from Western Buddhism involved a voluntary translation into lay terms of the original religious aims. Alfonso Perez-Agote (2013) defines secularization as "the process pertaining to modern societies, whereby religious doctrines and organizations experience diminished social influence because of the expansion of rationalism, science, and technology that accompanies the process of industrialization and urbanization" (p. 1). Individuation is a related concept, which Annette Wilke (2014) describes as "too narrow a concept of religion . . . possibly too much trapped in an ethnocentric and christocentric bias" (p. 264). Wilke also explains how current studies are more grounded in direct and embodied experience. However, she posits that they are still entrapped by terms such as "belief," "faith," and "transcendence." Wilke identifies how the terms *religion* and *spirituality* (the former being the institutionalization of the latter) cannot be easily separated from a belief in a transcendental reality, with or without a God. This is why a number of scholars prefer to use the term *contemplation*, which is intended to encompass the experience of meditation and prayer as related to the existential meaning of life (Giorgino, 2001, 2004).

Roth (2008) addresses the persistence of ethnocentrism in academic studies of religion as a major obstacle to a detached comprehension of contemplative practices. He argues that religion is deeply entrenched in everyday perspectives whether people embrace religion or not. Scholars seem to ignore that some fields of study—phenomenology being one—derive their concepts and understanding of the functioning of consciousness from processes that are empirically grounded in experience (Rehorick & Bentz, 2008).

There is another assumption implicit in the presupposition that European religious conceptions of human experience inherited by the Western world, along with philosophical and now scientific conceptions, contain the only possible "true" models. This further assumes that it is not possible for human experience to occur unless it is completely conditioned by preexisting cognitive categories.

This reductionism was born at the origins of the field of study, when the aims of value-neutral inquiry insisted on the separation of the chaplaincy from Christian theology (Roth, 2008). What was lost was the subjective experience in religion. Studies became based on rational, cognitive approaches rather than on actual experience. Looking at the U.S. academic situation, Roth argues that the historical development of this area of study gradually moved away from Christian theology; nonetheless, it continued to think in Christianity's conceptual categories: soteriology (how people are saved, which implies a Power who does the saving); metaphysics (which implies the existence of a nonphysical, world-transcending supernatural power); ontology (which implicitly posits an ultimate Being in the world); and cosmogony (which implies that the universe had a unique and discrete beginning). In the end, says Roth, "it is all about faith, belief, God and the supernatural" (p. 9). According to this conception, religious experience must never be studied from the insider, first-person perspective. The consequence of abandoning subjectivity is to leave it completely to religious practitioners. This leads Western religious studies to ignore a valuable source of empirical knowledge: first-person experience. The traditions of Asia, on the other hand, have developed this area more completely.

Finally, Roth (2008) poses an open question that might well be addressed to much of the critical sociology of the self:

> If human cognition can be effectively reduced to the product of preexisting historical, social, and political forces, then it can be valuable to study only as a product of these forces, and it provides no new insights in its own right....If people only experience what their culture imprints on them, how can anything new arise (p. 11)?

An echo of this concern in sociology can be found in Bruno Latour's (2005) book, *Reassembling the Social*, in which he criticizes sociological reductionism. He uses the example of the "invention of a believer" in the sociology of religion, calling for a social science that respects people's varying definitions of and experience of reality, no more treating them as incompetent of their own lives.

The Emergence of a New Paradigm.

As it continues to evolve, the field of sociology must move toward understanding that humans are embodied sentient beings and it is only through the basic tools that first-person research methods provide that we can "gather data" regarding the fullness of that experience, whether pleasures or suffering. Contemplative knowledge gives an original solution to this "hard problem" (Chalmers 1995).

These issues have been part of a challenging dialogue between Western scientists and Buddhist scholars that began at the end of the 1970s. This dialogue was significantly advanced with the publication of *The Embodied Mind* by Varela, Thompson, and Rosch (1991). The focus was on the dominance of Western cognitive theory, which produces a fragmented, disembodied self. The authors proposed the construction of an alternative approach called enactivism, which relies heavily on the conception of self coming from the Buddhist tradition.

A surface consideration of the meanings currently attached to the words *experience, expertise, expert, experiment, existence,* and *existential* might imply that they have little in common. A consideration of the etymologies, however, reveals how our culture through its language has separated what was once connected. Varela, Thompson, and Rosch opened an important dialogue for the new conditions of postmodern societies. Human experience is codified in light of different sources of knowledge: personal living experience, contemplative practices, and phenomenology (specifically that of French philosopher Maurice Merleau-Ponty).

Experiencing and first-person methods. These are contemplative practices from the wisdom traditions, social inventions designed to sustain humans in dealing with existential suffering, the common human experience. One main difference between the social sciences and contemplative practices, however, is that social science methods are about the *lived* experience. Whether textual or numerical, it is a methodology that can be performed only *after* the experience. Methods of contemplative knowledge, on the other hand, relate to the *living* experience (Giorgino, 2014).

Farb (2007) provides a distinction betwen *living* and *lived* experience. In this study, functional magnetic resonance imaging (fMRI) was used to investigate two aspects of awareness: extended self-reference that links experiences across time; and momentary self-reference centered on the present. The results suggest a fundamental

170

neural disassociation between these two forms of self-awareness, even though they are integrated processes. Attentional training can help reintegrate these so that the experience of the self across time and the self in the present moment are united.

Varela and Shear (1999) refer to these experiences as *first-person events*. The accounts derived from them are called *first-person methods*. In first-person methods, the *content* and the *processes* of mental acts are distinct. Using this method, data are collected and expressed in "I" form. Second-person methods, expressed in "you" form, result from techniques such as interviews. Second-person methods require training in order to elicit meaningful descriptions of experience, whereas first-person methods do not.

Varela and Shear (1999) also describe third-person methods, which describe the study of other natural phenomena. According to them, the three positions are structured according to the *manner in which they appear* instead of according to what content they address. They are inserted into a network of social exchanges and subjected to different modes of validation.

There are criticisms of first-person methods (see Petitmengin & Bitbol, 2009; Vermersch, 1999). The argument is that a person cannot divide himself into two, one who reasons and one who observes himself reason. This seems to be the question in the minds of some researchers as to how the object being observed can be the subject that is observing. Rather than attempt to reconcile these complementary processes of which humans are clearly capable, researchers in the positivistic tradition consider first-person methods null and void. Consciousness, a much-used term, then becomes a vague concept or it is understood in a reductive sense. The subjective aspect of experience is the hard problem; according to Chalmers (1995), it is consciousness that makes the mind-body problem intractable (see also Nagel, 1974).

The recourse to contemplative knowledge allows an *ad hoc* methodology. The originality and inspiration of Varela, Thompson, and

Rosch's (1991) concept of enactment is that it combines two different forms of knowledge, seen as traditionally antithetical or indifferent to each other. In this way, Buddhist practice can be a method for exploring experience, and fits within the flow of science without detracting from its existential value.

If we take first-person experience seriously as a method, we are met with considerable challenges. This means walking along a mostly uncharted but fruitful path. The central problem is that we must resort to meanings intended as texts—for example, in the Meadian tradition and in constructivism in general.. Some hints for an initial reflection are in Giorgino 2015). Other similar attempts to address this problem, such as introspectionism,[5] were proposed by William James and Wilhelm Wundt (see Vermersch, 1999). Today, contemplative practices are interpreted as forms of suspension of the individual's usual pattern, not only in terms of the action, but also in the preparation of the response plan that begins with recognizing the existence of a same pattern, followed by a redirection and a gesture.

The metaphor of no-self and its ethical function. The no-self is an attitude, not an alternative to the self. The idea is to see the self as an event or series of events, not a structure that I am or possess. This is described in the Majhima Nikaya.[6] From this process, the identity develops (Oldenzki, 2006). The self is momentary, a product of *grasping* that generates identity. The subject arises with a "wanting" (p. 257, 259). As the fifth-century Buddhist philosopher Vasubandru expresses, "without the afflictive dispositions [actions] are not capable of giving rise to a new existence. Thus, the afflictive dispositions should be known as the root of existence" (in Waldron, 2006, p. 186).

Human evolution depended on this attitude because it is connected to a certain aggressiveness in defense of life and for the procurement of food and shelter. The emergence of language enabled humans to shift from the sensory realities to a more symbolic world. This in turn contributed to the affirmation of a conception of the self as an enduring locus of experience. With this conception, the self could be experienced as existing relatively independently from momentary stimuli, favoring the conception of a separation between subject and object:

> Rather than being the starting point of experience, the essential agent needed to have experience, self is regarded as the end product of an elaborated process of assimilating data, constructing meaning and building a world of local experience. Rather than being an essential structure embedded in the psyche, self is regarded as a synthetic view that is fabricated every successive moment in the mind and body...The patterns of such response demonstrated by any individual are both regular and idiosyncratic enough to yield the illusion of a unique self...[Therefore] the construction of a personality—the fashioning of a self—only occurs when an attitude of possession or appropriation takes place...The "me" to which it all belongs does not actually exist—it is created for the occasion...Consciousness grasps one object after another to create "the stream of consciousness" of felt experience (Oldenzki, 2006, pp. 254-55).

In the Theravada tradition, "the concept of no self (*anatta* in Pali) is not even a force: it is a mode of cognition" (Roth, 2008, p. 4). Nevertheless, this redefinition of the self does not open the door to any form of essentialism, such as the discovery of the "original" or "pure" self. Citing Wallace (2001), Roth (2008) says that if each person is clearly an individual, the self is not an independent ego in control of body and mind: "Rather, the individual is understood as a matrix of dependently related events, all of them in a state of flux ..." (p. 8). We are influenced by and exert our influence on the context. When we do not recognize that this is our nature as human beings, we fall into the idea of a fixed self.

The Buddhist concept of nonattachment is cultivated by not confining oneself to a fixed perspective; this allows one to respond to

173

every situation with freedom because he is not attached to previous experiences or understandings. "The Way" in Buddhism is precisely this experience of the falling away of the dualities of subject and object. There are no metaphysics in this response, no deeper alternative reality or Truth because the perceived world is illusionary or designed from assumptions.

Objects are not separate from us because we develop cognition of them through our sensorial, or experiential, apparatus (Waldron, 2006). Thompson (in Varela, Thompson, & Rosch, 1991) emphasizes that "cognition is not the representation of a pre-given world by a pre-given mind but is rather the enactment of a world and a mind on the basis of a history of the variety of actions that a being in the world performs" (p. 9). The knower and the known stand in a relation to each other through what is called dependent co-origination: Experience is intersubjective not separated interaction, and "there is no unchanging agent as the principle of dependent origination" (Oldenzki, 2006, p. 254).

Enactivism, then, is a "two-way or reciprocal relationship between embodied conscious states and local neuronal activity" (Varela, Thompson, & Rosch, 2001, p. 418). More specifically, in neurophenomenology (NP), consciousness is downgraded at a methodological level as part of a pragmatic strategy in which first-person experience and neuro-data (via third-person methods such as fMRI) are joined together to achieve an integrated vision (Varela, 1996).

NP and enactivism sparked a wide-ranging debate around the original proposals of Varela and other authors, a debate that continues to this day. What generated this ongoing discussion is the proper positioning of first-person methods in partnership with third-person methods. Some authors (Kirchhoff & Hutto, 2011) criticize neurophenomenology for the strategy of combining experience and neuroscientific studies on the same level. They argue that Varela's pragmatic position is unsustainable:

> The fact that phenomenal descriptions neither reduce to, nor are entailed by, physical descriptions lends no support to the idea that we are dealing with two things rather than one thing differently described. The phenomenal might just be the physical described differently....Phenomenal experience is just dynamic activity grounded in agent-environment interactions. There are not two relata—the physical and the phenomenal, qualia and brain activity (p. 306).

Varela, Thompson, and Rosch's strategy of shifting from metaphysics to methodology does not work for Kirchhoff and Hutto because the gap between the two dimensions can only be overcome by grounding it on first-person data, which they reject. The philosopher Michel Bitbol (2012) reconstructs the concept, stating that neurophenomenology is not a theory of consciousness because it does not aim to have an ontological foundation. Rather it is a methodological stance in which first- and third-person methods can be considered together.

Eugene Gendlin's radical shift. In the rich debate about first-person methods a most encompassing theoretical and practical contribution comes from the phenomenological philosopher and psychologist Eugene Gendlin (2009). He contends that individual experience is socially determined because each individual lives in an environment. Gendlin bases his ideas on the insights of Husserl and Heidegger, giving a fresh perspective about the body, its tacit form of sensorial intelligence, and the felt sense that emerges in interaction. He criticizes the cognitive and representational (perception-oriented) model of experience in favor of an experiential approach based on human body as interaction. This suggests a different conception of what practice and science are, and their implied *intricacy*:

> The smaller entities are always richer in difference and complexity than their aggregates....In other words, society does not represent a higher, more complex order

than the individual monad, and a brain, a soul, a body is itself composed of myriads of "little persons," or agencies, each of them endowed with faith and desire, and [each] actively promoting one's total version of the world (Gendlin, 1991, n.p.).

Gendlin's (1991/2009) position is articulated through a systematic critique of Western thinking, with the aim of building a modality of thinking beyond patterns, forms, concepts, definitions, categories, distinctions, and rules:

> Foremost is the assumption that order can only be something imposed on experience, that forms, distinctions, rules or patterns are the only order so that there is nothing else, no "other" and hence no possible interplay between the forms and something more. Supposedly, nothing but disorder talks back (p. 3).

Two of Gendlin's books that are especially relevant here are *Experiencing and the Creation of Meaning* (1962/1997) and *Thinking beyond Patterns* (1991/2009). Gendlin reminds us of Karl Marx's statement that human nature is "unfinished." At the basis of Gendlin's (1996) concept about how we build meaning is the human body:

> A body implies what it is about to become, if it can. Living things organize what needs to happen....[It] is a sort of thing that knows its next step.... And this tells us also what "situations" are—they aren't what's around in the space, nor inside us subjectively.... Living bodies are capable of quite new next steps when the circumstances around them change... For instance, hunger is the body itself doing the hungering, it's not a perception of hunger.... It's a being kind of knowing. It

doesn't require perception and pictures and representations....The body IS the light and IS the water, and IS
the interaction with the other person. It's from that one
that we know all the stuff. It's kind of knowing that
we do....A body lives its relationships, it IS interaction.
There is only ongoing interaction, not one body here
and an environment there.... (1996, pp. 15-21).

Gendlin (1991/2009) also describes how living bodies organize and activate their physical processes. For example, cellular processes relate
not only to physiology but to information and experience: "The cellular
carries human environment as well as animal environment in the actual
cells" (1996, p. 23). In addition, "The human individual is inherently
interactional. That doesn't mean the content of what we live is produced
by others; it means that life-events are inherently with, at, from, to and
about others and ourselves" (p. 28).

This complex perspective is critical of a cognitive-based approach to self and knowledge. The body does more than collect experiential data through its five senses; it also interprets that life experience
through both internal and external interaction. Gendlin (1991/2009)
redefines physiology and biology in these terms. He maintains that
knowledge is actually created *during* interaction and that it is a "felt
sense or a felt understanding or an experiential intricacy" (p. 10). This
explains how felt sense is not derived from culture. Therefore, we can
discover or rediscover in the situation at hand the existence of multiple
possibilities that may or may not come up:

...not as a set of fixed entities, that need only separating
out.... A situation is the implying of all the ways in which
it can be carried forward . . . A culture can be said to con-
sist of situations, that is to say of clusters of action-possibilities. Some situations that arise in our culture cannot
arise in another. It is not the same situation if it involves
a different scope of possible actions. A situation is the

implicit action-possibilities. But this implicit intricacy of
a situation exceeds the cultural story (p. 47).

Gendlin abandons constructivist reductionism, and, opening to the body, understands that it is possible to go beyond a patterned model. He does not deny the that use and functions patterns have in our society, but he limits their influence because he believes that meaning is not socially prescribed. There is nothing wrong, according to Gendlin (1991/2009), if science renders processes in terms of patterns (p. 56). Indeed, it is quite obvious that our lives have gained immense improvements from this form of science. The problem arises when we take the "space of pattern things as independent, as if the bodily situational environment were merely added on" (p. 6).

In everyday life, as in science, humans have to cope with experiential data based on sensorial elements; patterns do not always factor in, yet interpretative sociology shows an almost exclusive interest in patterns alone. It is interesting that, at the sensorial level, there is a space in which patterns are not yet built. At this point, situations are open to different solutions, as Gendlin shows. Our pre-conceptual world lies on a set of *felt sense*, and interpretation is helped by the community in which we are socialized. Thoughts and concepts are linked to specific gestures, and gestures have a more or less precise location in our bodies. A sort of permeability between the inner and outer world is often accompanied by a transformation of identity.

From this, it should be clear that in any situation there is unpredictability of experience and an understanding that can be identified and measured from the outside only—partly, and only through a perspective that recognizes the possibility of greater or lesser individual opening to oneself and beyond oneself. Thus, first-person methods are valuable, and enactment helps explain the interface of self and other.

Walking the Talk of the Social Transformation from Within

> Critical social scientists and activists
> "have only tried to change the outside world, in various ways.
> The point, however, is to change it from the inside out"
>
> *Anonymous*
>
> "Don't fill the blanks"
>
> Bruno Latour, *Reassembling the Social*

One might say that this describes the Western social science approach. In fact, social innovation seems to have mainly flowed in a one-way direction, from East to West, the latter appearing as a receiver exhausted from its own hyper-materialistic culture and almost collapsed under the weight of its moral poverty: a clearly unbalanced view.

The resulting *Buddhist modernism* in the West is still character-ized by an ambiguous relationship between tradition and sciences, and religious meditation and lay practice, in everyday life. The process, to be effective, requires a transformation of both: of which magnitude and of which quality is difficult to anticipate, but the current situation shows the signs of an uncompleted secularization. The Dalai Lama (2011) writes:

> In today's secular world religion alone is no longer ad-equate as a basis for ethics. One reason for this is that many people in the world no longer have any particular religion. Another reason is that, as the people . . . be-come ever more closely interconnected . . . in multicul-tural societies, ethics based on any one religion would only appeal to some of us; it would not be meaningful for all (p. xiii).

His authoritative and auspicious plea for a post-religious ethics, one based on compassion and interconnectedness, recognizes that formal religions have progressively lost the ability to speak to the whole of humankind. In fact, he states, not only are the institutions showing their limits, but religion itself is a social construction and it can no longer "tie" people together.[7] Furthermore, contemplative practices can be disconnected from religion because "...mental discipline itself requires no faith commitment. All it requires is a recognition that developing a calmer, clearer mind is a worthwhile endeavor and an understanding that doing so will benefit both oneself and others" (Dalai Lama, 2011).

The positive exit of religion and the consequent consolidation of the mindfulness initiative I have sketched have nonetheless provoked harsh critics to rise up from different sides, just "as in all cross-cultural marriages, both sets of parents have some concerns" (see Crane, in Wilks, 2014). Religious leaders and teachers raise doubts about the appropriateness of the lay version compared to the original ethical spirit of contemplative practices. On the other side, social critics see it as the inevitable outcome of a capitalist system that commodifies the most intimate and sacred aspects of human existence, or as the ideology that best fits with postmodern requirements based on self-responsibility and self-exploitation (Žižek, 2001).

Williams and Kabat-Zinn (2011) reflected on the developing field of the secular mindfulness approach, highlighting some risks and opportunities of its unexpected success. Among those is the unresolved question regarding the nature of the mind. Constructivists and innatists continue to differ in their understandings. In addition, there is the need to develop secular measuring tools that respect the original scopes of meditation and the role of compassion in teaching mindfulness, which at the same time are removed from religious structures.

There are at least two other interesting lines of reflection that are gaining ground in the last years. One originates within the secular mindfulness movement and the other from the Secular Post-Buddhism movement.

The first contribution is a specific criticism grown inside the mindfulness movement and it mainly relates to the need to challenge the reductionist approach dominating the field, a consequence of the growing intersection of the clinical culture and the neurosciences, in which contemplative culture can become ancillary rather than partner. McCown et al. (2011), on the basis of a long and dense experience of contemplative teaching in a variety of social settings, put their attention to the individualistic model on which mindfulness has been based so far, influenced by the medical and psychological culture: they suggest to incorporate in the new perspective the sets of interactions in which the practice is performed, so to give value and recognition to its co-creational aspects.

The second contribution comes from Stephen Batchelor (2015) as he goes back to the origins of Buddhism, before its transition into a religious institution. One obstacle in understanding contemplative knowledge from the Buddhist tradition is the difficulty of relying on original texts. For example, *The First Discourse* of the Buddha is notorious for not being a verbatim transcript. Indeed, it has at least 17 versions in four languages (Pali, Sanskrit, Chinese, and Tibetan). From that come countless translations into every language. Therefore, we must talk of "Buddhisms," a plural tradition instead of a singular one. Buddhism that is grounded in modern philological works has produced well-known concepts such as "noble truths," yet these are absent from the text cited above. They are nothing more than religious rhetoric or catch-phrases that developed to ensure a monopolistic market (Batchelor, 2010). It is a short step from this first interposition to the metaphysics of two truths—the conventional everyday truth and the Ultimate one.[8]

According to a fresh reading of a core passage of the *First Discourse* that grounds on the philosophy of Nagarjuna (150-250 A.D.), Buddhism involves four *tasks* more than *truths*; these are "the outline of a trajectory of practice rather than the conceptual foundation for a system of belief" (Batchelor, 2012, p. 98). The accomplishment of the four tasks (the awakening or nibbana) is not "a singular insight into the absolute, comparable to the transcendent experiences reported by mystics of theistic traditions, but a complex sequence of interrelated achievements gained through reconfiguring one's core relationship with *dukkha*, a rising, ceasing and the path" (p. 99). It is not the *truth* of suffering that we need to understand but suffering *itself*, our experience of it (Batchelor, 2015, p. 122). The last book of this author is also rich of sociological insights – tips for a systematic investigation - and precise elements showing how the development of an elite knowledge, as part of an emerging class of professional keepers of tradition, takes hold and legitimates the formation of a religious hierarchy with a separation between it and the laity. For this author, the dualities mentioned in orthodox Buddhism testify to this passage: sacred/profane, eternal/transitional, unconditional/conditional, and reality/appearance (p. 134).

Dukkha (suffering) is reinterpreted by Batchelor (2012, 2015) as a property of the world, not of the individual. In other words, it is not a consequence of ignorance because there is no such thing as "pure consciousness" (p. 180) or an unconditioned or pristine "knowing" that exists independently of the phenomenal world of discrete physical things and mental process" (p. 191). Throughout history, translations, selections, and adaptations to specific social contexts have been the means of the social construction of a closed apparatus. For example, Bachelor recommends removing the doctrine of reincarnation from secularized Buddhism (Wright, 2015). In addition, "instead of losing oneself in mystic union with the Absolute, one loses one's class identity in order to practice the dharma as free, self-creating person" (Batchelor, 2015, p. 205). He draws from Gotama's *Short Discourse on Emptiness* to explain: "To dwell in such emptiness means to inhabit fully the embodied space of one's sensory experience, but in a way that is no longer determined by one's habitual reactivity" (p. 9).

Self is considered illusionary because is identified with our attachments, but this does not mean that we do not exist as individuals or that we must work to nullify ourselves in an indistinctive magma. On the contrary, Varela (1999) adds, we can flourish as persons if we adventure on the road of awareness, if we cultivate attention to the present and develop compassion. An understanding of no-self is a complement to the self, where the expression of the former is a true, pure reality unencumbered by attachments: "Rather than being the negation of self, emptiness reveals the dignity of a person who has realized what it means to be fully human" (Batchelor, 2015, p. 8).

If we follow Batchelor in developing a secular approach to contemplative social science, we can see Buddhism as pragmatic training aiming to liberate ourselves from our reactive habits instead of as a science of mind. Buddhism did not originate in order to set up a theory of conscience, and it is not a "science of mind" as understood in the Western meaning. It is born instead to alleviate human suffering. Its observations and descriptions can be useful and possibly even collimate contemporary research, which is the core aim of social science and sociology.

Wallace (2001) states that "consciousness is empty, intangible, and unsubstantial...What obscures the fundamental brightness of consciousness are thoughts, mental constructs, dullness, excitation, and an endless array of mental contents" (p. 22). These create habits that clutter our perspectives. Contemplative practice is based on different methods to reach a basic state of consciousness, in which *nibbana*—rather than being seen as a state of perennial bliss or awakening—is a condition in this real and everyday world in which we are liberated from our habits. Karma, instead of being seen as the spiritual investment of helpful or harmful actions, is seen as the energy generated by mental content that leaves a "residue" that obscures the substrate consciousness. From a secular contemplative perspective, this energy must be redirected.

The concepts of compassion and care lie at the heart of the four tasks of Buddhism. Care is a social virtue "sustained by the matrix of relationships one cultivates with others who are likewise committed to realizing comparable values in their lives" (Batchelor, 2015, p. 105). Contemplative social scientists can be highly inspired by the contributions of Buddhism. With this paradigm of understanding, they are better equipped to take into account the post-modern shift toward a post-religious, post-credal society. This is a society in which the existential quest is still alive and kicking, perhaps as never before; there is an intensity resulting from the process of individualization that leaves a craving for connectedness (Beck & Beck-Gernsheim, 2002).

It is important to recognize that creative achievements are often produced outside of academies and institutional platforms. Significant new developments are within networks of digital social peer-to-peer webs, a form that is leading to new social, economic, and organizational models. These associations are not identifiable with the market or with the state. They are instead part of nonmarket social production (Benkler, 2006; Castells, 1996) or commons (Rifkin, 2014) in which structural hierarchies and intermediary powers lose ground.

One modern application of contemplative science is the development of *Buddhist economics*, a methodological and theoretical Buddhist approach in sociology (Bentz & Shapiro, 1998, and Immergut & Kaufman, 2014 are just two examples). One risk for social scientists is that they might blindly accept a transcendentalist view. This could lead to merely transplanting original religious and dogmatic language without mediation of any kind, which could easily lead to devotional science.

The following lines of secular contemplative social research seem to be the most urgent:

1. To explore and experiment with a nonindividualistic perspective in mindfulness practice, assessing its effects
2. To reconsider the definition of self and agency
3. To include methods of first-person inquiry as part of sociological methodologies; and
4. To develop a critical analysis of the context in which contemplative practices are coproduced, be it religious or not, for profit or not, paying attention to the interactional patterns, situation,

and context in which they are taught and learned

Perhaps we humans are still ignorant about what it is like to be a bat (Nagel, 1974), but collectively we seem to be taking effective steps toward learning how to be fully human.

Endnotes

[1] These are only a few of the better known among the many major contributors to the development of this field.

[2] I do not refer to the encounter between the ancient Eastern religious culture and the Western "discovery" of Buddhism dating from the beginning of the 19th century because of European colonial policies in Asia. In fact, this does not coincide with "a mosaic of disparate canons, doctrines, local social practices, institutions, beliefs and folkways" typical of the time (Higgins, 2012, p. 110). That period has been characterized by what was called *Buddhist modernism*, an attempt to meld tradition with some aspects of modernity but without a systematic reform.

[3] A very useful reconstruction can be seen in Chapter 2 of this book. McCown includes a brief overview of Buddhism in the West, specifically in the United States.

[4] One definition of mindfulness is "paying attention in a particular way on purpose, in the present moment, and non-judgmentally" (Kabat-Zinn, 1990, p. 4). More recently, mindfulness has been identified by three elements: intention; attention; and attitude. Intention means being aware of why one is paying attention. Attention means the direct knowing of what is happening as it is actually happening. Attitude refers to the way in which one pays attention; specifically, it means accepting, caring, and discerning qualities of mindfulness.

[6] The introspective method is restricted to verbal relations, a result of the dominance of behavioral psychology in the 1920s.

[7] *Majjhima Nikāya* is a Pali term that refers (in English: The Middle Length Discourses of the Buddha) to one of the major collections in the

Sutta Pitaka or "Basket of Discourses" belonging to the Pali Canon, on which is grounded the Theravada tradition, one of the three main monastic schools of Buddhism with Mahayana and Vajrayana.

[8] The term "religion" originated from the Latin *re-ligare,* "to tie" (see Hoyt, 2012).

[9] In this case, they do not occur in the Sutta or Vitaya baskets of the Pali Canon. They are just the basic layers on which the social construction of a religion as belief and belonging system is developed. It must be added that every school or church in Buddhism relies on only a small part of the canons. Batchelor further contends that a new platform grounded on secular foundations is required, a "secular Buddhism versus transcendental Buddhism" (p. 307).

References

Batchelor, S. (1997). *Buddhism without beliefs: A contemporary guide to awakening.* New York, NY: Riverhead.

-------. (2011). *Confessione di un ateo buddista.* Roma, Italy: Ubaldini.

-------. (2012). A secular Buddhism. *Journal of Global Buddhism, 13,* 87-107.

-------. (2015). *After Buddhism. Rethinking the dharma for a secular age.* New Haven, CT: Yale University Press.

Bauman, Z. (2001). *The individualized society.* Cambridge, MA: Polity Press.

-------. (2008). *The art of life.* Cambridge, MA: Polity Press.

Beck, U. (2005). How not to become a museum piece. *The British Journal of Sociology, 56*(3). doi:10.1111/j.1468-4446.2005.00063.x.

Beck, U., & Beck-Gernsheim, E. (2001). *Individualization: Institutionalized individualism and its social and political consequences.* London, England: SAGE.

Beck, U., Giddens, A., & Lash, S. (1994). *Reflexive modernization: Politics, tradition, and aesthetics in the modern social order.*

Stanford, CA: Stanford University Press.

Benkler, Y. (2006). *The wealth of networks: How social production transforms markets and freedom*. New Haven, CT: Yale University Press.

Bentz, V. M., & Shapiro, J. J. (1998). *Mindful inquiry in social research*. Thousand Oaks, CA: SAGE.

Bitbol, M. (2012). Neurophenomenology, an ongoing practice of/in consciousness. *Constructivist Foundations*, *7*(3), 165-173.

Bourdieu, P. (1999). *The weight of the world: Social suffering in contemporary society*. Cambridge, MA: Polity Press.

Castells, M. (1996). *The rise of the network society*. New York, NY: Wiley-Blackwell.

Chalmers, D. J. (1995). Facing up to the problem of consciousness. *Journal of Consciousness Studies*, *2*(3), 200-219.

Dalai Lama. (2011). *Beyond religion: Ethics for a whole world*. New York, NY: Rider.

Duerr, M. (2004). A powerful silence: The role of meditation and other contemplative practices in American life and work. The Center for Contemplative Mind in Society. Retrieved from www.contemplativemind.org/.

Farb, N. A. (2007). Attending to the present: Mindfulness meditation reveals distinct neural modes of self-reference. *Social Cognitive and Affective Neuroscience*, *2*(4), 313-22.

Gendlin, E. (1996). Making concepts from experience. Presented at the 1996 International Focusing Conference. Gloucester, MA (USA).

-------. (1997). *The process model*. Nyack, NY: The Focusing Institute.

-------. (1962/1997). *Experiencing and the creation of meaning*. Evanston, IL: Northwestern University Press.

-------. (1991/2009). *Thinking beyond patterns: Body, language, and situations*. Nyack, NY: The Focusing Institute.

-------. (2009). What first and third person processes really are. *Journal of Consciousness Studies*, *16*, 10-12.

Gergen, K. J. (2009). *Relational being: Beyond self and community*. Oxford, England: Oxford University Press.

Giddens, A. (1990). *The consequences of modernity*. Cambridge, MA: Polity Press.

-------. (1991). *Modernity and self-identity: Self and society in the late modern age*. Cambridge, MA: Polity Press.

Giorgino, V.M.B. (2001). Understanding and compassion: Towards an integration between spiritual and sociological knowledge. Presented at the Sociological Practice Association Annual Conference, August 18, 200. San Francisco, CA.

-------. (2004). Contemplative knowledge and sociological understanding. Presented at the Panel on Contemplative Understanding: A challenge to the sociological perspective, August 17. Sociological Practice Association (SPA) annual conference, San Francisco, CA.

-------. (2014). "Happiness is an art of living: Towards a contemplative perspective on economy as relational work." In *The pursuit of happiness and the traditions of wisdom*, V. M. B. Giorgino (Ed), Chapter 5. Dordrecht, The Netherlands: Springer.

-------. (2015). "Contemplative methods meet social sciences: Back to human experience as it is" *Journal for the Theory of Social Behaviour, 45*(4), December: 461–483.

Higgins, W. (2012). The coming of secular Buddhism: Synoptic view. *Journal of Global Buddhism*, *13*, 109-126.

Hoyt, S. F. (2012). The etymology of religion. *Journal of the American Oriental Society*, *32*(2), 126-129.

Immergut, M., & Kaufman, P. (2014). A sociology of no-self: Applying Buddhist social theory to symbolic interaction. *Symbolic Interaction*, *37*(2), 264-282.

Kabat-Zinn, J. (1990). *Full catastrophe living*. London, England: Piatkus.

-------. (2005). *Coming to our senses: Healing ourselves and the world through mindfulness*. London, England: Piatkus.

-------. (2011). Some reflections on the origins of MBSR: Skillful means, and the trouble with maps. *Contemporary Buddhism, 12*(1), 281-306.

Kirchhoff, M. D., & Hutto, D. D. (2011). Never mind the gap: Neurophenomenology, radical enactivism, and the hard problem of consciousness. *Constructivist Foundations, 11*(2), 302-309.

Latour, B. (2005). *Reassembling the social: An introduction to Actor-Network-Theory*. Oxford, England: Oxford University Press.

McCown, D. (2011). *Teaching mindfulness: A practical guide for clinicians and educators*. Dordrecht, The Netherlands: Springer.

Nagel, T. (1974, October). What is like to be a bat? *The Philosophical Review, LXXXIII*(4), 433-50.

Nauriyal, D. K., Drummond, M., & Lal, Y. B. (Eds.). (2006). *Buddhist thought and applied psychological research: Transcending the boundaries*. London, England: RoutledgeCurzon.

Oldenzki, A. (2006). The transformative impact of non-self. In D. K. Nauriyal, M. Drummond, & Y. B. Lal (Eds.), *Buddhist thought and applied psychological research: Transcending the boundaries* (pp. 250-261).

Perez-Agote, A. (2013). *Secularization: Drawing the boundaries of its validity*. Madrid, Spain: Sociopedia. Retrieved from http://www.sagepub.net/isa/resources/pdf/Secularization2013.pdf. doi:10.1177/205684601075.

Rehorick, D., & Bentz, V. M. (Eds.). (2008). *Transformative phenomenology: Changing ourselves, lifeworlds, and professional practice*. New York, NY: Lexington Books.

Rifkin, J. (2014). *The zero marginal cost society: The Internet of things, the collaborative commons, and the eclipse of capitalism*. New York, NY: Palgrave Macmillan.

Roth, H. (2008, October). Against cognitive imperialism: A call for a non-ethnocentric approach to cognitive science and religious studies. *Religion East and West*, 1-26.

Varela, F. J. (1996). Neurophenomenology: A methodological remedy to the hard problem. *Journal of Consciousness Studies, 3*, 4.

-------. (1999). *Ethical know how: Action, wisdom, and cognition*. Stanford, CA: Stanford University Press.

Varela, F. J., & Shear, J. (Eds.). (1999). *The view from within*. Bowling Green, OH: Imprint Academic.

Varela, F. J., Thompson, E., & Rosch, E. (1991). *The embodied mind: Cognitive science and human experience*. Cambridge, MA: The MIT Press.

Vermersch, P. (1999). Introspection as practice. In F. J. Varela & J. Shear (Eds.), *The view from within* (pp. 17-42). Bowling Green, OH: Imprint Academic.

Waldron, W. S. (2006). The co-arising of self and object, world and society: Buddhists and scientific approaches. In D. K. Nauriyal, M. Drummond, & Y. B. Lal (Eds.), *Buddhist thought and applied psychological research: Transcending the boundaries* (pp. 175-208). London, England: RoutledgeCurzon.

Wallace, A. B. (2000). *The taboo of subjectivity: Toward a new science of consciousness*. Oxford, England: Oxford University Press.

-------. (2001, December). The potential of emptiness: Vacuum states of space and consciousness. *Network: The Scientific and Medical Network Review*, 77, 21-25.

-------. (2007). *Contemplative science: Where Buddhism and neuroscience converge*. New York, NY: Columbia University Press.

Weber, M., & Gerth, H. H. (1958). *From Max Weber: Essays in sociology*. Oxford, England: Galaxy.

Wilke, A. (2013). Individualization of religion. *International Social Science Journal*, *64*, September-December, 263-277.

Wilks, J. (2014, October). Secular mindfulness: Potential & pitfalls. *Insight Journal*. Retrieved from https://www.bcbsdharma.org/

article/secular-mindfulness-potential-pitfalls/.

Williams, J.M.G., & Kabat-Zinn, J. (2011) Mindfulness: Diverse perspectives on its meaning, origins, and multiple applications at the intersection of science and dharma. *Contemporary Buddhism*, *12*, 1-18.

Wright, D. S. (2015, January). A philosophical assessment of secular Buddhism. *Insight Journal*. Retrieved from https://www.bcbsdharma.org/article/a-philosophical-assessment-of-secular-buddhism/.

Žižek, S. (2001). From Western Marxism to Western Buddhism. *Cabinet Magazine, 2*, Spring. Retrieved from http://www.cabinet-magazine.org/issues/2/western.php.

Vincenzo M.B. Giorgino, PhD, is Professor of Economic Sociology in the Department of Economic and Social Sciences, Mathematics and Statistics, University of Turin, Italy. His research interests include analysis of co-production and self-production as forms of relational work in the economic field; and practices of health and well-being at the individual, organizational, and community levels. He is interested in the integration of social sciences and contemplative practices, first-person methods, action research, clinical sociology, and grounded theory.

PART TWO

CONTEMPLATIVE RESEARCH AND PRACTICE: APPLICATIONS

Meditation as Epistemology: How Can Social Scientists Profit From Meditation?

By Krzysztof Konecki, Ph.D.
Department of Sociology of Organization and Management,
University of Lodz, Poland

Abstract

The practice of meditation can explain a lot about society. Although we seem to be alone while meditating, concentrating on something or nothing, we understand society based on the experiences and diverse interpretations of meditation. In this chapter we consider what we as social scientists can get from the practice of meditation and philosophies of meditation. We will explore the main advantages of meditation as an epistemological practice. The main aim is to gain insight that helps us see the changing nature of the mind and its creative nature, which is without essence, observing how mind work yields many inspirations to analysis of the connections between the mind, the self, and society and its "empty nature" (no-mind, no-self, no-society). The consequences of these practices will be very important to reconstructing/deconstructing our concepts and theories (deconstruction based on emptiness). Meditation not only increases a person's sensitivity for deconstructing and constructing concepts; it also increases sympathetic introspection, the ability to have empathy for others. Moreover, following Buddhist inspiration we can infer implications for social research methods and analysis of data in deconstructing and constructing the existing sociological procedures and concepts. It is important in inquiry that a person assumes irony in this approach in order to be open to other possible explanations and falsifications.

Epistemology of the Middle Way

The concepts inspired by Buddhism are present in sociological literature. The first major article on this subject was written by Inge Bell (1979), who attempted to look at the limitations of sociology from the perspective of Buddhist assumptions and practices. She analyzed the possibility of applying Eastern philosophical achievements concerning the meaning of "I" (self) to the theory of self in the Western context. She emphasized the necessity of sociologists being open to different methodologies and research practices, including their own ethical dimension. Some sociologists developed their theoretical concepts of the "self" and "no-self," inspired by symbolic interactionist theory (Immergut & Kaufman, 2014). Still others focused their investigations on the practical dimension of Buddhist assumptions to teach sociology—for example, by developing ethnomethodological experiments aimed at "de-socializing," where the purpose was to determine how individuals experienced social influences or forces (McGrane, 1993a, 1993b). Still others sought to acquire environmental awareness (Schipper, 2012). Some researchers have also used meditative and contemplative practices in their studies (Schipper 2008, 2012).

Robert Moore, in "Dereification in Zen Buddhism" (1995), suggested that contemplative practices can be considered in terms of attempts to increase the methodological and epistemological awareness of social scientists. The purpose of his article was to further develop the phenomenological concept of dereification following Alfred Schutz's (1970) analysis. Dereification means to cease thinking of any human activity in terms of the manifestation of the forces of nature, the dispositions of the universe, or expression of the divine will, as if it were an isolated and independent element of its creator (p. 701). This dereifying perception can be achieved through concentration on "emptiness," through the practice of "nonconceptual mind" or "no-mind" (Moore, 1995, p. 699). As individuals we perceive illusions that can be traps for our minds: "Any *thing* perceived as existing independently of the perceiver can be dereified by recalling the subjective experiences out of which the object was constituted and by apprehending the reflexive connections of the object to its extent" (p. 703).

A similar goal was chosen by another sociologist, Janine Schipper (2012). She attempted to improve qualitative methodology through the development of conscious awareness (mindfulness), combining individual internal experiences with external social influences (social forces) to improve the sociological imagination.

How is sociological knowledge created? This epistemological problem requires more reflection. Sociologists often use concepts or descriptive categories; the assumptions of rational activity; and interpretative procedures that are rooted in everyday language, thought, and common sense thinking (Cicourel, 1970; Garfinkel, 2007; Goode, 1994). Buddhism could be an inspiration to elaborate on sociological concepts, research and analysis of data, or analysis of a society without data. This would involve greater detail and broader perception.

Generally, Buddhist epistemology "problematizes" mundanely accepted ways of producing knowledge. It shows that knowing is almost impossible if we treat as real our mundane concepts and cognition using theoretical concepts. This is in the sense that we reference "real" existing objects and they are treated as separate categories regarding internal essence. However, by adopting this kind of thinking we experience doubt at the base of every type of cognition—even Buddhist thinking—so that any epistemology becomes impossible. This is the error of *petitio principia*, or begging the question.

However, there is light at the end of the tunnel if we come back to meditation practice. Meditation could be the base of cognition, because it shows the processual character of minding, the temporality of mind perception, the temporality of mind conclusions and inferring, the phenomenon of no-perception, and the stability of knowing in not-knowing. Meditation on interconnectedness and inter-being shows the illusionary character of distinctions such as internal and external, micro and macro, self and other, solidarity and anomy, mine and yours, and so on. Although constructionist and postmodernist perspectives in social sciences adopt a similar position, they do not follow the consequences of that position.

Buddhist epistemology accents the unity of mind and reality; it does not simply refuse cognitive distinctions as illusions. In fact, the argument of the illusionary character of life has its roots in the basic texts of Buddhism. What is not clear is how this might be adopted without filters in the *realm* of social sciences. It is the human way to know and act by making distinctions. If we deny that, we support an essentialist and absolute model of truth, which is highly questionable from the Buddhist perspective.

Buddhist ontology is a "middle way" when considering the problem of determinism. The structure of reality is strictly connected with perception and "valid cognition." If valid cognition must fulfill some condition, then it is strictly connected with epistemological questions, or how reality is perceived and what the conditions of this perception are.[1] The ontological problem of Buddhism is connected with the dilemma that oscillates between eternalism and nihilism. On the one hand, we can say that everything exists as it is; on the other hand, we can say that nothing exists at all (Griffith, 2010).

The Madhyamaka ("middle way") school, represented mainly by Nagarjuna, a Buddhist philosopher (150–250 A.D.), says that we should refuse the language of existence and nonexistence. The change of language leads us to another kind of ontology that is connected with the mind. We are also led to the problem of existence and to cognition, so we come finally to another epistemology. The mind, as a cognitive *device*, perceives objects and interprets their meaning at the same time. Objects exist as a mental construction in the same way as dreams exist. In this Buddhist school of thought, only the mind exists. We can conclude that, according to Buddhist ontology, things are not as they seem (Kohl, 2007). This leads us to important aspects of epistemology in Buddhism.

Sociologists and, in general, humanists consider "shared formal symbolic language as a distinguishing feature of human beings and of being human" (Goode, 1994, p. 96). Further, in sociology, "so entrenched is this notion that it is found in introductory textbooks as an obvious—and, I would add, completely unexamined—axiom about human society" (p. 96). Buddhist epistemology, however, suspects that there are more ways to knowing than merely through language and symbols. D. T. Suzuki (1964) writes:

> Zen thinks we are too much slaves to words and logic....Zen deals with facts and not with logical, verbal, prejudiced, and lame representations. This consideration has compelled one to plunge oneself deep into the abyss of the "Nameless" and take hold directly of the spirit as it is engaged in the business of creating the world. Here is no logic, no philosophizing; here is no twisting of facts to suit our artificial measures; here is no murdering of human nature in order to submit it to intellectual dissections; the one spirit stands face to face with the other spirit like two mirrors facing each other, and there is nothing to intervene between their mutual reflections (p. 61).

So, how we can get to the cognition of the "true reality"? An epistemological approach to Buddhism suggests concentrating on the process of forming beliefs. This is the production of knowledge that is only available to human beings. Buddhists concentrate on sensory perception and reasoning. Some other Indian traditions of thought also emphasize testimony, but Buddhism refuses this as an appropriate way of knowledge production.

Direct sensory perception is possible through, for example, meditation. However, we should stress here that sensory perception, or bare percept, is difficult to translate into Western scientific language and its concepts. Researchers in the West sometimes attempt to apply the inspiration of Buddhist epistemology to Western science, but to do so is very difficult. At the same time, we should stress that ethnomethodology is very similar to the position of some Buddhist theses. There is no need for formal language to understand the Other. When we concentrate our analysis on the features of interaction in context, we notice that the routines, the activities in the concrete layout of the space, the likes and dislikes, and the body might be enough to understand people who do not use words—for example, someone who is deaf or blind and therefore does not share a vocabulary for experiences of sight and sound that are not shared (Goode, 1994).

Concerning reasoning, Buddhists generally look for fallacies in the arguments of others. According to Suzuki (1994), "The second major function of reasoning ('reasoning for oneself') is to provide action guides, whether in day-to-day interaction with the physical world, or in abstruse matters of meditational practice or ethical decision-making" (p. 18). Buddhist reasoning helps us infer some happenings in the physical world without stating that this physical world exists at all. What is important here is that we see the epistemological tool as the reasoning, which is helpful for meditation. This should be practiced according to some rules, elaborated by reason. This will get us to the reality, or to the mind and minding. We will come back to meditation practice later to explain this in detail.

Generally, Buddhism's aim is to promote different perspectives of reality that are not based on the traditional sense of logical inference or logical categorizing of the world. Suzuki states that "Zen wants us to acquire an entirely new point of view whereby to look into the mysteries of life and secrets of nature" (p. 59). This is because "Zen has come to the definite conclusion that the ordinary logical process of reasoning is powerless to give the final satisfaction to our deepest spiritual needs" (p. 59). Spiritual needs, needs related to caring for one's well-being, can be associated with looking for the sense of life and the answer to the fundamental question "Who am I?"

Eightfold Path: Ethics and Cognition

Buddhism is an internally diverse tradition, so choosing concepts and interpretations that represent it is a delicate matter. Here we will follow the interpretation and teaching of Zen Buddhism presented by Vietnamese monk Thich Nhat Hanh. We will consider the ideas of Buddhism as described in his writings (see http://www.thichnhathanhfoundation.org/ for more information). Hanh's teachings are based on a combination of Zen Buddhism and Theravada Buddhism concepts (Hanh, 1976, 1999, 2006). We will also use some inspirations from the teachings of Seung Sahn, a Korean Buddhist teacher in the Kwan Um school (1976, 1982). Further, we support our reconstruction by Suzuki's interpretation (1964, 1994).

Suffering is the basic concept of Buddhism. We know this from the four noble truths: suffering; creation of suffering; cessation of creating suffering; and the noble Eightfold Path. The eightfold "right practices," as the Chinese call it, can stop a person's suffering. These eight aspects of living should not be considered as separate; instead, they are interconnected as a single path.

There are eight assumptions we make in order to see things as they are. Notice that these assumptions are strongly connected to a specific social context; thus, we can see that the link between Buddhist assumptions and societal obligations is both relative and context specific.

The following are brief definitions of these assumptions: First, we have the Right View. This refers to the view of the phenomena, objects, and concepts that reduce suffering and do not increase suffering.

Next, Right Intention and Thinking relates to the intent of self-improvement when, in every moment, a person tries to be a better person, tries not to do harm to others, and wants to be more compassionate.

Right Speech guards against using words in ways that cause suffering for other people. We should avoid bad words with wrong intentions, and abstain from false speech and idle chatter.

Next, Right Action means we avoid harming other living creatures, stealing, and sexual misconduct. This rule is associated with the general assumption of Buddhism that we not contribute to increased suffering in the world.

Right Livelihood means we avoid harming others in the way we earn our living (e.g., by butchery or trading arms or drugs).

Right Diligence means putting in much effort to reach an understanding of the Fourth Truths,[2] engaging the mental energy to be disciplined and to have compassion for suffering of all sentient creatures.

Right Mindfulness means that we are aware that many people see the world as it is filtered through their own conception. We are also aware of our consciousness as it is going on during our life events, moment by moment.

Finally, Right Concentration means paying attention to one object or point for a long time in order to settle our minds and understand better. We can concentrate, for example, on the noble truths or on one aspect of the Eightfold Path.

"Rightness" means to be correct, not solely in a moral sense but also being straight, not bent, seeing reality as it is and not as we want it to be. It is clear that ontology is tightly connected with epistemology. The structure of the world is such that we see it through our minding. All eight aspects also have moral character, a morality strongly associated with cognition and thinking processes. Seeing the world in some way, we also create it and shape the path to its future.

Because in this chapter we are interested in epistemological issues, we focus our consideration on the assumptions that are directly connected with cognition: right view; right mindfulness; and right concentration. These qualities help us see reality without considering other quasi-ontological assumptions, especially those taken from the everyday life world and common sense thinking that state reality as an objective sphere.

We cultivate the *right view* through contemplation and meditation. When we do, we see the temporary nature of ideas and concepts. Meditation means, among others things, observing the thoughts that relate to objects through concepts or feelings. We can also observe the *karma* results,[3] or the causes of our concepts and feelings. Why does suffering arise? What is responsible for this? For sociologists interested in applied sociology and with the moral responsibility for their research, these questions are fundamental.

Meditation on problems can make a person more mindful of the conditions necessary for causing the phenomenon, as well as sufficient conditions to create the suffering situation (which can sometimes become intervening variables). A variable, often used as a noun in sociology, is a concept that reflects the quality of changeability. However, we should add to this one more meaning: the temporality of existing phenomena is also *variable*, as an adjective, indicating liability and potentiality for change. The variable becomes one entity with variable objects. The researcher and analysts should not rely on other explanations or theories to understand the world. She should use the intuitive thought created during contemplation and meditation to understand the *karma* of phenomena and their changeability in the creation of suffering. The right view is deepened by right concentration and right mindfulness.[4]

Right concentration is a very important skill for the sociologist. To achieve the skill, she must practice meditation. Each of us has a lot of layers that cover reality, and we see reality as filtered through them. We should unlearn the primary and secondary knowledges to which we were socialized. By this I mean that every person has acquired status quo knowledge, not only for living everyday life, but also in the set of concepts and methods of research and analysis in which she was trained. The concept of what qualifies as "empirical data" is an assumption or "layer" that must be deconstructed and reconstructed in order to allow for a broader understanding of reality. We must acknowledge that "seeing reality" is a process of creating it by *a priori* categories that we apply in typical situations of our everyday lives, including research situations. If we learn to suspend our existing knowledge, stereotypes, and categories, we can concentrate on the objects in this present moment. This will be direct knowledge rather than inherited from the history of perception of the object. In this way, we try to see the present social reality without preconceptualization. This is the aim of Grounded Theory methodology (Strauss, 1987).

In right concentration, we can see the *one in many*, or the whole in the part. The concentration on the no-self when one is supposed to have a sense of self, for example, allows a person to become open to the inter-being of all human beings, and the interconnectedness of the social worlds in which they participate.[5] It is difficult to express the experience of the no-self. It happens sometimes during meditation. If we contemplate self, asking the question "Who am I?" we can also get a direct view of the self/no-self. In a moment, we may be able to see the absurdity of both the question and the answer that is not directly suggested by the question.

The autoethnography method is very helpful for developing this practice.[6] When we do "research" on ourselves, we can see how self changes over time instead of being certain as a social and psychological object. It is easy to reduce self to the impressions in specific contexts that come and go, but in autoethnography we see the impermanence of the concept of self. We will return to this for further explanation.

The first impulse to go deeper and recognize no-self in the existential sense often comes from feelings of the impermanence of self that arise in a discrete situation. Autoethnography is a form of contemplation that does not necessarily extend beyond methods of obtaining objectively proven knowledge; it looks deeper into inner and outer knowledge as that knowledge appears in the practice of mindful concentration on self. Cultural patterns are seen as they connect with the self-image and subjective experiencing of the external pressure of culture and internal wills to oppose or adapt to it.

Right mindfulness further enhances right view. This means being mindful of the whole of life in thinking and doing. The Sanskrit word for mindfulness, *smriti*, means "remember." Mindfulness is remembering to come back to the present moment. The character that the Chinese use for "mindfulness" has two parts: the upper part means "now" and the lower part means "mind" or "heart" (Hanh, 1999, pp. 64-65). The full meaning is to be present here and now.

Right mindfulness helps us identify the body as a construct (*rupa*) by being mindful of all the parts of the body and contemplating them while intentionally scanning the body's experience. Paying attention to the heat of one's body, the weight of one's body, and one's breathing give the same effects. Mindful breathing is a major practice of mindfulness. In this way a person can experience his body both as in parts and in totality. This depends on the perception in each moment. Corporality, as it is researched by sociologists, is not always described only by societal concepts, norms, values, and influences. Direct cognition of one's body also plays an important role in going beyond the concepts of external influences and determinants because these are constructed concepts rather than real ones. These constructions are the layers that cover one's body and obscure it, like a thick coat of concepts that blocks the perception of reality and the experiencing of it.

The second base of right mindfulness is awareness of feelings (*vedana*). Identifying feelings and naming them (for example, anger, hate, love) helps a person to see them more deeply and to deconstruct their empty nature. During meditation and contemplation, we should not cling to feelings, whether they are pleasant, unpleasant, or neutral. Meditation helps a person see them as they are–as impermanent, created, not determined externally, induced by minding and volition.

The third establishment of mindfulness is the mind (*chitta samskara*). Mind formations (*samskara*) mean that everything is formed from something else–the tree is a formation, our hate is a formation, prejudices are formations, volition is formation. Hanh (1999) writes, "The basic unwholesome mental formations are greed, ignorance, pride, doubts, and views" (p. 74). If we instead observe wholesome feelings and thoughts, we create positive connections because they give a direct, clear view of what is real.

We can see the sociological sense of mindfulness in the interconnectedness of the individual and collective. We can do research on individual consciousness and at the same time research community: "Individual consciousness is made of collective consciousness, and the collective consciousness is made of individual consciousness. They cannot be separated. Looking deeply into our individual consciousness, we touch the collective consciousness" (Hanh, 1999, p. 75, 181).

Consciousness is a product of interaction between society and individual mind. Mindfulness helps us discover the connections. It also allows looking deep inside one's consciousness to see the mental formations that may arise at some moments. The mindfulness of phenomena is the fourth establishment (called *dharmas*). Hanh (1999) writes that "phenomena are objects of our mind. Each mental formation has to have an object" (p. 76). Perception comes from our mind: If a person looks at a table, the image of "table" arises in his mind. The objects of his thinking are minds (*dharmas*). Hanh goes on to say, "In Chinese, the character for perception [想] is composed of the ideograms for sign and mind. A perception is a sign, an image in our mind" (p. 76).

Right mindfulness is the essence of the path to right view and can be important to sociologists for right research and analysis. We can analyze data, but we should remember that data are in our minds; we can contemplate ideas that are socially important to see their true nature, to see them as they are and what is behind them. If we want to understand "society," we should deconstruct the elements of "being." This involves declassification, enumerating, and observing their connectedness, in order to see their origin and temporal character. In addition, we will finally see what we get from having such a concept as "society" in our work and life as sociologists.

Usually, researchers do not use inspirations from this perspective as conceptions in research. A contemplative perspective is useful for deeper understanding of our research and for getting a sense of the importance of the results. However, might we improve the lives of the human beings upon whom we conduct research? Can research lead to an end to suffering? Can we analyze and find the causes of suffering? How do we use such concepts? What are the reasons for the effort to maintain concepts such as society, integration, or anomie? Are these reasons epistemological, ontological, or methodological? Are they common sense reasons, or are they simply ideological reasons? Is it a nonsense statement in our modern society to say that society does not exist? Is that contrary to the "common sense" of the society?

We may even use the term "contemplative practice" without noticing that it has already been devalued. The concept of contemplative practice must be deconstructed and reconstructed in the same way that we treat other sociological concepts such the concepts of self and mind. Being mindful of concepts, here and now, in every moment of research practice, may enrich the research. It can help the researcher see the "researched" or "co-researched reality" as it is, not as she assumes it is.

Meditation Practice for Sociologists

There are many books, even scientific books, and websites that provide instructions for how to meditate (Engler, 2009, p. 469). Many of the techniques of meditations are included in Hanh's books (for example, see Hanh, 1976). We can also find many examples on www.youtube.com.

Here, I will simply summarize some guidelines and tips from many sources, as well as my own experience. I hope to show non-meditating persons how to meditate in a Buddhist tradition of "sitting meditation" (*zazen* in Zen Buddhism).[7]

Sit with your spine straight. You can sit on the floor using a cushion or on a chair. Your legs may be crossed in the lotus position or in the common position, or you can sit on your heels as Japanese Buddhists do. If you sit on a chair, try to sit on the front one-third of the chair and keep your spine straight. It is necessary to keep your spine straight to avoid sleeping. Your position should be comfortable enough to concentrate on your breathing as you breath rhythmically from your diaphragm.

Concentrate your sight on one point on the floor about one meter in front of you. Look at this point as if there is a line going from your nose to down to the floor.

Concentrate on your breathing as you count breaths from one to 10, then once again. Simply observe your thoughts that they come and go without concentrating on them.

Do this for at least 15 minutes. After one week, you might increase the time to 20 minutes, then 30 or even longer if you want. It is helpful to set a timer.

Pic. 1. Meditation.
Photo of author by Anna Kacperczyk

The goal is to meditate twice a day for at least 20 or 30 minutes each session. Of course, you can meditate more often and longer for better effects.

When a person meditates on the question "Who am I?" she can reach the point of understanding that the concept of "self" is merely a constructed image of how she sees herself and, as a constructed image, it is empty. This is a very important moment for a sociologist because in that moment there arises an empty hole. It is a common experience to find out we do not know who we are. In fact, we may have so many answers to the question that we cannot decide on one. All of the sub-stantive answers are connected with social roles, stereotypes, and our perceptions of the perceptions of others (this is the looking-glass self of Cooley, 1909). These are all temporary and do not touch the essence of what we would like to be. Desire mixes with reality, but reality is constantly moving. It is difficult to stop and see its essence. However, when we meditate, we should not try to fill this empty hole, even though we feel uneasy and uncomfortable because the mind wants to fill a hole that has no bottom:

> That's what we're doing when we meditate: we are "let-
> ting go" of all the physical and mental activity that dis-
> tracts us from our emptiness . . . unreality. Meditation is
> uncomfortable, especially at the beginning, because in
> our daily lives we are used to taking evasive action. So
> we tend to take evasive action when we meditate too:
> we fantasize, make plans, feel sorry for ourselves (Loy
> 2008, p. 21).

Eventually, we will see that self is constructed. We will also see that if the self is constructed and not real, we might uncover the emptiness of other concepts. Our presumptions are called into question and we broaden our thinking. The meditation of self might be a good exercise that leads us to develop a new way of deconstructing and reconstructing assumed knowledge. We can deconstruct the concept of self and finally see its true nature—one that is impermanent and which is connected to the no-self. One develops perception of the interdependence of things, even in a place that has been allocated to the concept of "I." Meditation teaches us that there is no "I," that in fact "I" is composed of many in-terdependent elements. "I" has no essence.

The experience of emptiness is very fruitful for a sociologist because he can build something new once he deconstructs the self. We can also see emptiness as a fullness, which seems to be a paradox. In re-ality, however, we can see more (fullness) from experiencing the empti-ness. The Buddhist term usually translated as emptiness (Pali, *shunnata*; Sanskrit, *shunyata*) has a double-sided meaning. It derives from the root *shu*, which means "swollen": "not only the swollenness of a blown-up balloon but also the swollenness of an expectant woman, pregnant with possibility" (Loy, 2008, p. 22). Loy suggests that a more accurate trans-lation of *shunyata* is "emptiness/fullness, which describes quite well the experience of our own empty core, both the problem and the solution" (p. 22). For Hanh (1999), the emptiness means interdependence and not having essence:

> We are empty of a separate, independent self. We cannot be by ourselves alone. We can only inter-be with every-thing else in the cosmos. The practice is to nourish the insight into emptiness all day long. Wherever we go, we touch the nature of emptiness in everything we contact. We look deeply at the table, the blue sky, our friend, the mountain, the river, our anger, and our happiness and see that these are all empty of a separate self. When we touch these things deeply, we see the interbeing and in-terpenetrating nature of all that is. Emptiness does not mean nonexistence. It means Interdependent Co-Aris-ing, impermanence, and nonself (p. 89).

Hanh also says, "'Emptiness' means empty of a separate self. It is full of everything, full of life. "The word emptiness should not scare us. It is a wonderful word. To be empty does not mean non-existent" (Hanh,

2012, p. 421). Rather than a nihilistic concept, emptiness is an optimistic view of the cognition of the world in co-arising. The emptiness here may be connected to three issues: co-arising; accenting compassion; and reference to naturalness. These three references are connected with exploration of *groundlessness* (Varela, Thompson, & Rosch, 1993, pp. 220-221).

It is important to meditate on one point, on breath, or steps during sitting or walking meditation. However, the meditation should be the everyday life practice in every activity. When we are mindful all the time, the concepts are not a barrier to seeing reality in oneness. The thick coat of concepts is removed:

> Another beautiful sight always followed. If you are the wave and you become one with the water, looking at the world with the eyes of water, then you are not afraid of going up, going down, going up, going down. But please do not be satisfied with speculation, or take my word for it. You have to enter it, taste it, and be one with it yourself, and that can be done through meditation, not only in the meditation hall, but throughout your daily life. While you cook a meal, while you clean the house, while you go for a walk, you can look at things and try to see them in the nature of emptiness. Emptiness is an optimistic word; it is not at all pessimistic (Hanh, 2012, pp. 426-427).

Sometimes we say that the good sociologist should be a sociologist all the time. It is the same with the practice of meditation. If we practice only in separate special spaces, we lose a lot of time through not-mindful living in our mundane, everyday life. It is important to develop this sense of emptiness for all experiences of life. If the practice of meditation is excluded to a separate, special place, awareness of the emptiness might be lost. I believe we see evidence in our world that people are deceived by false categories that are external, imposed, and unconsciously accepted. Thus, we lose the possibility of seeing the world as it is, the "suchness" of the world. Moreover, as sociologists we often use "common sense" concepts and thinking, or mind formations, to state scientific hypotheses. Mind formation, as we recall, is the third establishment of mindfulness. We can avoid the trap of assuming what is "common sense" by meditating on it.

Deconstruction and Reconstruction

Deconstruction of self and then reconstruction of a sense of self result from meditation practice. Here we do not understand deconstruction in the postmodernistic sense; we can see that this view is epistemologically nihilistic, and there are ethical consequences when there is deconstruction of all meanings (Bentz & Kenny, 1997). Deconstruction of concepts does not mean refusing their meanings, but rather contextualizing them and coming to new understanding. By contextualizing phenomena, named by concepts, in the here and now, we are offered a different view; the concepts are embodied in a lifeworld and we are able to construct new meanings.

When a researcher meditates, he becomes able to see beyond the phenomenon of text or language expressions; he is able to meet something much more basic to reality: it is in meditative practice that other deconstructive and constructive efforts start. Sociologists who meditate know this experience very well. Understanding the experience of meditation practice might change our methodological practice as well. For example, according to Buddhist thought, a person might be suffering because of his attachments to his sense of identity. If he contemplates his concept of self, he will come to realize that self is not his own concept, not is the sense of self stable over time. Instead, it is social, external, and impermanent. By understanding and experiencing impermanence of the self, he has taken the first step in understanding that traditional methods of researching and analyzing result in transformations of identity. It will become clear that his thought processes are a result of his context, and that his previous understanding of self was limited and barely touched on the problem of self (Strauss, 1959; Strauss, 1993, see chapter 5). When we see the fragility of self in everyday life and in every moment, we begin to sense the meaning of emptiness; the transformation of identity cannot happen because there is nothing to be transformed.

A substantive understanding of self lacks a deeper understanding of the diverse selves and identities existing in the world. Self is self and self is also everything that created it; this is the concept of co-arising. Self is shaped by and shapes all aspects of the lifeworld. Observing how self creates and is created in the here and now requires a new method of research that incorporates meditation practice.[8] This practice can highlight for sociologists the necessity for experiential techniques that are incorporated into the research methods used. The researcher who assumes all things can be objectively measured will not be able to account for data that is subjective. It is only through experience and awareness of the emptiness of external constructs that the researcher might open to broader understandings. In this awareness, the researcher is likely to see that linear cause is often not the reality of human lifeworlds. Instead, causality is reciprocal and co-arising. When deconstruction empowers methods of social research, epistemology becomes pragmatic and even practical.

What is important in the deconstruction process is looking for and analyzing the duality of perception—the self existing separately from context, as Western sociological thinking would have us believe. The Buddhist concept of *Anatta* (no-self), however, changes our options.[9] Meditation on and analysis of the self/identity reveals that a pure "self" is a delusion. Sociological thinking about the self is always in relation to an assumed other; self does not exist without the other. In the ontological sense, there is no-self, so there are no reasons to concentrate on the well-being of the individual self when in research, therapy, persuasions, pedagogy, and life in general. The suffering of the self is not caused by "the other"; it is caused by the perception that "I" and "other" exist separately. The sense that self and other are separate is a socialized experience, induced for *constructionistic* reasons: to create a sense of shame; to create a sense of guilt; to create a sense of sin; and finally to control an individual or a group, or to dominate both of them.

After the deconstruction of this duality, we can reconstruct the concept of self through contemplation. During the meditation a person can simply ask: "Who am I?" He repeats the question as a mantra during breathing in; he answers, "I do not know" during breathing out. Keeping a "don't know" mind means cutting off all discursive thoughts. This takes us to the wellspring of our true nature and brings us to the present moment.

Paying attention to this moment is what Zen practice is all about: "What are you doing just now?" For example, a Zen teacher might use a *kong-an* interview situation to understand a student's practice and guide the student toward the "don't know" mind. *Kong-an* allows the student to experience any hindrances he is having (Wu Bong, 1990).[10] Lacking a presumed answer presses the student to stop the thinking. He clears his mind and what arises is the concept that his self/identity is a false problem introduced by contemporary sociologists as one of the most important sociological concepts for understanding the modern world (see Goffman, 1956, 1963; Strauss, 1997).

Dualistic thinking about the self still prevails in social research, operating in the dimension of self-other duality and even I-Me duality related to the internal dialog (Immergut & Kaufman, 2014). Charles H. Cooley's (1909) concept of the "looking-glass self" is a good example of how constructivism helped shape modern sociology. This concept states that self does not exist without others' perceptions and our perceptions about their perceptions. This self is chronically anxious, constantly looking for the evaluations of others and afraid of negative estimations from them (p. 5). In the practice of not-thinking, this social conditioning of self disappears because a person is in an "identity vacuum." That is what is real; the rest is delusion. This might be one of the directions to pursue in developing an anti-essentialist sociology.

This is my interpretation of the meditation on identity. It is my experience. However, an interpretation for the experience itself is not needed. Meditation on self requests that I leave the state of my mind as it is, leave conscious thinking, and wait to feel the real sense of self. However, if I want to get something sociological from the meditation, I will draw more conclusions—unfortunately, and ironically, by thinking.

Research on identity should be done by uncovering and observing the natural narrations that oscillate around identity/self in the mind. We would need to show how the desired concept is maintained from moment to moment. The motive of identity creation is to fulfill a desire for permanent existence. Desires are often greedy motives associated with material props that uplift the egotist yearning for identity. Motives are also created by our history of being in social worlds. At the same time, these desires are social and interactive constructions, and they are empty because the vocabularies of motives are ideological narrations elaborated to educate citizens to conformity (Mills, 1940). We are educated to want to become what our context expects—managers, doctors, lawyers, officers, professors, and many other socially prescribed roles. Part of the narrative is that happiness can be achieved by being somebody valuable and useful to society. But if the society does not exist—as the self does not exist—the motives to achieve socially approved identities also have dubious existences. In consequence, if the motives are empty—that is, they are impermanent, constructed, not always valuable, creating suffering, and recognizable as mere concepts—so too is identity/self empty because it was created by false desires and values.

Apart from contemplating self/identity and no-self, sociologists benefit from the practice of *signlessness interdependence* (*animitta*). This contemplation practice gives us the sense of how subject and object interweave. Hanh (1999) states, "Every object of the mind is itself a mind" (p. 59) because we always have the object of our thinking. For example, when we contemplate society, the society becomes the mind. When we contemplate the body, the body becomes the mind. When we contemplate the self, the self becomes the mind. When we contemplate conflict, the conflict become the mind. When we contemplate anger or anxiety, the anger or anxiety becomes the mind. However, "when the object of knowledge is not present, there can be no subject. Meditate and see the interbeing of the subject and the object" (p. 59). Deconstruction becomes the reduction of objects to the mind.

Deconstruction is also connected with contemplation of signlessness. A *sign* is an object of our perception. Signs are the cause of our deceptions, illusions, and often our sufferings. By breaking through the signs, we can touch the reality that they are covering:

> As long as we are caught by signs—round, square, solid, liquid, gas—we will suffer. Nothing can be described in terms of just one sign. But without signs, we feel anxious. Our fear and attachment come from our being caught in signs. Until we touch the signless nature of things, we will continue to be afraid and to suffer. Before we can touch H_2O, we have to let go of signs like squareness, roundness, hardness, heaviness, lightness, up, and down. Water is, in itself, neither square nor round nor solid. When we free ourselves from signs, we can enter the heart of reality. But until we can see the ocean in the sky, we are still caught by signs (Hanh, 1999, p. 89).

Hanh (1999) recommends that politicians, economists, and educators practice signlessness. It would, for example, help them understand why so many people are in jails. I think that sociologists should do the same; they can understand that signs, words, and phrases commonly used in everyday life are misleading and deficient.

The practice of meditation is connected with the contemplation of interdependence when we deconstruct the phenomena as co-arising no-self beings. This is especially important in understanding crime and delinquency: If we analyze problems through the no-self, we can comprehend the realities of how crime is co-conditioned in a society. In fact, researchers themselves are delinquents in a society, the person whose picture is on the "wanted criminal" poster—I am that person; you are that person—because there is no separate being, no separate personality dissociated from the social worlds in which we participate. There is no individual personality in the sense of *being*. Instead, there are legislations, educational systems, families, religions, states and cities, politics, and media, all of which are interwoven and co-create the delinquent acts assigned to delinquent individuals. The concept of a delinquent personality is misleading and hides the real phenomenon. Personality is a person's mind; we see and experience our mind. All else is constructed.

Even more important for the process of deconstruction is a meditation on *emptiness*. We can meditate on the emptiness of names, signs, and representations. During this, a person usually draws conclusions about the role of language in the construction of what appears to be real; "real" is often understood as substantive objects with differentiable essences. We assume that there are definitive features that constitute objects in a logical way. It is certainly possible to do this during the special sitting meditation practices, but we can also meditate on it during everyday life activities. We can practice the mindfulness of all acts: walking, running, driving, cooking, eating, teaching, reading, working, dancing, doing hathayoga, and any other activity.

Meditation and mindfulness help us to see the emptiness of all ideologies expressed in language. This frees us from the delusions of ideologies. We should analyze the existing theories, ideologies, and discourses and refuse them in order to get to a higher level of cognition. On an even deeper level, contemplation is able to free us from even the Buddhist thoughts on which the practice is based (Loy, 2003, p. 26).

This does not mean that we should be attached to emptiness either. Such attachment is a trap in meditation; emptiness could be also delusion. We should meditate on this as well.

The concept of delusions is very important: "The role of delusion has a special meaning in Buddhism. The fundamental delusion is our sense of separation from the world we live in, including our alienation from other people" (Loy, 2003, p. 44). When we assume, for example, that "evil" is outside of our self, outside of our community, when we are attached to the dualistic concept of good and evil, we mistake delusions for reality. Evil often starts with our own self or community. We do not want to see that. However, having a vision of the interconnectedness of all things in the world can lead us to understand why evil comes to us, especially as we desconstruct concepts through our language. This suggests opposites and dualistic thinking[11]: "Buddhism encourages us to be wary of antithetical concepts: good and evil, success and failure, rich and poor, and even enlightenment and delusion" (p. 110).

Intuition for Sociologists

Sociologists try to create theoretical sets of statements that are logically connected. Definitions and axioms form the basis of connected hypotheses. The hypotheses are checked by empirical investigation. If verified—that is, found reliable—rational reasons for the validity of the hypotheses are established, which reinforces the findings and the certainty of the conclusions reached. This is the "scientific" way of thinking that developed as our positivistic, scientific heritage. Without a doubt this is a rational and logical way to obtain some types of data. However, this heritage leads to dualistic thinking about rational knowing and intuitive knowing; science came to see the latter as a matter of faith. This is a rational way to avoid analyzing the role of intuition in science, and refusing it as irrational. Petitmengin-Peugeot (2002) writes:

Examination of individual experience before thinking is extremely difficult because it is a subjective experience, discrete, direct, sudden and complete. The perceived research's difficulties and presuppositions, that we cannot explore the origins of intuition because it is pre-verbal, cause often rejection of this kind of research issues in modern science...However, the emergence of intuition takes time and is progressive in nature, if we accept this vision, a research of intuition is possible (pp. 44-45).

From an Eastern perspective, it is assumed that intuition goes beyond linear reason. Carl Gustaw Jung has been widely quoted as saying that intuition is "perception via unconscious." However, intuitions must also be informed by past experience and observations; these are what form the basis of knowing, even when the intuitive researcher is not fully aware of it. Sometimes intuition is called "sixth sense," so it can be considered a "cognitive faculty" or "a kind of perception," which is what Immanuel Kant wanted (Benedict, 2011). Intuitive statements are not irrational; they are instead a different kind of rational thinking with a different foundation.

Intuitive thinking refers to concentration and perception of the world as it occurs during flowing and indivisible time. This time is not the here and now, neither the past nor the future. Henri Bergson (2007) believes that it is generally continuous, but our modern world chops it up to make stop-frames, using photographic language.

Right mindfulness and right concentration help us cultivate intuition in flowing time. This is, of course, achieved by regular practice. The word "intuition" comes from the Latin *intueri*, which means "to look inside," without rational thinking at that moment. Because meditation helps us perceive the interconnectedness of all things in the world, observing and feeling these relations is very important in the creative work of interpreting data, a process that is about seeing connections between things. Seeing interconnectedness helps researchers find new relations. In Buddhism, intuition is connected with feeling oneness with nature (Seung Sahn, 1976), or sensing "inter-being" (Hanh, 1999).

Moreover, when we meditate, we lose attachment to the egoistic self that creates boundaries to our mind. Mind cannot work fully and associate things in the world when it is limited by thinking about the interests of a self, which is a delusion anyway. Intuition as a creative way of knowing is connected with no-attachment:

> No-attachment thinking means that your mind is clear all the time. When you drive, you aren't thinking; you are just driving. So the truth is just like this. Red light means Stop; green light means Go. It is intuitive action. Intuitive action means acting without any desire or attachment. My mind is like a clear mirror, reflecting everything just as it is. Red comes, and the mirror becomes red; yellow comes, and the mirror becomes yellow. This is how a Bodhisattva lives. I have no desires for myself. My actions are for all people (Hanh, 1976, p. 7).

What is important here is to see things-in-themselves. When the mind is included in perception, we see only the representations. When we see "homeless person," we see the person through a category that is socially predefined; "the homeless person" is a representation. We do not see the person-in-her-homelessness. We do not see her fully connected with all of the social surroundings. We do not see that she is we, because we see all things as separate. The assumption is that my identity is different from yours. Real compassion cannot arise in this way of thinking because separation invokes a feeling of pity but not empathetic understanding. Sociologists who do not practice meditation may have problems achieving an understanding of the researched objects because objects are assumed to be separate things and therefore each has definitive meanings. Reaching the level of sympathetic understanding is impossible without achieving the level of understanding the emptiness of concepts. (For example, the meaning of "homeless person/ non-homeless person," "determinants of homelessness," "personality/ identity of homeless person," and the like are empty contexts in and of themselves.) However, through sympathetic introspection, a methodological strategy in which the researcher takes the role of the other, the following is possible:

> ...putting himself into intimate contact with various sorts of persons and allowing them to awake in himself a life similar to their own, which he afterwards, to the best of his ability, recalls and describes. In this way he is more or less able to understand—always by introspection—children, idiots, criminals, rich and poor, conservative and radical—any phase of human nature not wholly alien to his own...This I conceive to be the principal method of the social psychologist (Cooley, 1909, p. 7).

Sympathetic introspection is contextual because it "emphasizes adopting the standpoints of social actors as the basis for empathetically understanding their behavior in a given situation" (Manis & Meltzer, 1978, p. 4; see also Bentz & Shapiro, 1998). Sympathetic introspection is used to understand the participants' worldviews and begin to understand the deeper level of motives, not merely actions (Manis & Meltzer, 1978, p. 22). This understanding is on the surface of the minding activity, where concepts turn into action.

The deeper understanding of taking the role of other means that I am other, and other is I. His suffering is my suffering and I participate in it, even if I do not have the awareness of this in the moment. If I am aware of it, I start sympathizing with the other. If I achieve this understanding, I can use the procedure of empathy, which is so important in social qualitative research methods such as sociological ethnography. Generally, we perceive reality through images and representations, although some researchers using first-person methodologies do not follow this model of generating knowledge (Bentz & Shapiro, 1998; Rehorick & Bentz, 2008; Seamon, 2000; Toombs, 1995; Varela & Shear, 2002; Varela, Thompson, & Rosch, 1993).

Preconceptualization is needed for standard scientific procedure as we prepare a set of concepts and hypotheses before beginning our research. However, the images through which our perceptions are formed might be wrong: We might see that what looked like a snake in a dark room is actually a piece of coiled rope; we might see that the drunkard staggering toward us is a person in need of help. Representations often have stereotypical meanings, and we might see enemies where people are friendly. Preconceptions might lead us to see the social structures contributing to suffering or happiness. We might see identity negotiations where there is only suffering that results from an egotist preoccupation on how self is perceived (Goffman, 1956). We might see social roles where there are attachments to delusions of presentation of self. Hanh (2006) writes that intuition is a form of knowing not based on thinking or imagining: "Yet even our mind consciousness can touch the realm of things in themselves from time to time. When we have a strong intuition, our mind consciousness is in touch with the realm of suchness" (p. 56).

Intuition seems to be a way of direct perception, bypassing the participation of minding (see Scheff, 1990, Chapter 9).[12] These intuitive skills can be practiced through meditation. Meditation creates an opportunity for this form of knowing because it releases us from categorical perceptions, shows the emptiness of concepts, and exposes false imagining of reality. Meditation is in essence the *form* of intuition as a way of perception. On the other hand, it is formless because you must sit/walk/

do only, and observe in order to go beyond mere form.

On an epistemological level, we can put an equals sign between the two experiences: meditation = intuition. In this way, the form becomes the content. By practicing the repetition of *koans* (the Japanese form of the Korean *kong-an* described previously), we get to direct and spontaneous intuitive actions:

> Any moment in our life can be understood as a kong-an. As we are able to penetrate the simple situations of kong-ans without being confused by our discursive minds, our intuition starts to grow. Eventually our intuition can grow so that when confronted with complex situations in our lives, the correct response will automatically appear (Wu Bong, 1990; see also Suzuki 1994).[13]

Meditation is helpful for seeing a problem in a broader context; at the same time (maybe a little earlier) we see things directly, without assumed categorical filters. Compassion develops at that moment and makes a sociologist less ethically detached and more engaged. Sympathetic introspection (Cooley, 1909) is not possible without including this ethical perspective in the sociological analysis. We know that sympathetic introspection is a very important tool in ethnography (Prus, 1996, p. 51). It is also helpful to artists who observe human experience and "report" on it through their art.[14] If we want to understand the "data" we collect through our participants and others collaborators, we have to know how to step into their shoes, how to understand lifeworlds through sympathetic introspection. Right view (seeing the temporary nature of the concept of other), concentration on other, and mindfulness of other are indispensable to be in the here and now with humans, animated objects, and unanimated objects.

A field researcher must be mindful of *otherness* all the time

(Bentz & Shapiro, 1998, p. 52). With meditation practice, the other and we will engage in real, interactive ethnographic research. Future consideration might be given to how method in ethnography—that is, the ethnographer, his sensitivities, and embodiment in the situation—may be decisive for the research results (Goode, 1994, p. 144).[15]

Conclusions

In trying to make our research trustworthy, we should not over-identify with any conceptual framework that we use to explain the social phenomena. Attachment is a first step to falling into a trap of delusion. Experiential knowing, by using the practice of meditation and contemplation, gives us the tools necessary for developing the insight of *shunyata*—the complementariness of emptiness/fullness indicates something that has to be approached experientially rather than cognitively. We can explain the concepts using words, but the experiential knowledge gives them direct understanding and meaning. Shunyata means neither a void nor a transcendent reality such as God or Brahman. It simply refers to the fact that things have no "essence" or self-being of their own. It is a useful concept because it can help us realize something while it does not itself refer to that something (Loy, 2008; see also Kohl, 2007).

This concept is an instrument of understanding the phenomena; it is useful and acceptable because of its practicality, not because it is discovering absolute truth about the essence of things or phenomena. We should not be attached to this concept either, because it also does not *exist objectively* and any referential objects of it are likewise illusive.

If we do field research on *Other* or in ethnography, or if we construct a grounded theory of *Other* or otherness, we will easily see the emptiness of the concept because it is constructed and not essentially "real." The *Other* is me. In fact, we do the study about ourselves when we research *Other*. Emptiness is a faculty of all phenomena. If we follow Rorty's (1989) idea of irony, it applies also to our assumptions. Our assumption of emptiness is temporary. Thoughts and minding become the problem to be solved pragmatically.

We can summarize the practical functions of meditation for social researchers as follows. First, meditation could be a very useful tool for developing the researcher's sensitivity and intuition. We can, in this way, make a research of our own consciousness that creates concepts and dichotomies. Describing our own experience of phenomena or sociological research *per se* we can locate the structures of the sociological mind during the empirical research. We can get to the essence of the experience. This kind of studying our own consciousness is similar to phenomenological research (Bentz & Shapiro 1998). However while meditating on any concept or experience, we try to understand what is appearing. Moreover, we want to get to compassion – not only understanding another person but acting compassionately in the world.

There are some similarities between meditating in this way and the phenomenological concept of *epoch*é (Bentz & Shapiro, 1998; Depraz, Varela, & Vermersch, 1999; Simpson, 2008). The pragmatic approach to *epoch*é could be characterized by three unfolding stages. The first is a phase of suspension of habitual thought and judgement. This is a basic precondition for any possibility of change in the attention which the subject gives to his own experience and which represents a break with a "natural" or unexamined attitude. The second is a phase of conversion or redirection of attention from the *exterior* to the *interior*. The third is a phase of letting-go or of receptivity towards the experience. First we decide to suspend the everyday knowledge. Next we redirect our attention from the content of perception to the act of perceiving. We could see how the mind works and could clear it by letting go of the all impressions that come to the mind. This second phase could be understood as concentration on the breath in Zen meditation. The third phase might be understood as a cutting ties and being not-attached to anything (detachment) that comes and goes. This consciousness that appears is prereflective, prediscursive, preverbal, and nonconceptual. We open our mind to all the things that could appear. In practical terms we do not refuse anything because we are not attached to any assumptions. So, Zen meditation could be understood as a practice of *epoché*.

Next, autoethnography could be a useful method to analyze the concept of self and its emptiness. Authoethnography is often an analysis of self by the researcher to discover how the self is maneuvering against cultural interpretations. This is called evocative autoethnography (Ellis, Adams, & Bochner, 2010). There is no mirroring of reality in the description of the objects; rather, there is a showing how the description is achieved. The mind process is revealed. The focus is not on the text as a final object and effect of scientific work; instead it is on the *process* of reaching the insight, which sometimes remains elusive. Impressions might be "copresent" and belong to the "things" happening "between" the researcher and his collaborators. There might be a sense of the loss of the physical, tangible, and lasting nature. Evocative autoethnography is therefore a kind of cognitive practice, which allows a person to generate knowledge in dyadic systems, such as the narrator/performer or the reader/viewer (Kacperczyk, 2014; Ellis, Adams, & Bochner, 2010). The emphasis here is on the moral responsibility of the researcher and the process of co-arising knowledge. He is not above "the researched objects," looking from the advantage point of an all-knowing expert. There is an emphasis on empathy and equal relations with collaborators of the research.

Grounded theory is another methodology that fits well within contemplative social science because it is based on the assumption of limited pre-conceptualization (Glaser & Strauss, 1967; Glaser, 1978; Strauss, 1987; Strauss & Corbin, 1997). Meditation practice could help in cutting the grounded theory researcher's mind away from concepts that might restrict the innovativeness and impose external categorical structure of seeing the social reality. In GT, codes are built from reflecting on and analyzing the empirical data. Analysis should be mindful and an analyst should be very attentive to the data; there is recognition that the context of their production and reception give the inspiration to constructing concepts and hypotheses. Hypotheses are not the a priori statements but are generated from the process of collecting and analyzing the data (Glaser, 1978).

Ethnography inspired by GT is also a form of field research that tries to be close to the in vivo codes collected during the participant observation of the community (Battersby, 1981; Charmaz & Mitchell, 2001; Konecki, 2011; Uhan, Malnar, & Kurdija, 2013). The concepts of an ethnographic study are derived from analysis of common sense language used by the observed co-producers of data. These concepts are analyzed by how they are used in contexts of everyday life activities. Sensitivity and mindfulness to the moments, contexts, and actions are very important skills for researchers. Experiencing of "the suchness" is possible when we have intuitive feelings and perceptions of the reality of which we are a part. Concepts are provisional consequences of such attitudes.

New approaches that rise within contemplative social research practices might be irritating for many sociologists. They challenge established paradigms, assumptions, and methods. As humans, researchers will also struggle to accept *shunyata* because we are accustomed to focusing on something concrete, something "real," even if our assumptions and methods are covering, transforming, hiding what we are trying to reveal and understand.

Through the contemplation of the interdependence of all things, we might see "the true nature" of the world, including social worlds. We do not create reality but rather experience it. Through contemplation we can see from a broadened perspective:

> If we look deeply at the bud on the tree, we will see its nature. It may be very small, but it is also like the earth, because the leaf in the bud will become part of the earth. If we see the truth of one thing in the cosmos, we see the nature of the cosmos. Because of our mind-

fulness, our deep looking, the nature of the cosmos will reveal itself. It is not a matter of imposing our ideas on the nature of the cosmos (Hanh, 1999, p. 59).

If we look deeply at (contemplate) the social relations included in our way of cognition, at our self as a researcher, at our concepts, at our emotions, at our embodiment of the social worlds, we can see how our sociological mind operates. Going beyond the extant methods and concepts, we can also directly observe the objects that we are interested in. How can we describe them? This is a topic for another time.

Endnotes

[1] The specific Buddhist ontology (inside the Buddhist theorizing) is something different and it treats the problem as "how is it possible to reach the enlightenment?" We approached the problem of ontology here from an "external" to Buddhism perspective.

[2] The four noble truths of Buddhism are: affliction/suffering (dukkha); accumulation of suffering (source of suffering); ways to alleviate suffering (cessation of suffering); and the right paths (Chuang & Chen, 2003).

[3] *Karma* means that our fate is caused by previous deeds and by our thinking. Karma concerning the body (body karma) also comes from thinking (Sahn, 1976, p 40). The creation of suffering comes from karma, and by meditating we can stop its activity. If a person sits Zen, he will make his karma dissipate and he will no longer be trapped in these actions. According to Sahn, "The only way to make karma disappear is for your consciousness to become empty" (p. 102, see also pp. 189-190; Loy 2003, p. 7).

[4] Meditating sociologists are practicing "engaged sociology." They possess the values of cessation of suffering, compassion, and helping others by their sociological research and analysis. Sociologists that meditate

know that suffering comes from social commitments to the self, social roles, social positions, ideologies, social groupings, cultures, property, and careers that are all temporary. It is very difficult to separate cognition processes (epistemology) from the ethical values (ethics) that inspire our perception of the world. However, "with mindfulness, we can change the world and bring happiness to many people. This is not abstract. It is possible for every one of us to generate the energy of mindfulness in each moment of our daily life" (Hanh, 1999, p. 59). Ethics can also be observed in contemplating distinctiveness when we think about the reasons for crime: "This denies the distinction we are usually quick to make between an offender and the rest of us" (Loy, 2003, p. 47). Usually we think in the categories of guilty and not guilty, but in reality legal cases are more complicated and guilt is determined on the side of the culprit as well as and negotiated in the court.

[5] See the idea of intersections and segmentation of social worlds by Anselm Strauss (Strauss, 1984). Social worlds as perspectives and set of activities focused on central activity and auxiliary activities might cross each other and produce new worlds or subworlds. New relations and interdependencies arise and new social objects co-arise.

[6] Autoethnography can be understood as an act of auto-narration based on introspection producing the document created by a narrator (Kacperczyk, 2014).

[7] Meditation in the Zen that belongs to Mahayana Buddhism can also be understand as following: "1) insight into the existence and nonexistence of the nature of the dharmas; 2) insight into the fact that there are no external, tangible characteristics, and that all is emptiness; 3) insight into existence, emptiness, and the Middle Way; 4) insight into the true aspect of all phenomena; 5) insight into the mutual interpenetration of all phenomena; [and] 6) insight that sees that phenomena themselves are the Absolute" (Sahn, p. 71).

[8] Autoethnography of the self may be a good choice to follow the stream

of minding that is elaborating on experience, which is not permanent but changing over time and through space. Observing self-fluctuations during meditation is an introduction to reconstruction of the self in details that finally create the whole picture. The whole picture is not the self, however, but the interconnectedness of the spot where we are socially and physically at the moment, and with the all the social worlds and natural worlds of material and living objects.

[9] The *anatta* "no-self" teaching denies this duality, which for Buddhism is seen as psychologically and historically conditioned. Our sense of a self apart from the world is a construct. "I" results from interacting physical and mental processes interdependent with the rest of the world. We are each, therefore, a manifestation of the world. The Buddhist path helps us realize our interdependence with all things, and to live according to that understanding: "This path is incompatible, therefore, with any economic system that treats the earth only as a commodity, or that works to reinforce our delusion of separation from it and from other people" (Loy, 2003, p. 86; see also Immergut & Kaufman, 2014).

[10] This practice of a *kong-an* comes from the Buddhist Zen meditation of the Kwan Um school. The following illustrates the practice:

> A student asked Zen Master Seung Sahn, "How can I get beyond just verbalizing the question, 'What am I?'"
>
> Soen-sa replied, "You want this question to grow. This mind is not good. This is attachment thinking. You must cut off this thinking, and only do hard training. It is not important for the question to grow. What is important is one moment of clear mind. Clear mind is before thinking. If you experience this mind, you have already attained enlightenment. If you experience this for a short time, even for one moment, this is enlightenment. All the rest of the time you may be thinking, but you shouldn't worry about this thinking. It is just your kar-

ma. You must not be attached to this thinking. You must not force it to stop or force clear mind to grow. It will grow by itself, as your karma gradually disappears.

"Clear mind is like the full moon in the sky. Sometimes clouds come and cover it, but the moon is always behind them. Clouds go away, then the moon shines brightly. So don't worry about clear mind: it is always there. When thinking comes, behind it is clear mind. When thinking goes, there is only clear mind. Thinking comes and goes, comes and goes. You must not be attached to the coming or the going." (Retrieved August 18, 2014 from http://www.kwanumzen.org/getting-started/how-to-practice/.)

[11] Loy (2003) explains it this way: "Realizing our interdependence and mutual responsibility for each other implies something more than merely an insight or an intellectual awareness. Trying to live this interdependence is love" (p. 108). The ethical dimension in Buddhism is always connected with cognition. This is the next step when we redefine our way of researching reality: We not only get to *know*, but we are also *engaged* ethically in what we research. Concepts that we use or deconstruct have meanings and are value-loaded.

[12] Intuition can be understood here as a first thought, as in the case of Albert Einstein who used his direct intuitive understanding to solve scientific problems (Scheff, 1990, p. 145). Moreover, intuition connects itself with spontaneity (p. 163) and *intuition* is a "virtually instantaneous and unlabored solution to problems insoluble in an analytic mode" (p. 58). Blaise Pascal proposed that science was based on the spirit of *geometrie*, which translates as *system*. On the other hand, nonscience, including religion, is based on the spirit of *finesse*, which translates as *intuition* (Pascal, 1657/2015). Pascal went on to say that a person might be a good journeyman scientist using only system, and a good everyday

artist using only intuition. But to advance knowledge or art, to progress to something new, she needs both. Being systematic seldom, if ever, results in new knowledge, unless it is testing a good idea. And good ideas come from intuition. However, intuitions need be tested; most may be either irrelevant or erroneous. Thomas Scheff writes:

> To appreciate Pascal's point, one need only to look at brilliant creators. One example would surely be the mathematician John von Neumann, whose work led to many advances, such as those that helped form the basis for computers. According to his family, he worked almost entirely on the basis of intuition. His colleagues have written that if he could not see the answer to a problem by simply looking at it, he would go on to the next problem. If he got stuck midway, he would sleep on it, often waking up with the answer. Similarly, as far as I know, almost all of Mozart's music was first draft: he seldom needed to revise (Scheff, 2012, para. 4).

Sahn (1976) also gives a good example using metaphor: "You have many *kong-ans*. But a *kong-an* is like a finger pointing at the moon. If you are attached to the finger, you don't understand the direction, so you cannot see the moon" (p. 44). However, "If you are not attached to any *kong-an,* then you will understand the direction. The direction is the complete don't-know mind" (p. 45). The goal is to cultivate a "don't know" mind in order to understand "like this." In fact, "the name for 'like this' is 'don't know.' If you understand 'don't know,' you will understand all *kong-ans* and you will soon understand 'like this'" (p. 45).

[14] In a very mindful way, Honore de Balzac (1836), in the short story "Facino Cane," shows what it means that observation can be supported by intuitive skills, together giving a person sympathetic introspection:

As I dressed no better than a working man, and cared

nothing for appearances, I did not put them on their guard; I could join a group and look on while they drove bargains or wrangled among themselves on their way home from work. Even then observation had come to be an instinct with me; a faculty of penetrating to the soul without neglecting the body; or rather, a power of grasping external details so thoroughly that they never detained me for a moment, and at once I passed beyond and through them. I could enter into the life of the human creatures whom I watched, even as the dervish in the Arabian Nights could pass into any soul or body after pronouncing a certain formula....As I listened, I could make their lives mine, I felt their rags on my back, I walked with their gaping shoes on my feet; their cravings, their needs, had all passed into my soul, or my soul had passed into theirs. It was the dream of a waking man. I waxed hot with them over the foreman's tyranny, or the bad customers that made them call again and again for payment ...Whence comes the gift? Is it a kind of second sight? Is it one of those powers which when abused end in madness? I have never tried to discover its source; I possess it, I use it, that is all (para 2-3).

[15] George Herbert Mead (1932) indicates that sympathetic understanding can happen only in the cooperative situation when the two persons really meet and "active sympathy" arises:

One does not put himself immediately in the attitude of the person suffering apart from one's own sympathetic attitude toward him. The situation is that of a person assisting the other, and because of that calling out in himself the response that his assistance calls out in the other. If there is no response on the part of the other, there cannot be any sympathy. Of course, one can say that he can recognize what such a person must be suffering if he could only express it. He thereby puts himself in the place of another who is not there but whom he has met in experience, and interprets this individual in view of the former experience. But active sympathy means that the individual does arouse in another the response called out by his assistance and arouses in himself the same response. If there is no response, one cannot sympathize with him. That presents the limitation of sympathy as such; it has to occur in a cooperative process (pp. 299-300).

However, sympathetic understanding may be the process that we induce based on our willingness to help others, not only based on the contextual interaction. We can sympathetically understand the other because, without attachment to self and direct physical reasons or motives, we might orient our efforts directly to help other persons, without any egoistic justifications. Ethics does matter in cognition.

[16] There are many kinds of autoethnography (Kacperczyk, 2014, p. 68). There is, for example, *analytic autoethnography*. It is an objectivistic way of describing reality through the experience of the researcher, who also checks his perceptions and interpretations with other sources of data from other observers, participants, and researchers. This kind of autoethnography is more detached and abstractive (Anderson, 2006; Kacperczyk, 2014). However, here we also start from the self, and this self-starting point needs to be deconstructed in order to be reconstructed.

References

Anderson, L. (2006, August). Analytic autoethnography. *Journal of Contemporary Ethnography, 35*(4), 373-395.

Battersby, D. (1981). The use of ethnography and grounded theory in educational research. *McGill Journal of Education/Revue des sciences de l'*éducation *de McGill, 16*(1), 91-98.

Bell, I. (1979). Buddhist sociology: Some thoughts on the convergence of sociology and the Eastern paths of liberation. In S. G. McNall (Ed.), *Theoretical perspectives in sociology* (pp.53-68). New York, NY: St. Martin's Press.

Benedict, G. (2011). *The five-minute philosopher: 80 unquestionably good answers to 80 unaswerable big questions*. London, England: Watkings Publishing.

Bentz, V. M., & Kenny, W. (1997). "Body-as-world": Kenneth Burke's answer to the postmodernist charges against sociology. *Sociological Theory, 15*(1), 81-96.

Bentz, V. M., & Shapiro, J. J. (1998). *Mindful Inquiry in Social Research*, London, England: SAGE.

Bergson, H. (2007). *The creative mind. An introduction to metaphysics.* Mineola, NY: Dover.

Cicourel, A. (1970). The acquisition of social structure: Towards a developmental sociology of language and meaning. In J. D. Douglas (Ed.), *Understanding everyday life: Toward the reconstruction of sociological knowledge* (pp. 136-168). Chicago, IL: Aldine.

Charmaz, K., & Mitchell, R. (2001). Grounded theory in ethnography. In P. Atkinson, A. Coffey, S. Delamont, J. Lofland, & L. Lofland (Eds.), *Handbook of ethnography* (pp. 160-174). London, England: SAGE.

Chuang, R. & Chen, G. M. (2003). Buddhist perspectives and human communication. *Intercultural Communication Studies, 12*(4), 65-80.

Cooley, C. H. (1909). *Social organization: Study of larger mind.* New

York, NY: Schocken.

de Balzac, H. (1836). Facino Cane. Retrieved from http://www.guten-berg.org/files/1737/1737-h/1737-h.htm. Originally published by Delloye et Lecou (1837).

Depraz, N., Varela, F. J., & Vermersch, P. (2000). The gesture of aware-ness: An account of its structural dynamics. In M. Velmans (Ed.), *Investigating phenomenal consciousness: New method-ologies and maps* (pp. 121-137). Amsterdam, Holland: Benja-min Publishers.

Ellis, C., Adams, T. E., & Bochner, A. P. (2010). Autoethnography: An overview. *Forum Qualitative Sozialforschung/Forum: Quali-tative Social Research, 12*(1), Art. 10. Retrieved from http://nbn-resolving.de/urn:nbn:de:0114-fqs1101108.

Garfinkel, H. (1967/2007). *Studies in ethnomethodology.* Upper Saddle River, NJ: Prentice-Hall.

Glaser, B. (1978). *Theoretical sensitivity.* San Francisco, CA: The Sociol-ogy Press.

Glaser, B., & Strauss, A. L. (1967). *Discovery of grounded theory: Strategies for qualitative research.* Chicago, IL: Aldine.

Griffith, P. J. (2010). Buddhism. In C. Taliaferro, P. Draper, and P. L. Quinn (Eds.), *A companion to the philosophy of religion* (2nd ed.). Oxford, England: Blackwell Publishing Ltd.

Goffman, E. (1956). *The Presentation of Self in Everyday Life.* Mono-graph No. 2. University of Edinburgh Social Sciences Research Centre.

-------. (1963). *Stigma: notes on the management of spoiled identity.* New York, NY: Simon & Schuster.

Goode, D. (1994). *A world without words.* Philadelphia, PA: Temple University Press.

Hanh, T. N. (1976). *The miracle of mindfulness: An introduction to the practice of meditation.* Boston, MA: Beacon Press.

-------. (1999). *Interbeing: Fourteen guidelines for engaged Buddhism.*

Berkeley, CA: Parallax Press.

Immergut, M., & Kaufman, P. (2014). A sociology of no-self: Applying Buddhist social theory to symbolic interaction. *Symbolic Interaction, 37*(2), 264-282. doi:10.1002/SYMB.90.

Kacperczyk, A. (2014). Autoetnografia: Technika, metoda, nowy paradygmat? O metodologicznym statusie autoetnografii [Autoethnography: Technique, method, or new paradigm? On methodological status of autoethnography). *Przegląd Socjologii Jakościowej, 10*(3), 32-74. Retrieved from http://qualitativeso-ciologyreview.org/PL/Volume27/PSJ_10_3_Kacperczyk.pdf.

Kohl, C. T. (2007). Buddhism and quantum physics. *Contemporary Buddhism, 8*(1), 69-82.

Konecki, K. T. (2011). Visual grounded theory: A methodological outline and examples from empirical work. *Revija za sociologiju, 41*(2), 131-160.

Loy, D. (2003). *The great awakening: A Buddhist social theory.* Somerville, MA: Wisdom Publications.

-------. (2008). *Money, sex, war, karma: Notes for a Buddhist revolution.* Somerville, MA: Wisdom Publications.

McGrane, B. (1993a). Zen sociology: Don't just do something, stand there! *Teaching Sociology, 21*(1), 79-84.

-------. (1993b). Zen sociology: The un-TV experiment. *Teaching Sociology, 21*(1), 85-89.

Mead, G. H. (1932). Mind self and society from the standpoint of a social behaviorist (C. W. Morris, Ed.). Chicago: University of Chicago.

Mills, C. W. (1940). Situated actions and vocabularies of motive. *American Sociological Review, 5*(6), 904-913.

Moore, R. J. (1995). Dereification in Zen Buddhism. *The Sociological Quarterly, 36*(4), 699-723.

Nagarjuna, A. (2014). Daabhumika-vibhasa. Traktat o Dziesiciu Stopniach. Retrieved from http://mahajana.net/teksty/nagarjuna_10st.

html.

Pascal, B. (1657/2015). *Of the geometrical spirit* [*De l'Esprit géométrique.*] (O. W. Wright, Trans.). Printed by CreateSpace.

Petitmengin-Peugeout, C. (2002). The intuitive experience. In F. J. Varela & J. Shear (Eds.), *The view from within: First-person approaches to the study of consciousness* (pp. 43-78). Thorverton, England: Imprint Academic.

Prus, R. (1996). *Symbolic interaction and ethnographic research: Intersubjectivity and the study of human lived experience.* Albany, NY: State University of New York Press.

Rehorick, D. and Bentz, V. M. (Eds.) (2009). *Transformative Phenomenology. Changing ourselves, lifeworlds, and professional practice.* Lanham, MD: Lexington Books.

Rorty, R. (1989). *Contingency, irony, solidarity.* Cambridge, MA: Cambridge University Press.

Scheff, T. (1990). *Microsociology: Discourse, emotion, and social structure.* Chicago, IL: The University of Chicago Press.

-------. (2012, December). Homage to Pascal. *New English Review.* Retrieved from http://www.newenglishreview.org/custpage.cfm/frm/128369/sec_id/128369.

Schipper, J. (2008). *Disappearing desert: The growth of Phoenix and the culture of sprawl.* Norman, OK: University of Oklahoma Press.

-------. (2012). Toward a Buddhist sociology: Its theories, methods, and possibilities. *The American Sociologist, 43*(3), 203-222.

Seamon, D. (2000). A way of seeing people and place: Phenomenology in environment-behavior research. In S. Wapner, J. Demick, T. Yamamoto, & H. Minami (Eds.), *Theoretical perspectives in environment-behavior research* (pp. 157-78). New York, NY: Plenum.

Sahn, S. (1976). *Dropping ashes on the Buddha.* S. Mitchel (Ed.). New York, NY: Grove Press.

-------. (1982). *Only don't know: Selected teaching letters of Zen Master Seung Sahn.* Boston, MA: Shambala Publications.

Simpson, S. (2009). Experiencing phenomenology as mindful transformation: An autobiographical account. In D. A. Rehorick & V. M. Bentz (Eds.), *Transformative phenomenology: Changing ourselves, lifeworlds, and professional practice* (pp. 51-64). Lanham, MD: Lexington Books.

Strauss, A. L. (1984). Social worlds and their segmentation processes. In N. Denzin (Ed.), *Studies in Symbolic Interaction* (pp. 119-128). Greenwich, CT: Jai Press. Retrieved from https://www.uzh.ch/cmsssl/suz/dam/jcr:ffffffff-9ac6-46e7-ffff-fffffd-f1b114/04.22_strauss_78.pdf.

-------. (1987). *Qualitative analysis for social scientists.* Cambridge, MA: Cambridge University Press.

-------. (1997). *Mirrors and masks: The search for identity.* New Brunswick, NJ: Transaction Publishers.

Strauss, A. L., & Corbin, J. (1997). *Grounded theory in practice.* Thousand Oaks, CA: SAGE.

Suzuki, D. T. (1964). *Introduction to Zen Buddhism.* New York, NY: Grove Press.

-------. (1994). *The Zen Koans as a means of attaining enlightenment.* Tokyo, Japan: Charles E. Tuttle.

Toombs, K. S. (1995). The lived experience of disability. *Human Studies, 18*, 9-23.

Uhan, S., Malnar, B., & Kurdija, S. (2013). Grounded theory and inductive ethnography: A sensible merging or a failed encounter? *Teorija in Praksa, 50*(3-4).

Wu, B. (1990, May 20). Only keep "Don't know" mind. Retrieved from http://www.kwanumzen.org/?teaching=only-keep-dont-know-mind.

Varela, F. J., Thompson, E., & Rosch, E. (1993). *The embodied mind.* Cambridge, MA: The MIT Press.

Varela, F. J., & Shear, J. (2002). *The view from within: First-person approaches to the study of consciousness.* Upton Pyne, England: Imprint Academic.

Krzysztof Konecki, PhD, is Chief of the Department of Sociology of Organization and Management at the University of Lodz (Poland), Editor-in-chief of *Qualitative Sociology Review*, and Chair of a section of Qualitative Sociology and Symbolic Interactionism of the Polish Sociological Association. He served as Chair and Vice-Chair of the Qualitative Methods Network of ESA. He is a member of the board of the Qualitative Methods Research Network of European Sociological Association and has published extensively on qualitative methods and grounded theory methodology. His research interests include the sociology of organization and management, human and nonhuman animal interactions, visual grounded theory, and contemporary forms of spirituality.

Contemplative Psychology and Imagery

By Annabelle Nelson, Ph.D.
School of Leadership Studies,
Fielding Graduate University, United States

Abstract

Imagery is a contemplative practice that can serve to distract the ego and simultaneously open the unconscious to release blocked emotions and create a gateway to insight from the spirit self. The transformation of the mind to spaciousness is marked by softness, humor. and warmth—marks of wisdom or the *buddhi*. The physiology of brain waves documents that theta waves accompany blissful spiritual states, and alpha waves reflect a passive focus of attention, which is what transforms a person's inner world over time. The limbic system, a rim-like structure in the middle of the brain, is the center of imagery, emotions, and expanded perception (Pribram, 1981). Using the imagery of archetypes, which captures the ego's attention, adds power to contemplative practice. This chapter includes exercises for visualizing emotions in the body, and visualizing an accompanying archetype.

Introduction

After being introduced to North America at the turn of the 20th century, Asian spiritual practices gained momentum primarily through the writings of two men. Shunryu Suzuki, author of *Zen Mind, Beginners Mind* (1970)*,* started the San Francisco Zen Center in 1959. The second, B.K.S. Iyenger (1995), was author of *Light on Yoga*, and taught in Ann Arbor, Michigan in 1956. Currently, yoga is taught in most health clubs in the U.S., and "mindfulness" is a marketing buzz word. There are many committed spiritual seekers in North America, but sometimes practitioners struggle with maintaining the "highs" during the emotional ups and downs of daily life. Contemplative psychology aims to blend the quest for spiritual awareness with emotional health, combining the yin of enlightenment with the yang of human happiness.

Contemplation is a spiritual practice that focuses the mind without grasping for an outcome. Yoga is an embodied practice that facilitates contemplation and the calm attention that allows what is. For example, in *virabhadrasa*, or the warrior pose, a person brings attention to the outer edge of the back foot rolling into the floor. With Zen meditation, a person notices the breath coming into the nostril and at the same time counts the breath up to 10, and then back down to one. The psychological process of imagery, or thinking in internal sensations such as pictures, can be contemplative as well because it creates an internal focus of the attention. It has the benefit of creating awareness and at the same time acts to release emotions.

The purpose of contemplation is to open the mind to spaciousness, so that a person is not reactive to sensations and buried emotions that skew perceptions. Instead, the mind becomes warm, soft, humorous, and friendly. This is the definition of wisdom given by Chögyam Trungpa (1991), Buddhist Riponche and founder of the Naropa University in Boulder, Colorado. This does not happen immediately; it takes contemplative practice with yoga, meditation, or focusing on images. The memory bank unwinds, the unconscious opens and releases blocked emotions, and there is space for keen insight from the spirit self. Brain physiology and the psychodynamics of archetypes proposed by Jungian psychology can fine-tune the use of imagery as contemplation for both spiritual and emotional awareness.

An Elephant and Wisdom

Figure 1. The elephant archetype represents the removal of obstacles.

240

There is an Indian legend of six blind men touching an elephant and then trying to explain what this creature was like.

It was six men of Indostan
To learning much inclined,
Who went to see the Elephant
(Though all of them were blind),
That each by observation
Might satisfy his mind.

The First approached the Elephant,
And happening to fall
Against his broad and sturdy side,
At once began to bawl:
"God bless me! but the Elephant
Is very like a wall!"

The Second, feeling of the tusk
Cried, "Ho! what have we here,
So very round and smooth and sharp?
To me 'tis mighty clear
This wonder of an Elephant
Is very like a spear!"

The Third approached the animal,
And happening to take
The squirming trunk within his hands,
Thus boldly up he spake:
"I see," quoth he, "the Elephant
Is very like a snake!"

The Fourth reached out an eager hand,

And felt about the knee:
"What most this wondrous beast is like
Is mighty plain," quoth he;
"'Tis clear enough the Elephant
Is very like a tree!"

The Fifth, who chanced to touch the ear,
Said: "E'en the blindest man
Can tell what this resembles most;
Deny the fact who can,
This marvel of an Elephant
Is very like a fan!"

The Sixth no sooner had begun
About the beast to grope,
Then, seizing on the swinging tail
That fell within his scope.
"I see," quoth he, "the Elephant
Is very like a rope!"

And so these men of Indostan
Disputed loud and long,
Each in his own opinion
Exceeding stiff and strong,
Though each was partly in the right,
And all were in the wrong!

Indian Legend retold by John Godfrey Saxe (1816-1887)

The point of this story is that each person has a piece of the truth, but none of them have the whole truth. This is how humans go through life, often thinking that what they perceive is the whole reality. Yet somehow the individual ego, in its effort to create a stable reality, keeps the person away from perceiving reality as it really is. In order to begin to see the whole of reality, each human can adopt a practice that changes the inner topography of the mind such that it becomes spacious toward wisdom.

Wise people have a realm of self beyond everyday ego. This is sometimes called ego integration, integrity, or transcendence (Adler, 2009). Several Western psychologists have attempted to document and explain the stages that lead to this transformation.

Robert Kegan (1998), a developmental psychologist at Harvard University, created a theory of cognitive development. He proposed a number of stages. The first one begins with "the impulsive mind," as children aged two through six react impulsively to the world around them. As people age, they move through five stages, ending with what Kegan terms a "self-transforming mind." He calls this the interindividual stage because a person develops ego transcendence. One's inner world changes to allow the perception of interdependence beyond a subjective individual perspective.

Erik Erikson (1994), another developmental psychologist, created a framework for understanding psychosocial growth throughout the lifespan. According to him, wisdom is not merely expert knowledge but also includes actual changes in consciousness. He formulated eight stages, and in each one humans have a "task" to move toward health and maturity. For example, "competence" is the stage for children aged six to 12 years. The task is to move from inferiority to industry. The final stage of life, according to Erikson, includes the task of moving toward ego integrity instead of despair. Ego integrity moves an individual away from a myopic view of the self and others. This leads to more mental space, because mental activity is freed from the fears and anxiety of a limited perception of the self. The goal of therapy or coaching is to help someone gain a clearer awareness of the self, which can allow insights and healing to take place. This eventually moves a person to wisdom.

Other Western psychologists link openness to wisdom. For example, Brian Les Lancaster and Jason Timothy Palframan (2009) say wisdom requires a person to have mental space to perceive the self beyond the everyday ego. When this happens, there is a continual movement of awareness into the unconscious to sense the spiritual dimension. Ego integration helps the mind to open in this way.

What is needed, then, is a contemplative practice that settles the ego (Bergsma & Ardelt, 2012) and allows mental space to perceive the whole of the elephant, or the whole of the reality. Sigmund Freud (1949) has said that the ego will fight tooth and nail to try to keep awareness out of the unconscious. A psychologically friendly technique to do this can be the practice of imagery (Achterberg, 1985).

A Child and Transforming the Mind to Happiness

Figure 2. The child archetype represents innocence and spontaneity.

Humans want to be as happy as a child emerging into the world with hope for the future. For a young child, the ego is helpful in organizing perceptual information and giving a sense of self. Over time, the ego starts restricting and limiting awareness (Walsh, 2011).

To transform the mind to spaciousness, the ego needs security, so that it does not try to control perceptions, suppressing memory and skewing perceptions to support a limited view of the self. There are models from Eastern religious philosophy that shed light on creating a wise mind. Vedantic Hinduism (Rama, Ballentine, & Ajanja,

1976) is based on the ancient books, the *Rig Vedas*, which were written around 1000 B.C. This tradition taught that the goal of spiritual practice is to transform the mind to enlightenment. This happens through the eight limbs of yoga, which begin with attitudes and *asanas* or postures, and end with *Samadhi* or enlightenment. In this philosophy, the mind is flooded with sensations and is overcome with memories that erupt automatically. The eight limbs of practice teach humans to focus the mind, and the *buddhi,* or wisdom, develops. Contemplative practice lets the memory banks empty and allows emotions and sensations to pass through unheeded.

This is reminiscent of Freud's (1949) view that emotional health requires the release of suppressed emotions. Carl Jung (1970) developed the psychodynamic model of opening the unconscious to release what is unknown in order to allow awareness of the Self, or the full being. Both models prescribed dream interpretation or identification with archetypes so that mental obstructions can move up and out of the unconscious. In the Vendantic system, contemplative practice develops the *buddhi*. This focus creates space, which allows clutter to be released from the mind. With the development of the *buddhi,* awareness can join with the spiritual Self, called the *atman, s*ince this part of the mind is connected to the collective unconscious. The whole mind is both emotionally healthy and spiritually aware. The mechanics of accomplishing this go something like the following (see Nelson, 2007):

A focus of attention relaxes the mind

The unconscious opens

Emotional material is released

The mind becomes spacious, allowing three things:

1. emotions are sensed and released
2. unconscious motivation is diffused
3. spiritual insight is freed

A Priestess and Transformation of the Mind

Figure 3. The archetype of the high priestess stands for spiritual insight.

To experience the essence of spirituality, and at the same time gain day-to-day happiness, a practice is needed. This shift to wisdom can be marked by five characteristics: synchronicity; kindness; heightened intuition; increased awareness of one's own behavior; and feeling love.

Synchronicity (Woodman & Dickson, 1996) refers to happy co-incidences. When these occur, it is a good sign. One walks to the right place at the right time. For example, an accidental turn can result in running into an acquaintance not seen for several years. This type of serendipity is a gentle nudge that one is opening to the spiritual Self inside, leading to timely intersections. This idea is similar to the story of a Buddhist monk, who leans down to smell a flower, and inadvertently misses a blow from an enemy's sword.

Kindness (Dalai Lama, Tsong-ka-pa, & Hopkins, 1977) is feeling compassion inside. Showing kindness to others becomes a natural, automatic extension of the inner transformation.

Heightened intuition (Gawain, 2002) develops so that one might find that she starts doing healthy things automatically—changing her diet, for example, or going on early morning walks.

Increased awareness of one's own behavior (Lancaster & Pal-framan, 2009) means that one notices interactional patterns in new ways. For example, if a person usually argues with a family member

246

and thinks it is the other's fault, all of a sudden one sees what in one's own behavior might prompt the attack. One's own participation in the negative interaction becomes vividly clear instead of blaming others.

Feeling love: Feeling connected to spiritual forces, and feeling unending compassion inside and out is an excellent pat on the back that the transformation inside has happened.

A Brilliant Sunset and Brain Waves

Figure 4. The archetype of a sun represents happiness and balance of the emotional and the spiritual.

Spiritual highs that are awakening experiences (Burkett, 2015) can come but may be fleeting. However, a contemplative practice works over time to actually transform the inner world to spaciousness. When the brain experiences different states of consciousness, it emits certain brain waves (Restak, 2010). Researchers have documented four primary waves—alpha, beta, theta, and delta. *Alpha* denotes waking with a relaxed focus of attention, while *beta* is an alert reality with "getting things done" energy. *Theta* is an expanded, creative dream-like state. These are sometimes accompanied by a sense of interconnection with all of life and, sometimes, feelings of bliss or peace (Wise, 1995). The most noticeable theta state happens during the drowsy period right before sleep when consciousness erupts with flashes of images; meditators often report seeing their guru's (teacher's) face. The fourth brain wave, *delta*, occurs in deep sleep. It is obviously an important state because without it humans cannot restore. It is not, however, a state that can be consciously evoked.

The highs of spiritual experience are most closely associated with theta waves. These could happen during the visions that accompany mystics' transformations or scientists' breakthroughs. Jean Houston (1997, 2000), a psychologist, has a metaphor to understand the purpose of these theta highs. She is an expert on opening the unconscious and proposes that some experiences act as "depth charges" from the spiritual realm, also called the energy field. Visions and ecstatic experiences are such explosions, and over time they can expand the mind by making the barriers to the unconscious more permeable.

Ramakrishna (Vivekanada, 1956) was Vivekananda's teacher. (Vivekananda was one of the great yogis. He was the philosopher who brought Hinduism to the West in 1893 at the Parliament of Religions in Chicago.) Ramakrishna described a vision that radically changed his worldview. When he was in the presence of a statue of the Hindu goddess Kali, he saw her as a huge earth mother radiating golden light and filling him with such brilliant and vigorous love that he was thrown to the floor. Needless to say, he became a lifelong devotee of Kali. Many spiritual practitioners recall similar overwhelming emotional experiences.

For the great masters, theta visions seem to permanently transform their consciousness. For us mere mortals, theta states occur but experience may not last. The next day we might present anger or frustration at the people and situations around us. Most commonly, the highs come and go, but a sustained spiritual state escapes us.

Practices that create alpha waves are the real key to ongoing spirituality. Visualization creates a relaxed focus and, as a result, generates alpha waves. Biofeedback practices show this (Green, 1975). Thinking in words in order to try to change blood pressure does not work. Worrying about how high the meter reads, or trying very hard to lower it does not affect the gauge. But thinking in pictures has the opposite effect and relaxes tension in blood vessels. To lower blood pressure, one could imagine floating in a beautiful pool of turquoise water, rocking gently in the water. It is a different process to think in pictures instead of words, because imagery opens the unconscious and creates alpha waves. This is what can maintain an open mind over time.

A Circle and Imagery in the Body

It is helpful to create a diagram (see below) showing how the mind can be transformed to wisdom by using a contemplative practice. I proposed four interconnected bodies of the human being (Nelson, 1993, 2014). These are spiritual, physical, emotional, and mental. The spiritual body is the kernel of being as well as the whole of it (see Figure 4. The limitations of two-dimensional space does not adequately capture the complementarity of the spiritual body).

The physical is closely aligned to the self as it responds to intuition, as in a gut feeling. Many spiritual practices also focus on the body. Examples are practicing yoga or following the breath in meditation. Therefore, bringing awareness into the physical body assists in the transformation of the mind to wisdom because all are interconnected.

The emotional body rests inside the physical body and is highly reactive, influenced by memories and sensations. It has a natural connection to the spiritual body through primitive intuition. If the mind becomes spacious and simultaneously has a focus, it can sense the emotions and the intuition they carry, as opposed to being overwhelmed by sensations.

The mental body is within the emotional one. Most people think they are the thoughts that are rolling through their minds, but this is because the ego restricts awareness from other parts of the mind in an effort to create stability. It does this by moving memories toward the unconscious. Awareness, or conscious thought is, for most people tied to the ego. Contact with the self is limited to bursts of insight that might make the way through the closed mental body.

To develop wisdom, the ego can be relaxed so that information from other bodies can pop into awareness. The mental body can transcend the ego to become a holder of awareness. Infants create a stable sense of self by having the ego close off the stream of consciousness from the spiritual body (Piaget, 1972). This is important. Over time, the ego shuts down connections with other bodies because of difficult life events. The path to wisdom is to relax the ego, so that insight can spring from the other bodies to consciousness so that we develop wholeness of being.

The emotional body expresses primitive intuition but can easily take over consciousness with its strong sensations. Relaxing the ego allows emotions to be sensed and then released. The physical body has a direct connection to the spiritual body because it is not inhibited by the ego (Masui, 1987). That is why yoga uses physical movements and focus on the breath. Imagery and focusing on pictures in the mind do this as well.

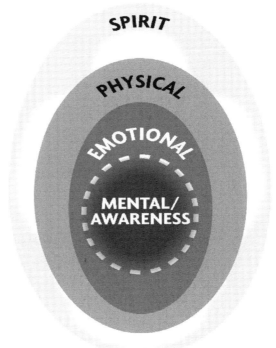

The Wise Mind-Body

Figure 5. The Wise Mind-Body Model shows how visualizing archetypes can quiet the ego and create space in the mind so that the emotional issues in the unconscious can be released, and how imaging in the body can help connect to the spirit self.

Imagery Exercise: Emotion in the Body

Take a few moments and feel yourself move into your body. Roll your shoulders, moving back, and bring them down slightly. Give your body a firm, positive suggestion to relax. Relax your toes in your right foot, your entire leg, see the ball and socket of your right hip; open it slightly with your mind's eye. Relax the toes in your left foot, your entire leg, see the ball and socket of your left hip; open it slightly with your mind's eye. Relax your groin area, your stomach, your heart, your lungs. Relax your right hand. Relax your left hand. Go to the small of your back; walk up your vertebrae as if your attention has fingers and restack them. Relax the back of your head, the top, your cheeks, your lips, your tongue; relax your eyes, your ears. Your whole body is heavier and warmer.

Now think about a time in the past several weeks when you have felt something you did not like. Imagine it as vividly as you can, as if it is a movie playing in your mind. You are there and it is happening right now. Where are you? Who is there with you? Try to notice some perceptual details. Do you notice colors, textures? Sounds? Now, where in your body are you feeling something? Do you feel something in your stomach, head, neck, legs, hands, or heart? Now take your attention to that spot in your body, and try to visualize it. How big is it? What shape? What color? Visualize it as clearly as you can. Do you like it? If not, give yourself permission to change it. You can change colors, change shapes; you can do anything you want with it. Take it out, burn it up, or simply and gently shift the color from black to green, for example. Let it transform.

Now come out of the imagery. Try to keep the sense of the trans-formation.

A Lotus and the Energy Field

Figure 6. A lotus is an archetype of spiritual insight. The crown chakra is pictured as a thousand-petal lotus.

Hidden in the unconscious is the spirit self or *atman,* and using the practice of imagery can focus attention within the body to open a gateway for creating a spacious mind. It allows insight from the energy field. Many Eastern traditions have called this the "subtle realm" or "subtle body." Jung introduced the "collective unconscious," which has become a Western way of understanding the subtle realm. All of these terms denote a dimension of interconnectedness beyond time and space.

Elders of the Hopi tribe describe *katsinas* (Walters, 1977), or spirits who come from the sacred mountains to bring gifts. According to these elders, the *katsinas* are right here next to us, invisible to the eye but active and felt by humans in their day-to-day lives. This is what the energy field is like—not a space above or below, but right here, underlying daily reality. If people have the capability, they can expand perception beyond the material reality to the energy field. Both realities coexist together, but a transformation of consciousness is necessary to sense information from the energetic realm. This happens by opening the conscious mind to the unconscious. In turn, the mind is transformed to wisdom, to become spacious so that the dualities of the material and spiritual world can intertwine into awareness.

In both psychological and spiritual traditions, scholars propose an element in the human psyche connected to this energy field. This is sometimes called the small, quiet voice within. The *atman* or spirit self designates the human faculty in the unconscious connected to the energy field. Humans are often cut off from this, because the ego in its natural quest for stability constricts consciousness.

The Brain and the Limbic System

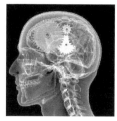

Figure 7. The archetype of judgment shows that the science of the brain can help understand how to use imagery to create a wise and spacious mind.

Neurophysiologist Richard Restak (2010), creator of the PBS series *The Brain*, has explained humans' amazing inner capacity. Restak showed that the sheer volume of what happens in the mind is breathtaking. There are more than 100 trillion neural connections in the brain, more than there are known stars in the universe. Humans are born with many, many brain cells. Different sources cite different numbers, but the most often cited is around 100 billion. The miracle of the brain is that new neural connections can grow, adding to the size and potential of the brain. Thinking in pictures can help people use more of their brains by accessing interconnected networks.

Achterberg (1985) underscores the importance of imagery, expanding the possibilities of what the brain can do. She worked as a psychologist at a Texas hospital's cancer center and her patients were all near death. She taught them imagery to increase their white blood cell counts and shrink their tumors. To her, imagery was a powerful tool to unleash the human potential locked in the unconscious, even at the cellular level. During the psychoneuroimmunology movement of the late 1980s, Candace Pert (1997) discovered neuropeptides such as dopamine, which showed that the nervous system is connected to the immune system. Neuropeptides fit like a key into an immune cell to change its direction and velocity. Imagery, or thinking in pictures, can change levels of neuropeptides.

Imagery is mediated in the brain by a small rim-like structure underneath the two cerebral cortices called the limbic system (Pribram, 1981). One part of this system, the amygdala, retrieves long-term memories. Together with the hippocampus, another part of the limbic system, these two areas have a primary role in regulating autonomic nervous system activity. Thinking in images opens up both memory and autonomic body functions, because they all happen in the same place, the limbic system (Achterberg, 1985). Imagery talks directly to the unconscious and opens it, retrieving long-term memories.

An Archetype and the Gateway to the Unconscious

Figure 8. Avalokiteshvara is the archetype of compassion that
is the marker of a transformed mind.

Imagery as a contemplative practice is empowered by wedding the process of imagery with the natural psychodynamic of the ego that identifies with archetypes. An archetype is a collection of characteristics that form a recognizable pattern, residing in the energetic domain. Examples are a sports hero, a seductive movie star, a martyr, or a criminal. From a psychological perspective, archetypes motivate human behavior in that an individual's ego identifies with an archetype as a way to organize its personality and motivate action (von Franz, 1985).

Imagining an archetype is a key skill for transforming the mind to spaciousness. Archetypes make the change process easier because they tap the mind's natural workings. They reside in the energy field of the unconscious, and at the same time are connected to the ego in the conscious. Archetypes lighten the load of the spiritual path, because one can use intuition and a playful mode to find them.

There is no specific set of archetypes, nor is there a magical list to choose from. Different traditions manifest different archetypes. Power animals given by a shaman—a bear, coyote, whale, or eagle—are not exclusive, nor is the list of Greek deities such as those in Jean Shinoda Bolen's (2004) book the *Goddesses in Every Women: Powerful Archetypes in Women's Lives.* It does not matter which archetype one chooses, and the choice can change as the intuition guides. A person can stay with an archetype as long as the fascination is there, and let go of one, making room for another, at any time. Marie Louise von Franz (1985), a renowned Jungian writer, explains that each archetype contains every other one because of the interconnectedness of the human experiences and qualities each represents. Therefore, one can experiment and try out different archetypes.

One of my colleagues, Judith Stevens-Long, shared with me her theory about psychological development: She believes that an emotionally mature person has an ego like a prism. A person's internal lens has different facets, changing focus depending on the situation and showing flexibility. The facet idea is similar to von Franz's (1985) view of archetypes. She believes that each face of the lens may be a different archetype but that focusing on any one creates a window to open the mind. One need not worry too much about getting the correct archetype. They can come and go, since they all lead to the same place. Not trying too hard and being playful will help a person find the right one. Meditation facilitates this experience.

Even though archetypes have a strong unconscious effect on humans, most people are unaware that they are being influenced by them. Archetypes usually operate on the unconscious level. If people can become aware of how the unconscious controls behavior, then they can have more choice and awareness about their actions. They can choose to develop intentionally and spiritually, for example, instead of being controlled by energies erupting from the unconscious. We sometimes wonder why very important people jeopardize their careers and relationships by doing unwise things such as shoplifting or having an affair. These seemingly aberrant behaviors are no mysteries to some psychologists. Something is going on in the unconscious outside of conscious awareness, which results in behaviors that are not in the person's best interest.

Imagery Exercise: Archetype

Take a moment to relax. Feel your whole body getting heavier and warmer. Uncross your legs and relax your hands. Take a breath. See your ribs moving out toward your arms, making space in your lungs. Relax your heart. Relax your lower back, your middle back, your upper back. Relax your neck; think about the point where your cranium sits on your top vertebrae. Relax that spot on your neck that holds so much tension. Feel your shoulders let go. Feel your whole body getting warmer and heavier.

Imagine that you are outside in a place that you have been before. Imagine the scene is playing right now in your mind's eye like a movie in present time. Notice colors. Then reach out and touch something. Move in this setting. Smell. What do you hear? You are feeling okay in the image. Now find a spot where it feels okay to sit down and rest for a bit. Imagine that a positive archetype is coming to you—an animal, a deity, or a person. Off in the distance you notice a movement. Wait and watch. Let the imagery move. See what the archetype does or says. Let the imagery complete itself. Is there anything you want to bring forward from the imagery? Slowly come back to the here and now.

The World

Figure 9. The world archetype represents all things in balance and fulfillment.

Opening the mind to wisdom is not an easy task. It is a complex and simultaneously subtle endeavor. The ego's hold on stability is sacrificed for the connection to spirit that brings peace and joy. The delusion of control and separation erodes to a softer, warmer, and friendlier awareness. The sense of self is not constricted to fragmented thoughts or overwhelming emotions. Trust does not rest with control of the inner world, but with the sense of interconnection. Stability comes from a focus of attention, not from a defensive posture.

The Wise Mind concept foreshadows a reality where there is not a division between mind and spirit, but where humanity and spirituality are the same. Wise people see the big picture of the interconnection of all of life and can act for the benefit of the whole.

References

Achterberg, J. (1985). *Shamanism and modern medicine.* Boston, MA: Shambhala.

Adler, A. (2009). *Understanding human nature: the psychology of per-*

sonality. London, England: Oneworld Publications.

Burkett, T. (2015). *Nothing holy about it: The Zen of being just who you are.* Boston, MA: Shambhala.

Bergsma, A. & Ardelt, M. (2012). Self-reported wisdom and happiness: An empirical investigation. *Journal of Happiness Studies, 13,* 481-499.

Bolen, J. S. (2004). *Goddesses in everywoman: Powerful archetypes in women's lives.* New York, NY: Harper Paperbacks.

Dalai Lama, Tsong-ka-pa, & Hopkins, J. (1977). *Tantra in Tibet.* Ithaca, NY: Snow Lion Publications.

Erikson, E. H. (1994). *Identity and the life cycle.* New York, NY: W. W. Norton & Company.

Freud, S. (1949). *An outline of psycho-analysis.* New York, NY: W. W. Norton.

Gawain, S. (2002). *Creative visualization: Use the power of your imagination to create what you want in your life.* Novato, CA: New World Library.

Green, A. M. (1975). Biofeedback: Research and therapy. In N. O. Jacobson (Ed.), *New ways to health* (pp. 1–10). Stockholm, Sweden: Natur ock Kultur.

Houston, J. (1997). *The possible human: A course in enhancing your physical, mental, and creative abilities.* New York, NY: Jeremy Tarcher.

-------. (2000). Myths of the future. *The Humanistic Psychologist, 28,* 43-58.

Iyengar, B.K.S. (1987). *Light on yoga.* New York, NY: Schocken Books.

Jung, C. G. (1964). *Man and his symbols.* Garden City, NY: Doubleday.

-------. (1970). *Analytical psychology: Its theory and practice.* New York, NY: Vintage Press.

Kegan, R. (1998). *In over our heads: The mental demands of modern life.* Cambridge, MA: Harvard University Press.

Lancaster, B. L., & Palframan, J. T. (2009). Coping with major life events: The role of spirituality and self-transformation. *Mental Health, Religion & Culture, 12*(3), 257-276.

Masui, T. (1987). *The patient's efforts and psychotherapy: The images of symptoms.* Presented at the 3ʳᵈ International Imagery Conference, Fukuoka, Japan.

Nelson, A. (1993). *Living the wheel: Working with emotions, terror, and bliss with imagery.* York Beach, ME: Samuel Weiser.

-------. (2007). The spacious mind: Using archetypes for transformation towards wisdom. *The Humanistic Psychologist, 35*, 235-246.

-------. (2014). *Archetypal imagery and the spirit self: Techniques for coaches and therapists.* London, England: Jessica Kingsley.

Pert, C. B. (1997). *Molecules of emotion.* New York, NY: Simon and Schuster.

Piaget, J. (1972). *The child and reality.* New York, NY: The Viking Press.

Pribram, K. H. (1981). *Languages of the brain: Experimental paradoxes and principles in neuropsychology.* Englewood Cliffs, NJ: Prentiss-Hall.

Rama, S., Ballentine, R., & Ajanja, S. (1976). *Yoga and psychotherapy: The evolution of consciousness.* Honesdale, PA: Himalayan International.

Restak, R. (2010). *Think smart: A neuroscientist's prescription for improving your brain's performance.* New York, NY: Riverhead Trade.

Saxe, J. G. (1963). *The blind men and the elephant; John Godfrey Saxe's version of the famous Indian legend.* New York, NY: Whittlesey House

Suzuki, S. (1970). *Zen mind, beginner's mind.* New York, NY: Weatherhill.

Trungpa, C. (1991). *The heart of the Buddha.* Boston, MA: Shambhala.

Vivekananda, S. (1956). *Raja yoga.* New York, NY: Ramakrishna-Vivekananda Center.

von Franz, M.-L. (1985). *Aurora consurgens.* Princeton, NJ: Princeton University Press.

Walters, F. (1977). *The book of the Hopi.* New York, NY: Penguin Books.

Walsh, R. (2011). The varieties of wisdom: Cross-cultural and integral contributions. *Research in Human Development, 8*(2), 109-127.

Wise, A. (1995). *The high-performance mind: Mastering brainwaves for insight, healing, and creativity.* New York, NY: Jeremy P. Tarcher.

Woodman, M., & Dickson, E. (1996). *Dancing in the flames: The dark goddess in personal transformation.* Boston, MA: Shambhala Publications.

Annabelle Nelson, PhD, is a professor at Fielding Graduate University, and formerly at Prescott College. She has given presentations around the world, visiting sacred sites as she traveled in Japan, India, the UK, Cuba, and Mexico. She has taught from preschool to graduate school, and created a dynamic storytelling curriculum. Her yoga and Zen meditation practice blends with her expertise in consciousness studies, expressed in her book *Archetypal Imagery and the Spirit Self: Techniques for Coaches and Therapists* (2014) and other publications. Committed to child advocacy, she created the WHEEL (Wholistic, Health, Education, and Empowerment for Life) Council. She also publishes research on storytelling and health education.

Retracing the Labyrinth: Applying Phenomenology for Embodied Interpretation

By Luann Drolc Fortune, Ph.D.
Program Director in Mindbody Medicine, Saybrook University

Abstract

This paper describes how, in the course of conducting phenomenolog-ically based research, I was able to tap into a fuller range of whole body insights. I reoriented the phenomenological stage of imaginative variation by using labyrinth walking to inform my interpretation. As a researcher concerned with bodily topics as well as process, my work intentionally includes concrete techniques geared to collect embodied data. While conducting an applied phenomenology study, I strove to structure my framework to include somatic techniques. Yet in one such study, I found that somatically geared data collection alone failed to reveal the full depth of the findings. Including labyrinth walking to support my analysis opened up a fuller range of somatic awareness in conjunction with somatic and spiritual awareness.

Introduction

My discovery of the labyrinth as a tool for discernment and imaginative variation (Wertz, 2011) demonstrates one case of employing bodily movement, sensation, and reflexivity toward more authentic research. By *authentic* research, I intend what Les Todres (2007) describes as an "aesthetic dimension" (p. 30), whereby the researcher conveys meaning that deepens personal insights and inspires sense-making at the level of the reader's lived body. Research tactics that invite the embodied lived experience of research participants as well as the researcher are better able to convey this aesthetic dimension to others. In the process, the research assumes a richer level of validity and trustworthiness.

In this chapter research findings identified during the labyrinth walk are interwoven with my report. Furthermore, the details provide

261

the reader with a basis for an inter-embodied experience (Todres, 2007) of my discoveries, intended to awaken further intersubjective validity in my reader. This approach contrasts with the predominant approach of researching and reporting the examined topic in the field of manual therapy, where the gold standard for research is sanitized random control trials (Moyer, Rounds, & Hannum, 2004). The full results of the in-depth study in which I explored the work process of massage therapists are published elsewhere (Fortune & Hymel, 2014).

My phenomenological design for that study was constructed to capture experience as it unfolded without changing its essence. My purpose was to identify foundational assumptions about the executing and experiencing of somatically based (massage) therapy work. Intending to capture real-time experience, I video-recorded therapy sessions as they were naturally conducted. Immediately afterwards, I interviewed therapist and client using the videos to stimulate recall (Gass & Mackey, 2000). Also, as an experienced therapist, I wanted to capture nonverbal somatic elements of the participants' experiences as well as allow my own somatic awareness into the data collection process. To that end, I incorporated steps orchestrated to access nonverbal, body-based perceptions in data collection, such as including a body awareness exercise before each session. Somatic presensing exercises (Fortune, 2011) before and during data collection can promote a more mindful atmosphere and supported bracketing (Rehorick & Bentz, 2008).

During data analysis, I also used bodily postures, movement, and awareness to enhance my insights. My data analysis was an exercise in taking the work apart, strand by strand, to reveal its organic material cells. In parallel I received and gave multiple sessions of deep tissue massage during this phase. My initial thematic analysis produced complex and authentic findings. But despite my various attempts to name the essence of the experience, the thematic results failed to materialize into a structural description (Wertz, 2011). Using a precedent for a secondary phenomenological analysis (Ferrero-Paluzzi, 2002), I conducted a second turn with the data from the primary perspective of my somatic perceptions. At this point, I brought my inquiry to the labyrinth. The resulting interpretation literally began through a labyrinth with a walking meditation into an *epoché* facilitated by somatic awareness.

Phenomenology and Somatics

Phenomenology and somatics enjoy a generative partnership. I use *somatics* here to refer to the internalized perception and sensing of one's bodily self (Hanna, 1988). Hanna maintained that the body and mind were intrinsically interrelated and that, viewed from the first-person perspective, feelings, movements, and intentions are experienced in subjective wholeness. Some phenomenologists (e.g., Carmen, 1999) argue that Husserl's seminal teachings do not invite somatic perspective into inquiry. But tenets forwarded by Maurice Merleau-Ponty (1945/1962, 1968) and subsequent scholars (Behnke, 1997; Gendlin, 1978; Hanna, 1988; Leder, 1990; Shusterman, 2008) place the corporeal body squarely in the center of all reflection. The persistence of discourse on embodiment topics (Rehorick & Bentz, 2008) highlights the importance of somatics in applied phenomenology.

Applied phenomenology supports somatics research through the rich philosophical history but also because of successful outcomes. Aside from an obvious application to research on body-based topics (Allen-Collinson, 2011), various studies report memories, emotions, and trauma as being revealed and released in body memory and perceptions (Bentz, 2003; Young, 2002). Clinically, the physical body not only reflects therapeutic outcomes, but research demonstrates that it offers a resource for healing and transformation (Price, 2006). In addition, somatic awareness and considerations stand to improve research quality and authenticity when introduced directly into the inquiry process: embodied research.

Various scholars have called for more embodied research (Bakal, 1999; Finlay, 2006; Todres, 2007). Donald Bakal (1999) proposed that somatic awareness communicates the highest degree of authenticity because it can capture primary information from the authority of the first-person perspective. But somatic perceptions are, by definition, nonverbal experience. Nonverbal experiences are associated with *background emotions*, which are "closer to the inner core of life . . . more internal than external . . . [and] richly expressed in musculoskeletal changes, body posture and shaping of body movement" (Damasio, 1999, pp. 51-52). These elude capture through conventional methods (Todres, 2007), and the medium of scholarship is, conventionally, the written word.

Implementing embodied research techniques demands a cornerstone of phenomenology: a suspension of judgment and disbelief. In my quest to assume a fresh phenomenological perspective, I moved my body in a way and setting not natural for conducting data analysis.

In the quiet majesty of a cathedral, I walked a formal labyrinth while meditating on my data. In so doing, I experienced insights guided by the stages of the labyrinth ritual. Furthermore, I noticed that stages of the labyrinth ritual resemble steps in phenomenological inquiry.

Phenomenology and the Labyrinth

As a contemplative tool, a labyrinth is designed to facilitate individual insight and communion through movement. Physically, it is a unicursal path arranged in a pattern that winds around itself to a center. One walks the path to the center and then follows the same path out again. Ranging in form from simple to elaborate, the labyrinth in any form is replete with mystical and ancient roots. The labyrinth is meant for discovering "the product of the creative imagination, found inside ourselves" (Artress, 1995, p. 17).

The labyrinth has appeared in world religions since ancient times (Artress, 1995). A physical structure constructed of various materials, it is usually circular and contains a path arranged in concentric patterns. Various patterns and materials, each with their own significance and history, have been carved into cathedral floors (e.g., the Cathedral of Chartres, France), constructed from seashells on beaches, and sewn into canvases for traveling. Labyrinths are believed to be mystical, based on sacred geometry, "created in the realm of the collective unconscious, birthed through the human psyche and passed down through the ages" (Artress, 1995, p. 45). There is one defined path that leads to the center that the walker reverses to come out.

Labyrinth walking is a calm slow-moving trek usually done silently. In Christian tradition, labyrinth ritual is a three-fold practice, preceded by a time of *centering* one's intentions at the mouth of the entry. The first stage of walking inward, or *purgation*, involves releasing control and suspending judgment. This could apply to a specific issue or a generalized state. The second stage occurs at the center. Termed *illumination*, it is the source of insights. Walkers sometimes remain in the center in quiet reflection or meditation. The final stage is retracing the path outward. Referred to as a time of *union*, this stage integrates insights into greater meaning (Artress, 1995). After stepping out of the labyrinth, walkers often turn back and bow or offer some expression of thanks. There is no time limit, and walkers are expected to travel at their own pace.

For my purpose, the labyrinth offered a physical portal for entering a mind-body reflection on my research. It revealed itself to be more than another antagonist to the natural attitude; it exhibited resonance with phenomenology in ways I had not expected. Like the labyrinth, phenomenology is enmeshed in intersubjective communions of meaning (Applebaum, 2011). While excavating to progressively deeper layers of an experience's essence, the phenomenologist travels through stages much like those outlined in the labyrinth ritual: centering; purgation; illumination; and union.

Mirroring the stages of labyrinth walking, phenomenological inquiry is an intentional three-fold process: a) *epoché*; b) *epoché* of the natural attitude or reduction; and c) *eidetic analysis* or imaginative variation (Applebaum, 2011; Wertz, 2011). Giorgi (1989) stressed that the steps are progressive and nonarbitrary, each satisfying a specific theoretical demand. Clark Moustakas' (1994) model claims that a fourth stage is required: synthesis. Here, the researcher integrates the resulting textual and structure descriptions into a unified statement that reflects the experience's essence—a final statement of meaning for the researcher.

Journey to Illumination: Walking the Labyrinth

Valerie Bentz (2003) suggests that in phenomenology, "the uniqueness of an individual subject's account of any phenomenon is co-presented with intersubjective patterns and themes that emerge from analytical work" (p. 14). My time in the labyrinth was analytic work that identified such intersubjective patterns intertwined with my unique perspective. My labyrinth walk also served as a *sensory bracketing device* (Bentz, 1989, pp. 63-65) for my own sensorial recall of the data collecting experience. In the process of walking, I arrived at new insights about my researched phenomenon's texture and structure. The insights, like the walk, unfolded in stages that tended to wrap back around themselves.

The *Epoché*: The Stage of Purgation

The phenomenologist is called to create an *epoché* as a container for her inquiry by assuming a newly cultivated sense of wonderment (Husserl, 1975). Similarly, I took my first step into the labyrinth with a sense of wonderment about what I was possibly doing here that concerned my research. But I adhered to the ritual for the first stage and focused on releasing to achieve a state of openness. With each solitary step on the inward path of the labyrinth, I realized I had dwelt in this stage for prior days while I debated making this labyrinth walk. I tried to release my doubts—about this tactic and about my ability to find new knowledge. I tried to hold a felt sense of naïve expectancy about the phenomenon I explored. I then imagined that my earlier suspended assumptions, ones I had set aside much earlier in the data collection process, were in a safe-box. I unlocked them, allowing them to swirl around me and inform my interpretation of the protocol, the data I collected, and the assumptions themselves. As I allowed myself to revisit that which I thought I had suspended, images and words appeared to me with each slow step. It seemed I had to revisit my preconceptions if I were to re-release them.

As I was still walking inward, the repetitive pattern, the back and forth of the labyrinth's inward path, shifted my focus back to the data. I planned to employ imaginative variation, to formulate my description when I got to the labyrinth's center. Labyrinth ritual claims that illumination occurs in the center of the winding trail, after the inward journey (Artress, 2006). I struggled between staying in the nonverbal present moment of the narrow path of the walk and being drawn into the thick text of my data. Then my first insight appeared along my inward path. Focusing on my felt sense while I traveled the path, I could name the familiar strain between the nonverbal states and the verbal descriptions. I identified a tension while balancing elements from two realms: the life of words, reason, and cognition versus the vague space of the precognitive, sensorial, and nonverbal. As Merleau-Ponty (1968) said, "There are two circles, or two vortexes, two spheres, concentric when I live naively, and as soon as I question myself, the one slightly de-centered with respect to the other" (p. 138). In an instant, I found a meaning I had previously not realized. I called it *Holding a Tension Between Somatic and Cognitive.* It was written into my findings, supported by the data, but arose from that moment in the labyrinth.

I was relieved to reach the labyrinth's center, where I planned to rethink my earlier findings. According to neuroscience, humans do have an imperative to "name it," to cognitively affix reason to their experience (Kandel, 2006). The brain is hard-wired to assign cognitive meaning to events that would otherwise be limited by sensorial perception. Or as Merleau-Ponty (1968) said, a person needs to honor "the need to speak, the birth of speech as bubbling up at the bottom of his mute experience" (p. 126). Propelled by an innate imperative, I was compelled to name and analyze my work.

While thinking hard, I noticed that standing in the center of the labyrinth and staying balanced, as others moved about me on their own trek, required an inner strength. I associated this sense with my research participants' strong and controlled posture while they conducted the work I was researching. This led me to see how the phenomenon held an essential quality that presented bodily as the warrior posture performed in yoga (Iyengar, 1979). By assuming this strong posture, the therapists symbolically created a temporary sanctuary where their clients could relax and release tension. The data supported this insight, which I called *Assuming the Warrior Archetype.* Furthermore, through my felt sense of remembering the data, I realized that nurturance accompanied an essential quality of empowerment. The work's effectiveness relied on the clients' internal control of their own releases, essentially empowering the receiver to determine the effectiveness of the work, partnered *nurturance* and *empowerment.*

After a time in the labyrinth's center where I summarized my thoughts, I took the return path, hoping for union and synthesis. Retracing lines and patterns, I saw that the universal structure was the soma, the "living body" (Hanna, 1988, p. 20). It was my participants' soma and my own. My imaginative variations reduced down to the common essence of the internally sensed self. I sensed how I shared with those I studied an inescapable sense of mortality that unconsciously accompanies intimate contact with another while on a quest for essence. The resulting insight, *encountering sacred dominion*, represents the sacred nature of somatic therapies. In the labyrinth's turns, I felt a connectedness through the ultimate mortality that unifies us and inspired a sense of the sacred.

Exiting the labyrinth, I gratefully registered success. I was elated by my insights, which I immediately wrote down along with a *protocol* (van Manen, 1990) describing my labyrinth experience. But my persistent somatic awareness reminded me of boundaries and helped me remember that ultimately, at this depth, I could only speak impeccably for myself. One of my research participants described how she surrendered the outcome of her work to a higher power, "I try really hard, not to hold or not to be in charge of or responsible for her outcome. . . . I'm just a conduit, I am nothing more. And that's an honor." While no single quote encapsulates all permutations, the felt sense of gratitude, blessing, and joy in serving appeared repeatedly in the textual data. I realized the same felt sense applied to me in this work that I was doing as researcher.

Discussion and Implications

I initiated this labyrinth experiment because my somatic markers heralded a sense of incompleteness in my initial findings. My value for somatic awareness guided me during the entire study and particularly allowed me to make my leap into the labyrinth. As a result, I arrived at new insights that led to a structural description that satisfied me. It stated that the phenomenon I researched resided on two planes: a physical dimension of biomechanics, sensorial experience, and touch; and a symbolic dimension of intersubjectivity, consciousness, and relationship. The work expressed its full potential at intersections. While I supported this description with my data and findings (Fortune & Hymel, 2014), I also know it was conceived in capturing the empirical experience but birthed in a labyrinth.

My study's conclusions provided a device to theorize about the work for a particular audience (Fortune & Hymel, 2014). While the mind-body split is not necessarily a universal experience, it remains a rubric for modern medicine and represents a prevalent worldview. Similarly, whether or not the symbolic is experienced as separate from the physical is individually constructed and based on complex variables, including culture, personal history, and individual psyche. Popular understanding often refers to massage as an alternative practice to reunite body and mind. But to participants in this study, it was not a given that mind and body are inherently divided, although they worked in a field that widely accepted mind-body separatism. To the extent that "we interact with the world is as though it's separate" (Fortune & Hymel, 2014), the body can serve as an integrator to reunite us so that we can again experience our lives from the perspective of a whole entity. In the words of one of the study participants:

> By the way [we] chose to live, we have separated something that started out as one thing . . . that every-thing is all one and then divided into two, but really it's all one. I think we make body and mind separate even though they're not. But it is the way we function, the way we think, the way we interact with the world is as though it's separate. So it's, I mean, it's so inherent in our language and our culture that we would really have to transform ourselves not to do that.

Walking the labyrinth allowed me to transform my felt sense of the data and findings to a manageable set of findings appropriate for a particular audience but authentic to my understanding of the lived experience. It also taught me some things about how I conducted phenomenological inquiry. For one, my stages were not tidily discrete, but rather blended in to one another. Although the stages were progressive, they entwined. For instance, after I invoked purgation (*epoché*), I continued to touch back to it during illumination and unity. Walking the labyrinth's pattern embodied pattern-seeking in my data interpretation, and seeking con-textual meaning.

Using the labyrinth engaged my full capacity as a researcher. But I acknowledge limitations. Some will question the veracity of my phenomenological method, particularly because I juxtaposed proper order (Giorgi, 2006). Applied too broadly, phenomenological method characterizes "any work in research, theory, or practice that emphasizes first-person experience" (Wertz, 2011, p. 52). Some researchers who claim to have practiced phenomenological methodology fail to fully grasp the underlying epistemology and hence misunderstand the requisite steps: "not all variations can be justified" (Giorgi, 2006, p. 305). According to Giorgi (1992), phenomenology is first a descriptive methodology. Description is essentially different from interpretation, and the two should not be confused. My labyrinth walk was primarily an interpretive process that occurred distant from the phenomenon I researched.

Because I was fascinated with parallels between the stages of phenomenological method and labyrinth ritual, I stretched to match one footstep of labyrinth walking with the stages of phenomenological inquiry, conveniently dismissing the critical condition of empirical data collection. My labyrinth walk did not include gathering descriptions or data collecting in an empirical setting. In reality, essential descriptive parts of my research, the long months of data collection and organization, preceded my labyrinth walk.

In summary, proponents of embodied research suggest that intellectualizing should partner with bodily awareness (Shusterman, 2008; Todres, 2007). Several phenomenologists have proposed methods for capturing more embodied descriptions and dimensions (Finlay, 2006; Todres, 2007). But specific guidelines are still limited, and researchers should experiment. To the best of my knowledge, my use of labyrinth walking as a research investigative model is unprecedented. Like phenomenology, the labyrinth is supported by a rich and long history of cultivating contemplation, discernment, and resolution. In partnership, this history offers generative possibilities worthy of further experiments.

References

Allen-Collinson, J. (2011). Feminist phenomenology and the woman in the running body. *Sport, Ethics, and Philosophy, 5*(3), 297-313.

Applebaum, M. H. (2011). Amedeo Giorgi and psychology as a human science. *Neuroquantology, 9*(3), 518-528. doi:10.14704/

nq.2011.9.3.463.

Artress, L. (2006). *Walking a sacred path: Rediscovering the labyrinth as a spiritual practice*. Berkeley, CA: Riverhead Trade.

Bakal, D. (1999). *Minding the body: Clinical uses of somatic awareness*. New York, NY: Guilford Press.

Behnke, E. A. (1997, April). Ghost gestures: Phenomenological investigations of bodily micromovements and their intercorporeal implications. *Human Studies*, *20*(2), 181-201.

Bentz, V. M. (1989). *Becoming mature: Childhood ghosts and spirits in adult life*. New York, NY: Aldine de Gruyter.

-------. (2003). The body's memory, the body's wisdom. In M. Ithonon & G. Backhaus (Eds.), *Lived images: Mediations in experience, life-world, and I-hood* (pp. 158-186). Jyvaskyla, Finland: Jyvaskyla University Press.

Carman, T. (1999). The body in Husserl and Merleau-Ponty. *Philosophical Topics*, *27*(2), 205-226.

Damasio, A. (1999). *The feeling of what happens: Body and emotion in the making of consciousness*. New York, NY: Harcourt Brace and Company.

Ferrero-Paluzzi, D. M. (2002). *The body in medicine: A performance of choice* (Doctoral dissertation). Carbondale, IL: Southern Illinois University.

Finlay, L. (2006). The body's disclosure in phenomenological research. *Qualitative Research in Psychology*, *3*(1), 19-30. doi:10.1191/1478088706qp051oa.

Fortune, L. D. (2011). Essences of somatic awareness as captured in a verbally directed body scan: A phenomenological case study. In R. L. Lanigan (Ed.), *Schutzian research: A yearbook of worldly phenomenology and qualitative social science*, Vol. 3 (pp. 105-118). Bucharest, Romania: Zeta Books.

Fortune, L. D., & Hymel, G. M. (2014). Creating integrative work: A qualitative study of how massage therapists work with existing clients. *Journal of Bodywork & Movement Therapies, Advance online publication*. doi:10.1016/j.jbmt.2014.01.005.

Gass, S. M., & Mackey, A. (2000). *Stimulated recall methodology in second language research*. Mahwah, NJ: Lawrence Erlbaum Associates.

Gendlin, E. T. (1978). *Focusing*. New York, NY: Bantam Books.

Giorgi, A. (1989). Some theoretical and practical issues regarding the psychological phenomenological method. *Saybrook Review*, *7*(2), 71-89.

-------. (2006). Concerning variations in the application of the phenomenological method. *The Humanistic Psychologist*, *34*(4), 305-319.

Hanna, T. (1988). *Somatics: Reawakening the mind's control of movement, flexibility, and health*. Cambridge, MA: Da Capo Press.

Husserl, E. (1975). *The Paris Lectures* (2nd ed.). The Hague: Klumer Academic Publishers.

Iyengar, B.K.S. (1979). *Light on yoga* (Revised ed.). New York, NY: Schocken Books.

Kandel, E. (2006). *In search of memory*. New York, NY: Norton.

Leder, D. (1990). *The absent body*. Chicago, IL: University of Chicago Press.

Merleau-Ponty, M. (1945/1962). *Phenomenology of perception* (C. Smith, Trans.). New York, NY: Routledge Classics.

-------. (1968). *The visible and the invisible* (A. Lingis, Trans.). Evanston, IL: Northwestern University Press.

Moustakas, C. (1994). *Phenomenological research methods*. Thousand Oaks, CA: SAGE.

Moyer, C. A., Rounds, J., & Hannum, J. W. (2004). A meta-analysis of massage therapy research. *Psychological Bulletin*, *130*(1), 3-18. doi:10.1037/0033-2909.130.1.3.

Price, C. J. (2006). Body-oriented therapy in sexual abuse recovery: A pilot-test comparison. *Journal of Bodywork and Movement*

Therapies, 10(1), 58-64.

Rehorick, D. A., & Bentz, V. M. (2008). Transformative phenomenology: A scholarly scaffold for practitioners. In D. A. Rehorick & V. M. Bentz (Eds.), *Transformative phenomenology: Changing ourselves, lifeworlds, and professional practice* (pp. 3-31). Lanham, MD: Lexington Books.

Shusterman, R. (2008). *Body consciousness: A philosophy of mindfulness and somaesthetics.* New York, NY: Cambridge University Press.

Todres, L. (2007). *Embodied enquiry: Phenomenological touchstones for research, psychotherapy, and spirituality.* New York, NY: Palgrave Macmillan.

van Manen, M. (1990). *Researching lived experience: Human science for an action sensitive pedagogy.* State University of New York Press.

Wertz, F. J. (2011). A phenomenological psychological approach to trauma and resilience. In F. J. Wertz, K. Charmaz, L. McMullen, R. Josselson, R. Anderson & E. McSpadden (Eds.), *Five ways of doing qualitative analysis: Phenomenological psychology, grounded theory, discourse analysis, narrative research, and intuitive inquiry* (pp. 124-165). New York, NY: Guilford.

Young, K. (2002). The memory of the flesh: The family body in somatic psychology. *Body & Society, 8*(3), 25-47. doi:10.1177/135703 4X02008003002.

Luann Drolc Fortune, PhD, is a faculty member at Saybrook's College of Integrative Medicine and Health Sciences (HCS). She is also Director of Instructional Excellence and the Practice and Health Care Systems (HCS) Specializations at Saybrook, fellow at Fielding University's Institute of Social Innovation, and on the executive committees for the Interdisciplinary Coalition of North American Phenomenologists (ICNAP) and the Society for Phenomenology and Human Sciences (SPHS). She has many years' experience working in organizational development as well as wellness and somatic therapy. Her research interests include integrative wellness practices; somatic awareness and embodiment techniques for scholarship, research, and practice; and human development related to mid-life scholar practitioners and family caregivers.

Toward Embodied Digital Technologies

By David Casacuberta, PhD
Professor of Philosophy of Science,
Universidad Autonoma de Barcelona, Spain

Abstract

Affordances are a basic design tool for digital interfaces and technologies. The original concept, as created by the psychologist James Gibson (1982), was based on a naturalistic background that was later lost, as Donald Norman's (1999a) convention-based proposal became the dominant view in the realm of interface design and user experience. In this chapter I will 1) analyze the main differences between the Gibsonian, ecological approach and the conventional approach by Norman; 2) show the social implications and the augment of suffering which this conventional, disembodied approach lead to; and 3) argue for a new understanding of digital technologies based on an ecological approach to affordances, the general framework of an enactivist approach to mind and cognition, and the Buddhist approach toward dukha and nonattachment.

Introduction

As writer Neal Stephenson (1999) stated, in the beginning was the command line. Human-computer interaction was based on writing commands in a symbolic language – such as UNIX, text-based GNU/LINUX, or MS-DOS – to a terminal. However, it is clear that one of the main reasons for the extensive use of computers and software nowadays is a result of the development of graphical interfaces, which started to become relevant with the Macintosh in 1984. Most users no longer even know how to use terminals in Windows or Apple operating systems. Actually, most do not even know there is a terminal to start with.

This importance of interfaces has been magnified by the overall movement of users from computers to smartphones and tablets, where interface is even more significant and intimate. It has become nearly impossible to think of digital technologies without some associated graphical interface.

There is plenty of research on the benefits, obstacles, social constraints, hidden agendas, and biopolitical principles behind interface development. My aim in this chapter is to analyze affordances, one of the principles behind interface design. Further, I will consider how it developed historically and what the implications are for the reduction of *dukha* (suffering or dissatisfaction). I will also see how digital technologies can help in the construction of the economies of becoming.

Donald Norman's Conception of Affordance

If you ask any UX (user experience) expert, or even someone who has thought a little about how an interface should be properly developed, she will for sure identify Donald Norman as the person who coined the concept and made it relevant for digital technologies. According to Norman (1988), an affordance informs a user of how an object or an interface has to be used:

> The term affordance refers to the perceived and actual properties of the thing, primarily those fundamental properties that determine just how the thing could possibly be used...Affordances provide strong clues to the operations of things. Plates are for pushing. Knobs are for turning. Slots are for inserting things into. Balls are for throwing or bouncing. When affordances are taken advantage of, the user knows what to do just by looking: no picture, label, or instruction needed (p. 9).

Norman is highlighting one of the main characteristics of affordances: that they can be understood more or less intuitively. As software develops, and as more and more apps are generated for the ecosystem of smartphones, we see how this idea of intuitive, no-instructions-needed use is adopted by more and more developers and users.

How are affordances created? Affordances, according to Norman (1999), are a combination of intrinsic properties that actually belong to the object and relational properties that the user perceives. A doorknob has physical, intrinsic properties that help to create a specific perceptual image, which indicate to the user that he needs to turn it in a specific direction to obtain the desired effect. When he decides, while using an e-commerce website, that a salient button colored in green has to be clicked in order to send an online form, it is those perceptual properties that turn the virtual button into an affordance.

The other relevant property of an affordance is that the user has to be able to perceive it. The fact that this sounds obvious is another example of how deep in our minds are Norman's (1999) conception of affordance and interface. In digital technologies, Norman argues, most affordances are mostly perceptual and are created through a convention. There is no material reason why a hyperlink should be blue and underscored, but that is the conventional norm that was created in the beginning of the World Wide Web. It is a basic affordance that most people understand and are able to use. That means that interfaces can be designed in whatever way we like. We can use any convention we fancy; the only requirements are that the convention is easy to recognize and understand without any need for instructions, and that the convention can be easily perceived by the user.

There are two implications of this understanding of affordance that will become relevant later. First, affordances in interfaces are mostly a cultural disposition: A user needs to share certain cultural concepts, habits, and practices in order to use an interface properly. Second, affordances do not need to physically exist; as long as they are perceived to exist, that should be enough.

James Gibson, Affordances, and Direct Perception

It was, however, James Gibson (1979), not Norman, who originated the concept of an affordance. It was the basis for his concept of ecological perception. Gibson and Norman ╒s ideas of affordance are different in some details that are relevant for our understanding of current digital technologies. According to Gibson (1979):

> The affordances of the environment are what it offers the animal, what it provides or furnishes, either for good or ill. The verb to afford is found in the dictionary, but the noun affordance is not. I have made it up. I mean by it something that refers to both the environment and the animal in a way that no existing term does. It implies the complementarity of the animal and the environment (p. 127).

Joanna McGrenere and Wayne Ho (2000) explain that an affordance is "an action possibility available in the environment to an individual, independent of the individual ╒s ability to perceive this possibility" (p. 2).

According to Gibson (1982) it is not only objects that have affordances, but "also substances, places, events, other animals, and artifacts have affordances" (p. 403). There is therefore no need for a user to perceive the affordance in order for it to exist. Being an affordance is a real property of an object, based in how it interacts with the environment, in an ecological context. So, for example, an apple tree full of apples that are covered with foliage has the affordance to feed a primate, even if the primate fails to see it. However, in Norman's (1999) account, if the apples are not visible to the primate, there is no affordance to consider.

According to Gibson (1979), in order to have an actionable affordance, we need the existence of the affordance and information in the environment helping the user to locate it. For Gibson (1979), a basic affordance, such as walkability, indicates whether a surface can be walked upon or not. In order to have walkability, we need a surface that can physically support an actor, as well as visual clues that the surface is opaque, of certain materials, in a specific position, and has other characteristics. Gibson (1979) calls this process "direct perception" (McGrenere & Ho, 2000).

Despite this – that affordances do not need to be perceived in order to exist – they are still relational. That is, they depend on the type of user or actor. A surface that may be walkable by a squirrel might not support an elephant. An apple that is reachable by a little monkey might be out of reach for us. This also extends to specific individuals. A person of standard height can usually reach any button of an elevator, but a person of smaller size, or a child, might not be able to reach the buttons of the upper floors in most lifts. In Gibson's (1979) words:

> I assume that affordances are not simply phenomenal qualities of subjective experience (tertiary qualities, dynamic and physiognomic properties, etc.). I also assume that they are not simply the physical properties of things as now conceived by physical science. Instead, they are ecological, in the sense that they are properties of the environment relative to an animal. These assumptions are novel, and need to be discussed (p. 403).

There are three obvious implications of Gibson's (1979) understanding of affordance. First, affordances are independent of the perception or understanding of the user. They either exist or not. Second, affordances are relational. What is an affordance for one person might not be for another. Third, actor and environment are one and cannot be separated in a direct perception process.

Gibson's (1979) strong point is a cognitive one: We do not perceive objective external things as color stains or masses in motion; we perceive affordances. That is, our direct perception of the world is not intellectual and objective, but based on our purposes. Another way to put it is: we do not see only things; we see values. Returning to our apple tree example, we do not see a round red stain, we see a fruit that can be eaten.

This, of course, is perfectly in synch with the main ideas of perception in Buddhism. According to Buddhist psychology, any mental act can be viewed from the perspective of five *skandas*, or aggregates, which represent a certain point of view. Any mental act is a combination of those aggregates. A brief description of the five skandas and their relevance for this discussion will be helpful. This description will be following Geshe Tashi Tsering (2006) and Red Pine (2005). The five *skandas* are form, perception, sensation, formations, and consciousness.

Form (*rupa*) is the trickiest one, philosophically speaking. It is usually identified as the external world, and includes the body. However, it would make more sense to interpret it phenomenologically, as how the world appears to us and not as how the world really is. Another way to put it is to say that form is whatever appears to the five senses. Form is therefore a subjective appearance, which may change from individual to individual.

Sensation (*vedana*) is how humans evaluate forms. According to Buddhist psychology, any perception we have includes an evaluation of how the phenomenon relates to our plans and aims. This sensation can be positive (it is in line with our purposes), negative (it is against our purposes), or neutral (not relevant to our purposes).

Perception (*sanja*) is how we conceptually categorize the world. Long before the "theory laden" paradigm the in philosophy of science, and against any naòve empiricism, Buddhists perfectly understood that we do not perceive only neutral forms but are always processing and categorizing what we see, hear, smell, taste, or touch using concepts and language.

Formation (*sanskara*) is usually translated as "memory," but memory is only a part of *sanskara*. Habits, dispositions, beliefs, and so on are also *sanskara*; therefore, I follow the more recent tendency in Buddhist scholarship of using a neutral term such as "formations." Within a Buddhist philosophical framework, *sanskara* are a sort of karmic repository. Whatever we have thought, said, or done gets imprinted in the *sanskara* of our mind, and they will be responsible for what we will do, say, or think later. Karma is not some sort of prize and punishment given by a deity according to our behavior; rather it is a natural law akin to gravity: If you do good deeds, they will lead to positive states of mind in a natural way. If you behave in a wrong way, that would lead to negative states of mind sooner or later – a moral statement suggesting to the individual to act for the good to avoid bad consequences.

Most Buddhist schools adhere to some sort of reincarnation model of the mind, so when you die, part of your mind is still alive and can resurface inside another body, which may not necessarily be human. Within that part of the mind that survives there is also *sanskara*. When we reincarnate, the marks of good deeds and bad deeds are still present in us. The main aim of such a philosophical device is to work as a moral motivator. If you behave well, your prize will come. It may not come in this life, but it will come out in future ones. You may see some people behaving very badly in the world and getting no punishment for it; on the contrary, they seem to enjoy a fantastic life. But we are not to worry; they will find their punishment in future reincarnations for sure. This is a part of natural life rather being seen as given from a deity.

If we set aside the concept of reincarnation and only consider the theory of karma as occurring within this one life, it is not as farfetched as it sounds. In the end, this theory states that, for example, if you are angry and you do not try to bypass it, anger will lead to more anger: you will have angry thoughts; start to act and speak aggressively; and sooner or later you will do something you will regret. On the other side, if you try to feel happy, patient, and in harmony with your surroundings, you will feel relaxed and at peace, and you will have nice thoughts. You will behave and speak in a friendly manner, and this will generate a relaxing and happier environment for you and those surrounding you.

However, must we assume that anger – or any experience – is always negative? What if you are angry because you have lost your job and, to your surprise, are asked to leave immediately? Must this anger be translated into something more harmonious, especially when harmony seems far away from your current condition? Do you not have the right to express your anger, recognizing all aspects of the experience? If you will not now have money to pay the bills, should you have to look for relaxation? Does that not sound "unnatural"? Is it not more "natural" to think to about killing your boss? If you concentrate only on your reaction with a full abstraction from the social situation at hand, are you not voluntarily caging yourself? Does this not seem to be an individualistic perspective?

Consciousness (*vijanana*) is our ability to be aware of what we are doing, saying, or thinking. In consciousness, we develop the basic operation of separating object and subject. We could call it, if we prefer, "discrimination". Within Buddhism there is no such thing as a Cartesian self-consciousness; it is more of a "consciousness of." There are six different consciousnesses, each one attached to one of the six senses, which are the five physical senses (sight, hearing, smell, taste, and touch) plus one mental sense. This mental sense refers to our ability to realize that we feel hungry, bored, tired, happy, and so on. So, there is nothing "extrasensorial" about this sixth sense.

According to Buddhist psychology, only one type of consciousness can work at a certain time. If a person is conscious of the color of a piano, he cannot also be conscious at the same time of the sound it is emitting, or the haptic feeling in his fingers as he plays it. "Consciousness of" is activated and disconnected in a very fast way, so we shift attention from one type to another very fast. We have the idea that we can appreciate the colors, the sounds, and the surface of the piano at the same time; in reality, we are only paying attention to one thing at a time, but in a very fast way.

Please keep in mind that we are not talking about separate elements that, combined, generate a mind and a self. *Skandas* are more like perspectives: Any mental process is holistic; and the five *skandas* (with the possible exception of consciousness) are happening together. We do not experience in a clear sequential manner. It is not that we first perceive something, then color it with some sensation, and then check our minds for any relevant information in our memory, habits, and so on. It all happens at the same time. However, when we are trying to understand the mind better, it is useful to have these perspectives as differentiated.

The more relevant *skanda* for our discussion now is sensation. Affordance is one of the ways that our minds connect the external world and our purposes. Therefore, according to Buddhist psychology, any perception is marked as positive, negative, or neutral. Looking for the positive while trying to avoid the negative is one of the main forces of *dukha*, and it keeps us in a permanent state of dissatisfaction.

Some Socio-Political Implications of Our Current Understanding of Affordances

Let us take a second look at the main characteristics of Norman's (1999) view on affordances, since that is the way designers currently envision them while designing interfaces. As we saw previously, affordances do not have to exist or be backed by any physical properties of the real world. They only need to be perceived as such by a user. Second, affordances implied in interface design and user experience are mostly conventional. Third, to perceive an affordance implies a minimum understanding of the cultural basis in which the designed affordance is based. And fourth, in order to work, affordances need to be perceived intuitively, without the need for any type of instructions.

This understanding of affordances is clearly based in a Cartesian view of reality, in which mind has a differentiated existence from the body. More specifically, it is based in the symbolic approach to mind, also known as the first generation of cognitive sciences (Varela, Thompson, Lutz, & Rosch, 1991). In this paradigm, thinking is understood using the computer as the main metaphor: The brain is the hardware, and mind is software. Because of the multiple realizability premise (which states that a mental kind – property, state, or event – can be realized by many distinct physical kinds), the type of hardware we are using is not very relevant, and software can be understood by itself, based on a formal analysis.

From within this paradigm, thinking is simply processing symbols. The meaning of those symbols does not matter, as long as certain formal rules and transformations are applied properly. This fits nicely with what we have been discussing so far: An affordance is a series of symbolic, syntactic rules that specify how, after a specific operation (clicking on an underlined blue text), a new behavior will take place (a new window will open and show us the webpage at which the link pointed).

We can therefore specify the relevant cultural background as a series of abstract objects (texts, images, buttons, forms, links) and syntactic rules (what to expect if you click in a certain place, what to type in a search box), which links those objects with actions from the user.

One might at this point feel some tension: If affordances are conventional, how can they be intuitive? The answer to that question is to realize that intuitive here simply means it is close enough to the shared cultural background. As Norman has pointed out several times (Norman, 1988, 1999, 1999b), contrary to Gibson (1979, 1982), there is nothing natural about most interfaces. There are no underscored blue texts in nature. The fact that clicking on them will lead us to a new page is a pure convention that we have learned after some practice. After all, what we call intuitions are relative to practice and progressive familiarity. For example, learning to read is a very anti-intuitive process, but after some time we get so used to it that it becomes natural. From those unnatural black stains on a white background, meaning comes intuitively. It is the same intuition that Gary Kasparov, champion chess player, shows while playing chess – his intuition is the result of his familiarity with the rules and conventions of that game, developed through years and years of deliberate practice (Ericsson, Krampe, & Tesch-Römer, 1993; Simon, 1996).

So far so good. But what are some implications of considering interfaces under the symbolic paradigm?

First, it reinforces the Cartesian view of a mind separated from the body. Using a computer program or a smartphone is simply a question of understanding a series of formal rules, a pure intellectual affair, in which the body does not have any role to be considered beyond the structure of our hands in order to design keyboards and devices these particular hands can use properly.

Second, it perpetuates the belief that culture is simply code, a series of instructions and rules. Culture is therefore infinitely malleable and liquid, and it can be conventionally rearranged in any way we see fit (Lessig, 1999). Because of the need to create intuitive interfaces, this process cannot be done in a great bold movement of creating brand new technologies. It must be done in a series of small steps, called *remediation* (Bolter & Grusin, 2000). In a remediation process, relatively new media are built based on a former one that is culturally shared. One typical example is the first webpages, which have the same structure as newspapers; the only new element is the hyperlink. Another example is two-dimensional video games such as the Zelda series, which can be played easily because they are based on the common experience of finding your way with a map (Cogburn & Silcox, 2009).

It will be beneficial to consider how this process of remediation has watered down our expectations of what an innovation is. For example, we call a service such as Uber "innovative" when it is really only a wise regrouping of technologies we are quite familiar with: GPS; smartphones; crowdsourcing; and collective intelligence. Recent talk about how Facebook is changing interfaces and user experience design (UX) also comes to mind. Two of the oldest digital technologies, older even than the World Wide Web, are Instant Relay Chat and chatbots. The *Messenger* application (Turban, Strauss, & Lai, 2016) is a newer application of those digital technologies. In fact, if we take a detailed look at most "innovative" start-ups, we will see this recombination process of media that are already working and people who more or less intuitively understand this process. They then use existing software to create a flashy service that no one really needs but that is more easily accessible than what was available. According to Ries (2011), that is the way we should view innovation in the 21st century –using innovation to make technology more accessible.

Consider how different this is from sending a man to the Moon, or how Bells Labs changed telecommunication by developing second-order innovation. In a first-order innovation, we create something that does not yet exist. From a real analysis, discovery, and design process, there are some new ideas and not simply reordination of older ones, though based on existing technology. We can consider the Google Search Engine as a first-order innovation. The designers used several existing technologies, but they found a novel way to process the relevance of information depending on the query (Levy, 2011).

In second-order innovation, we have a first-order innovation that needs some technologies that do not exist yet. Engineers, designers, and others have the obligation to create this new technology. This is what happened when Bell Labs developed the transistor. Transistors were invented in order to substitute relays and vacuum tubes in telecommunication networks because these were not reliable or fast enough (Gertner, 2013).

Our third implication of considering interfaces under the symbolic paradigm is that, whether digital or physical objects, they are simply structures to be observed. It is the mind/software that does all the work, while the external world is simply there, passively allowing the mind to analyze it. The eyes receive some light rays, the optic nerve sends some electric signals to the brain, and our neocortex does all the relevant work.

Finally, our fourth implication is that interfaces are neutral. They are simply formal rules based on conventions. One can find any convention that seems to fit and develop it. There are no hidden sociological or cognitive effects in interfaces.

If we consider these four implications from a Buddhist perspective, we can see that they are built on false Western premises, on ignorance of basic realities of human behavior. They generate a "ghost in the machine syndrome," in which the body is irrelevant. This leads to the Silicon Valley ethos of working long hours and eating simply as a form of fuel for the brain, ignoring the impact on the body. Consider, for example, the stories of Silicon Valley *Übermenschen* getting scurvy because they feed only on Coca-Cola and pizza. Then, consider the subsequent praise of *Soylent Green*, a nutrient that seems to have all the needed nutrients, proteins, and vitamins so you do not have to "lose any time eating" and even that "you don't have to leave the office to get sunlight as it has plenty of D vitamin" (Hurley, 2008).

Believing that anything from your culture is merely convention is a sure formula for nihilism (Vattimo, 1988): Nothing makes sense anymore because some other convention may substitute the ones that make sense to you now. It is also the recipe for believing in technological determinism: When a disruptive technology emerges, humans cannot do anything but follow it, and social activities are deeply transformed. Fortunately, we know that the process is more complex and that there is a continuous feedback loop between society and technology developers. In the end, it is society that decides the final use of a technology (Casacuberta, 2003). Believing that interfaces are neutral makes it impossible to discuss the dissatisfaction they might bring to humans if they are not really neutral.

Another Interface is Possible

I would like to consider an alternative. What if we reflect on affordances from Gibson's (1979; 1982) point of view, instead of Norman's (1988; 1999a)? The main difference to consider is that affordances have an objective existence, independent of whether humans can perceive them or not. This is a very different paradigm from where interfaces emerge. Instead of a conventional cultural code, infinitely malleable to back digital affordances, we have a series of physical properties that are the basis of more complex affordances. These affordances are not intrinsic, but relational. They are the result of complex interactions between the mind of the subject, its body, and the environment.

This alternative view of affordances is rooted in another paradigm of cognitive sciences, what Varela, Thompson, Lutz, and Rosch (1991) called "the third generation of cognitive sciences" or "neurophenomenology." It is currently called "enactivism."

According to Evan Thompson (2007), in this paradigm, thinking is not merely processing formal symbols, but acting. Thought implies agency, and – we might liken this to the hardware department – it involves the whole body, not only the brain. This is the main reason this paradigm is called "enactivism": Cognition is an expression of our agency; of our capacity to build meaning; and to make sense of things as we interact with the world.

Therefore, mental activity takes place when different constraints in the environment are constituted in order to activate an autonomous, self-organized system. In enactivism, this is called "auto-poiesis": Goals are not introduced by some other agent, as happens in our current software, but are self-generated by the system as it continuously interacts with the world (Thompson, 2007; Varela 1996).

This means that knowledge is ontologic as well as symbolic. Knowledge is the result of the interaction between an organism and a system, a covariation between the two. Knowledge is embodied in this process, and cannot be considered the result of a series of formal manipulations by a software system.

Under this new light we can reconsider what affordances are. Let us rewrite the four main claims presented previously, but now from an enactivist or Gibsonian view:

a)   Affordances exist independently of whether the subject perceives them or not, and are backed by physical properties of the real world.

b)   Affordances are not conventional but relational. They result from the interaction of the cognitive agent with the environment.

c)   What we call culture is one of the main resources a cognitive agent has access to in order to make sense of its surroundings. This culture allows us to interpret the environment in a certain way, and interaction with the environment allows the transformation of some principles, concepts, and guidelines of such culture.

d)   Affordances will be intuitive as long as they refer to relevant ways in which the cognitive agent makes sense of its surroundings.

Changing our assumptions implies a transformation of the main social and political implications of affordances and interfaces. By switching from a pure symbolic approach to a enactivist one, we have a new paradigm that asks us to consider the body as a relevant agent in the whole cognitive process. First, engineers have to pay close attention to questions of motor perception, of how a person moves around a space, how a person tilts his head, or what the structure of the room is like. This transforms the way we make sense of our surroundings (Noë, 2004). Second, and more importantly, we need to forget the image of a brain in a vat processing symbols; instead, we must think of a real human being with a real body that has purposes and affects, and that likes certain things while disliking other things.

We also need to reconsider the idea of culture as something infinitely plastic and transformative. We need to remember and consider that each person has a certain type of body, and that we each live in a certain environment that makes certain types of cultural customs, actions, and beliefs more common and usual. At the same time, we must recognize that other cultural environments are much more difficult to access and comprehend. This also frees us from the dictatorship of re-mediation and having to build an interface that is always based on a former one. Instead, we have the opportunity to use an already-existing affordance that humans understand well but have not used before because nobody has had that insight yet. Asking interface designers to base their work on existing interfaces does not put their creativity at risk. It gives them even more and better opportunities to excel in innovation.

Perception, understanding, and action are always in evolution and transformation with each other; we are in constant interaction with our environment. As it changes, we change; as we change, it changes. Nothing is "set in stone," so to speak. Perception is not a passive reception of what is "out there," but an active and continuous reconstruction of what is around us that also implies an active and continuous reconstruction of our selves.

And, of course, interfaces are not neutral. They are the results of such interactions. They include several cognitive, social, cultural, and political principles that have to be analyzed and addressed. Because such processes are not obvious, there is a need for detailed cultural and philosophical analysis of such interfaces to understand the demands and implications involved.

A very relevant example of such a problem is how social networks are developed. They are designed to fit, as much as possible, within the attention economy paradigm (Crogan & Kinsley, 2012). Users in general are not willing to pay for services that are offered free in the online world. The fight, therefore, is to keep the attention of the user inside the limits of the service as much as possible, so that she will see the biggest number of ads. This is called the "walled garden strategy" (Tufekci, 2008). The aim is to keep us "hooked" on Facebook, Twitter, Google+, and other social media, so plenty of mechanisms are developed to generate dependence. Users producing content use similar strategies, developing "listicles" such as "five things all successful people do before breakfast." Sensationalist and titillating titles such as "You won't believe what this mother of seven children did in order to raise them" and the bizarre "Seven sexual fetishes you wouldn't believe exist" are designed to impact the reader and hold his attention so that he sees more advertisements. As more people go online, online advertising becomes more attractive to companies. We see a virtual race to be the first to offer clickbaits, shorter and shorter text, and more ridiculous content. As the saying goes, the Internet is becoming an ocean of wisdom, three inches deep.

The Gibsonian Eightfold Path to Interfaces

There is a set of principles that can help define a different type of interface, one based on a Gibsonian understanding of affordances. I am inspired by another basic epistemic Buddhist tool, the Eightfold Path, in order to explain these principles.

The Eightfold Path is described in the *Dhammacakkappavattana Sutta* (translated by Thanissaro Bhikkhu [2013] as "Setting the Wheel of Dhamma in Motion"). This text is traditionally considered the first teaching given by the historical Buddha. In it, the Buddha uses a common rhetoric device popular with doctors in India at that time: In a ritual way, he presents the name of a sickness, the cause of that sickness, whether there is a cure for such a sickness, and if so what the cure for it is.

In the *Dhammacakkappavattana Sutta*, Shakyamuni Buddha indicates that every human being is afflicted with the sickness of *dukha*, that is, of perpetual dissatisfaction. The cause of such dissatisfaction is not how the world is, but our clinging to it. We are dissatisfied because of our desire to keep the good things going on forever while wishing bad things to stop. Fortunately, there is a cure, he says. That cure is the Eightfold Path. These can be inspiration for principles as we rethink interfaces. The Eightfold Path consists of eight interconnected aspects of living. These are:

1. Right understanding, which implies a way of thinking about the universe and its relation to humans that realizes that everything is connected. Any separation between the world and a subject is something a person is creating through misunderstanding the nature of things. A person must understand that there is no substantive self separated from the myriad of things that make her surroundings.

2. Right intention, which is to have the resolution and motivation to act according to right understanding. When deciding what to do next, a person needs to remove herself from the equation and simply do the right thing. She must do what is the best for the whole situation, independent of her own beloved wishes, goals, and plans.

3. Right speech, which is the invitation to use language in a kind way – not lying, not being rude, not speaking ill of others, and no idle chatter.

4. Right action, which is captured in the five Buddhist vows to not take life, not lie for profit, not take what is not given, not engage in sexual misconduct, and not abuse legal or illegal intoxicants.

5. Right effort, which is not the Protestant work ethic that requires a person to keep working as much as possible; instead it is to put effort where it really matters.

6. Right livelihood, which means working and getting our nourishment and sustenance in a way that does not create suffering. For example, a Buddhist cannot be an executioner, a soldier, a drug smuggler, or a hunter.

7. Right mindfulness, which is to pay attention to the present moment, being open to whatever is happening instead of being lost

in our inner world, typically fixed on what has happened or what might happen.

8. Right concentration, which is being able to intensely focus the mind on the task at hand.

These principles can guide us toward a reinterpretation of affordances, as Gibson (1979) understood them, in order to build new types of interfaces that are less prone to bringing dissatisfaction to the world:

1. Have the right knowledge of what the basis for proper affordances is, look for basic natural affordances, and develop interfaces based on them.

2. Do not assume that an interface is "neutral." Make as transparent as possible the possibilities and limitations of the interface so that the user can understand the intention that is behind it.

3. When opening the dialog to other applications, social networks, and so on, try to include indications on how a message can be distorted, and on how certain options allow the user to cheat, pretend, or misrepresent.

4. Consider how the interface will interact with the environment and the people, and what effects it may produce. Designers have social responsibility, too. Check out whether the interfaces align with moral values, individual or cultural.

5. List and consider the cultural values the interface entails, whether it enforces or obstructs any social practices. Again, check out whether the interface aligns with moral values.

6. Choose existent, physical, easy to understand affordances that make the interaction process clear. Avoid making peculiar, experimental interfaces simply to show how bright you are.

7. Any real affordance should be able to show how the surroundings are, instead of masking them. Be sure that the affordance is as transparent as possible, and allows the user to see the present moment as it really is.

8.   Digital technologies based on conventional affordances generate plenty of distractions. Be sure that any source of distraction in the interface can be disconnected easily. Provide affordances to help the development of deep work and concentration.

Conclusions

We are taking for granted so many aspects in the process of developing digital media. This should not be so. There are significant epistemological and even moral assumptions embedded in the way we currently understand affordances that have not been properly analyzed, and many that have not even been challenged. Those assumptions reinforce the older view of the mind as a mere processor of symbols, and of cultural artifacts as mere conventions that are infinitively plastic as well as utterly neutral.

This is not only a philosophical problem. It is an ethical – and even practical – one as well. Smartphones, social networks, e-commerce websites, word processors, and search engines can be a source of productivity and entertainment, but they can also become vehicles for suffering. The most rampant effect, it seems, is how the attention economy is lowering standards of what type of content one should expect in digital media, especially those of social networks. It is not difficult to see a connection between this and the unexpected success of caricaturesque representations of, for example, important political issues. In this case, not only has social media popularized outside-of-the-box politicians like Donald Trump, but the networks use soundbytes and look for the basic instincts of the users. One goal is to "go viral," to become the most watched as quickly as possible. Another goal is to generate as many likes, retweets, you-name-its as possible. An example of the proliferation of social media is that Facebook is used daily by 1.13 billion people worldwide. The main focus of social networks has been redefined –from pure entertainment and to see what friends are doing to a news aggregator system that more and more people use as their main source of what is going on in the world right now.

Because of the way interfaces are designed in such systems, users who trust social networks or portals such as Google Search or Amazon.com as their main source of information are slowly entering what Eli Pariser (2012) calls "the filter bubble." Most of these systems aggregate information into a common site and use filters based on what a person previously searched for, viewed, or liked. These filters, tailored to a person's preferences and activities, screen what each person finds – which means that we end up only reading or watching what most closely meets our prejudices and expectations. Over time, you may end up thinking that everyone sees the world the way you see it.

We need to rethink how interfaces are designed. This is a multi-disciplinary work in which sociologists, economists, philosophers, psychologists, and other humanities scholars have to work together with computer scientists, designers, and engineers. We are talking here about a very relevant cause. We are not simply searching for novel ways to attract the attention of users with some sort of clickbait. Reimagining interfaces involves interdisciplinary deep and systematic consideration of what an interface is and how it affects humans cognitively, economically, and spiritually.

Buddhism is clearly an important and relevant tool for this. Its own philosophical principles are in synch with the original way in which affordances were described by the ecological psychology paradigm. This paradigm recognizes that the continuous covariation between individual and environment is essential. It also incorporates the relevance of the whole body – not the brain and fingers exclusively – when analyzing how humans relate to an interface.

References

Bhikkhu, T. (Trans.). (2013, November 30). Dhammacakkappavattana Sutta: Setting the Wheel of Dhamma in motion (SN 56.11). Access to Insight (Legacy ed.). Retrieved from http://www.accesstoinsight.org/tipitaka/sn/sn56/sn56.011.than.html.

Bolter, J. D., & Grusin, R. (2000). Remediation. Cambridge, MA: The MIT Press.

Casacuberta, D. (2003). Creaciùn colectiva. Barcelona, Spain: Gedisa.

Cogburn, J., & Silcox, M. (2009). Philosophy through video games. Abingdon-on-Thames, England: Routledge.

Crogan, P., & Kinsley, S. (2012). Paying attention: Toward a critique of the attention economy. Culture Machine, 13, 1-29.

Ericsson, K. A., Krampe, R. T., & Tesch-RÜmer, C. (1993, July). The role of deliberate practice in the acquisition of expert performance. Psychological Review, 100(3), 363-406.

Gertner, J. (2013) The idea factory: Bell Labs and the great age of American innovation. London, England: Penguin.

Gibson, J. J. (1979). The ecological approach to visual perception. Boston, MA: Houghton Mifflin.

-------. (1982). A preliminary description and classification of affordances. In E. S. Reed & R. Jones (Eds.), Reasons for realism (pp. 403-406). Hillsdale, NJ: Lawrence Erlbaum Associates.

Hurley, K. (2008). Food in the future: Does futures studies have a role to play? Futures, 40(7), 698-701.

Lessig, L. (1999). Code and other laws of cyberspace. New York, NY: Basic Books.

Levy, S. (2011). In the plex: How Google thinks, works, and shapes our lives. New York, NY: Simon & Schuster.

McGrenere, J. & Ho, W. (2000, May). Affordances: Clarifying and evolving a concept. Proceedings of Graphics Interface 2000, Montreal, Quebec, Canada (pp. 179-186). Retrieved from https://www.interaction-design.org/literature/conference/proceedings-of-graphics-interface-2000.

Noæ, A. (2004). Action in perception. Cambridge, MA: The MIT Press.

Norman, D. A. (1988). The psychology of everyday things. New York, NY: Basic Books.

-------. (1999). Affordance, conventions, and design. Interactions, 6(3), 38-43.

-------. (1999b) The invisible computer. Cambridge, MA: The MIT Press.

Pariser, E. (2012). The filter bubble: What the Internet is hiding from you. London, England: Penguin.

Pine, R. (2005). The heart sutra. New York, NY: Counterpoint.

Ries, E. (2011). The lean startup. New York, NY: Viking Press.

Simon, H. A. (1996). The sciences of the artificial. Cambridge, MA: The MIT Press.

Stephenson, N. (1999). In the beginning was the command line. New York, NY: William Morrow.

Thompson, E. (2007). Mind in life. Cambridge, MA: Harvard University Press.

Tsering, G. T. (2006). Buddhist psychology. Sommerville, MA: Wisdom Publications.

Tufekci, Z. (2008). Can you see me now? Audience and disclosure regulation in online social network sites. Bulletin of Science, Technology & Society, 28(1), 20-36.

Turban, E., Strauss, J., & Lai, L. (2016). Marketing communications in social media. In Social commerce: marketing, technology, and management (pp. 75-98). New York, NY: Springer International Publishing.

Varela, F. J. (1996). Neurophenomenology: A methodological remedy for the hard problem. Journal of Consciousness Studies, 3, 330-350.

Varela, F. J., Thompson, E. Lutz, A., & Rosch, E. (1991). The embodied mind: Cognitive science and human experience. Cambridge, MA: The MIT Press.

Vattimo, G. (1988). The end of modernity. Cambridge, England: Polity.

Zephoria Digital Marketing. (2016, July). The top 20 valuable Facebook statistics–updated July 2016. Retrieved from https://zephoria.com/top-15-valuable-facebook-statistics/.

David Casacuberta, PhD, is Professor of Philosophy of Science at the
Universidad Autÿnoma de Barcelona (Spain). His current line of research is artificial emotions, considering both their use in software applications especially, those that are media-related, as well as theoretical
research. He is also project manager for Transit Projectes and scientific
coordinator for the EU Projectes. He is a member of the Spanish think-
tank Edemocracia, which is devoted to the study of how ICT can improve democratic processes such as voting and participation. He serves
as secretary of the Spanish chapter of Computer Professionals for Social
Responsibility and is the Spanish representative in the International Coalition of European Digital Rights.

Designing for Consciousness: Outline of a Neuro-phenomenological Research Program

By E. Christopher Mare, PhD
Director, Village Design Institute, Eugene, Oregon, United States

"Once grasped, a great truth becomes self-evident."
~ Theodosius Dobzhansky (1956, p. v).

Abstract

The modern quest for "sustainability" is often framed as achieving a condition of steady-state material maintenance: "meeting the needs of current generations without sacrificing the needs of future generations." Such a goal will never be attainable under an economic system that converts land into "real estate" that may be exchanged as private property for market value. Such a system creates a patchwork pattern of private individual holdings that never has a chance to congeal into a coherent whole at the scale of the landscape. When land becomes "real estate," it is converted into an abstraction that loses any meaningful relationship with its underlying ecology—and a healthy ecology is always the basis of a robust economy. Village Design remediates these problems by organizing and managing land at the scale of the landscape. The perennial Village is symbiotically integrated into its local ecology, neatly conforming to and enhancing the characteristics of it local topology. Under these conditions, "sustainability" ceases to be an issue: attention may be turned *beyond sustainability*, toward creating conditions under which the people may *thrive*. Villages may even compete with each other to see who can create the most beautiful living conditions possible. This striving for "beauty" instead of "sustainability" naturally spawns a renascence of the Spirit: Human potential is maximized as human beings grow into their next level of evolution.

Introduction

The built environment is the structural milieu through which human beings move to conduct the daily affairs of living. From the dualistic Cartesian perspective—which shaped the epistemologies that have informed the construction of the modern world—the qualities and characteristics of the built environment are not overly important. The mind itself is encapsulated inside the head and the environment is "out there." Each of these operates according to its own separate set of reductionist properties.

A very different sort of picture emerges, however, with a study of ecological psychology, environment-behavior research, and the enactive approach to cognition. Mind is increasingly regarded as a *function* of the body and as an *interface* with the environment; it begins to make more sense to speak of a mind-body-environment continuum. Design and construction of the built environment become more important with such an understanding because the qualities and characteristics of this environment—particularly its geometry and morphology, its topology, and circulation patterns—can be perceived as intimately influencing mind and, by association, consciousness.

Design of the built environment is entrusted to the professional practice of planners, architects, and landscape architects. In the modern world, each of these professions has become progressively more dependent on the use of computer technology, not only in the production of working drawings but in the actual process of design thinking itself. Considering a mind-body-environment continuum, then, what does this dependence on machines and mechanistic processes imply for the quality and characteristics of the built environments so produced? By extension, what sort of consciousness can be associated with a population that must move through and conduct their affairs *within* such mechanistically conceived environments? Further, what is happening to the creative potential of a generation of designers whose imagination is limited to the pop-up contents of software programs?

Questions such as these have prompted the emergence of a research program to empirically test assumptions and document effects.

It is generally assumed that reliance on computer technology is an improvement over previous methods, so the built environments produced by the associated mechanistic processes must be inevitable validations of progress. The emergent research program, by contrast, proposes a *radically embodied* design methodology as a literal application that has profound implications of the mind-body-environment continuum. This research program is characterized as "neurophenomenological" because explanations are possible at the level of the nervous system in correlation with direct experience.

This chapter introduces and outlines this "designing for consciousness" research program by providing sections on theory, methodology, and method, with an abundance of supporting literature. Also included is final documentation—in the form of a conceptual site plan—from an initial case study that was conducted on the campus of a yoga college located near Portland, Oregon.

Theory

A theory can be considered as a lens through which to view the world. The lens is there to magnify or highlight some particular aspect of a phenomenon over others for descriptive purposes. A theory may be more or less inclusive, more or less encompassing; yet, whatever its scope, "Theory ought to create the *capacity to invent explanations*" (Stinchcombe, 1968, p. 3, emphasis in original). Theory is not intended to pose as objective reality but rather to represent only one angle on that reality, and this angle is there to serve a specific purpose. Within the context of a research program, the purpose of constructing theory is to provide an account for the empirical data that is produced by the associated research methods.

The core hypothesis of the Theory of Designing for Consciousness is that *it is possible to design the built environment in such a way that the consciousness of users is enhanced simply by moving about the place* (Mare, 2016). This hypothesis is supported by a previously established theory, the theory of "structural coupling," first introduced by Chilean biologist Humberto Maturana in his 1974 paper "The Organization of the Living: A Theory of the Living Organization." Since Maturana (1974) was developing a *systems* biology, he sought the language and ideas to explain ontogeny (individual development) and phylogeny (species development) in terms of *relationship*; that is, as a "dialectical process" (Levins & Lewontin, 1985) of mutual interaction and unfoldment between organism and environment. The theory of structural coupling was thus a direct counter-statement to the prevailing separatist notions of Cartesian dualism.

The key relational concept of the Theory of Structural Coupling was later paraphrased by Francesco Varela, Evan Thompson, and Rosch (1991, p. 174): "The organism both initiates and is shaped by the environment...We must see the organism and environment as bound together in reciprocal specification and selection." Systems theorist Erich Jantsch (1975) expressed the phenomenon this way: "As humans shape the systems in and through which they live, they are in turn shaped by their human systems" (p. 61). Or, in the stately words of Winston Churchill, "We shape our buildings, and afterward our buildings shape us" (in Dubos, 1968, p. 190).[1]

The Theory of Structural Coupling is a biological theory, and so the "reciprocal specification and selection" between organism and environment occurs in the nervous system. The nervous system, in fact, *is* the operational interface between the volitional actions of an organism and the environment to which it is coupled. Maturana and Varela (1987) state clearly that the nervous system arose in the process of evolution to facilitate *motility*. Behavior, therefore, is a consequence of "the different ways in which these two surfaces (sensory and motor) are dynamically related, via the intraneuronal network, to constitute the nervous system" (p. 153).

The brain is the concentrated locus of the intraneuronal network, and within the brain there are two regions in particular involved in the process of "spatial cognition," or the activity of guiding the organism successfully through the environment: These regions are the parietal cortex and the hippocampal formation. The neuroscience of spatial cognition thus provides the detailed knowledge with which to construct the Theory of Designing for Consciousness.

The parietal cortex processes multimodal sensory information to form an *egocentric*, or body-centered, representation of the environment: "The posterior parietal cortex . . . receives input from different sensory modalities . . . and combines this information to form multimodal representations of extrapersonal space" (Cohen & Andersen, 2012, p. 99). The hippocampal formation, on the other hand, creates *allocentric*, or environment-centered, representations of topological space in the form of "cognitive maps" (Nadel, 2008; O'Keefe & Nadel, 1978). Hippocampal neurons are "exquisitely sensitive to the spatial geometry of the environment" (Smith & Mizumori, 2006, p. 717), and it is now commonly accepted that the phenomenon of "place cells" in the hippocampus is what stores spatial information (Ekstrom, Kahana, Caplan, Fields, Isham, Newman, & Fried, 2003; Jeffery, 2007; Muller, 1996): "Place cells are *neural correlates of spatial memory*" (Kentros, Agnihotri, Streater, Hawkins, & Kandel, 2004, p. 283, emphasis added).

Hence, while egocentric spatial processing is very short-term—limited to the current orientation and viewpoint of the observer and depending on multimodal sensory cues happening in the moment—the allocentric cognitive map provides the opportunity to store the locations of multiple viewpoints, and the content of these viewpoints may be physically stored in the place cells for decades. This sort of understanding derived from the neuroscience of spatial cognition gives stark new significance to the structure of the built environment, knowing that this structure is being stored as cognitive maps that are translations of topological space. The structure of the built environment is therefore not arbitrary or incidental—something happening "out there"—because it is making direct impressions upon regions of the intraneuronal network, namely in the configuration of place cells in the hippocampus.

There is one more important neural phenomenon to address to complete the theoretical component of the research program, and that is what may be called "distributed neural networks." In the mechanistic-reductionist worldview, the brain was considered to be composed of an assembly of specialized centers, with each center performing a distinct function separate from all other centers. This "modular" view was a result of the "computational" paradigm, where the operation of the brain was equated to that of a digital computer. Within this paradigm there was believed to be a central "command" module, for example, and another module controlling consciousness. Fortunately, though still predominant, this mechanistic-reductionist worldview has begun to be supplanted by theories supporting a network form of neural organization (see Gardner, 1993; Goldman-Rakic, 1988; Selemon & Goldman-Rakic, 1988; Tononi & Edelman, 1998).

Researchers have been accumulating empirical evidence demonstrating the existence of these distributed neural networks. The Laboratoire de Neurosciences Cognitives et Imagerie Cerebrale (LENA) in Paris, for example, conducted a series of experiments at the turn of the century to test the hypothesis that the onset of a cognitive act may be the result of the "synchronization of oscillating neuronal discharges" widely distributed across the brain and brought together into a "coherent ensemble" (Lachaux, Rodriguez, Le Van Quyen, Lutz, Martinerie, & Varela, 2000; Lachaux, Rodriguez, Martinerie, & Varela, 1999; Rodriguez, George, Lachaux, Martinerie, Renault, & Varela, 1999; Varela, Lachaux, Rodriguez, & Martinerie, 2001).

Results from this laboratory can be encapsulated in the following statements: 1) "Cognitive acts require the *integration* of numerous functional areas widely distributed over the brain" (Lachaux, Rodriguez, Martineric, & Varela, 1999, p. 194, emphasis added); and 2) "The emergence of a unified cognitive moment relies on the *coordination* of scattered mosaics of functionally specialized brain regions" (Varela, Lachaux, Rodriguez, & Martinerie, 2001, p. 229, emphasis added). Based on findings like these, it may safely be hypothesized that any time one of these brain regions involved in the act of synchronous integration happens to be the parietal cortex or the hippocampal formation, details of topological space are making their way into consciousness.

Specific modes or manifestations of consciousness can also be proposed here. The connection between spatial context and episodic memory is unequivocal (Ainge, Dudchenko, & Wood, 2008; Bird & Burgess, 2008; Burgess, Becker, King, & O'Keefe, 2001; Burgess, Maguire, & O'Keefe, 2002); it can be asserted that any time a conscious experience includes content of an autobiographical nature, the quality of the built environment is entering consciousness. Evidence is also available to suggest that the quality of the built environment is influencing the propensity for subjective recall, relative to the intensity of feeling evoked when an experience was first embedded (Bird & Burgess, 2008; Kentros, Agnihotri, Streater, Hawkins, & Kandel, 2004; Mare, 2016). Additional evidence can be shown relating the content of cognitive maps to the quality of *imagery* that may be produced (or reproduced), thus leading to speculation about a connection between the quality of spatial information stored with episodic memory and imagination more generally (Becker & Burgess, 2001; Burgess, 2008; Jeannerod, 1994; Nadel, 2008). Further, since any cognitive map has been imprinted from a specific "viewpoint," a question can be raised about the possibility that "points of view," or more generally "worldviews," can also be traced back to the quality of spatial imagery stored in the hippocampal formation (King, Burgess, Hartley, Vargha-Khadem, & O'Keefe, 2002; Mare, 2016).

This last possibility becomes even more intriguing when considering the work of George Lakoff and Mark Johnson (Johnson, 1987; Johnson, 2007; Lakoff & Johnson, 1980; Lakoff & Johnson, 1999), who have studied the use of language based on metaphors that are employed. An extensive survey reveals that a broad range of thinking utilizes metaphors based on embodied sensorimotor experience. A vivid example comes from the quote that was offered as the epigraph to this chapter: "Once grasped, a great truth becomes self-evident" (Dobzhansky, 1956, p. v). Here, the act of comprehending the essence of a great truth is equated with firmly holding it in one's hand. Other examples are legion, yet of particular interest here are metaphors that reference the spatial context of experience. These are referred to as Orientational Metaphors, because most of them have to do with spatial orientation: up-down; left-right; over-under; inside-outside (Lakoff & Johnson, 1980). These Orientational Metaphors are based on an egocentric perspective, and thus are coming from the multimodal processing of the parietal cortex—which, it must be remembered, is always in contact via theta rhythms with the long-term storage of maps in the hippocampal formation (Buzsaki, 2005, 2010; White, Congedo, Ciorciari, & Silbertein, 2012).

The use of metaphors based on sensorimotor experience even extends to the realm of reason:

> Reason is not, in any way, a transcendent feature of the universe or of disembodied mind. Instead, it is shaped crucially by the peculiarities of our human bodies, by the remarkable details of the neural structure of our brains, and by the specifics of our everyday functioning in the world (Lakoff & Johnson, 1999, p. 4).

The Theory of Structural Coupling makes sure to insert that "our everyday functioning in the world" is intimately associated with a specific environment with which we are co-evolving through mutual selection and specification. The Theory of Designing for Consciousness goes a step further by hypothesizing that the particular *qualities* of this environment—qualities that include details of spatial geometry—are influencing the quality of conceptual reasoning. This is possible by way of accessing the substrate of sensorimotor experience stored as cognitive maps. In other words, a concept could not be contemplated, and metaphors could not be employed to facilitate this contemplation, if there were not some neural precedent already instantiated. One of the most vivid instantiations of neural precedent is in the form of cognitive maps that are created simply by the act of moving through the geometric structure and topological arrangement of the built environment.

This overview of the theoretical component of the research program of designing for consciousness implies powerful responsibility being imparted to designers of the built environment. When it is realized that a *topological isomorphism* exists between environmental structure and neural structure, and that the configurational characteristics of this topology have direct influence on cognitive acts of consciousness—and by extension on human potential—then it can no longer be blithely assumed that methodologies are without consequence. Recognition that a mind-body-environment continuum exists would suggest that mechanistic design processes will have mechanistic consequences, both in the minds of the designers and for the users of the environments so produced. In an effort to take this responsibility seriously, and to use the understanding of topological isomorphism to an advantage—to in fact prepare a research program that may explore the possibility of *enhancing* consciousness through a thoughtful, well-informed design protocol—a new methodology must be developed. This methodology will ask practitioners to go deeper into the subject matter, as well as deeper into their bodies, than ever before.

Methodology

A research methodology is a study of the ways knowledge may be generated and knowledge claims evaluated relative to the proposed goals and purposes of a research program. The methodology developed in support of the research program of designing for consciousness is derivative of the correlation that can be established between the respective goals of the philosophy of phenomenology and the philosophy of yoga.

The philosophy of phenomenology, as formulated by Edmund Husserl (1913, 1960), is the foundation of the research methodology. To be literal, phenomenology is the study of "phenomena" (from the Greek *phainomenon*, "an appearance") or that which is revealed to awareness. Phenomena may be any stimuli impinging upon the nervous system as sense impressions, or they may be nonsensual in the form of intuitions, feelings, wishes, memories, cogitations, and so forth. Phenomenology seeks to comprehend these phenomena in their *essence*, as they are directly *experienced*, before they are filtered down and modified through the imposition of prior judgment, expectation, belief, or theory. Successful practice phenomenology requires a new way of "being-in-the-world" (Heidegger, 1962): experiencing the world openly, fresh, anew, and free of preconceived categories, limiting conclusions, or ready-made answers. The philosophy of phenomenology therefore seeks to legitimize *direct subjective experience* as a valid perspective from which to conduct research. This sort of position, of course, stands contra to the prevailing ideal of objective science, which is prepared to solely legitimize a postulated pure and detached form of knowledge untainted by subjective experience.

Phenomenology is ideally suited to complement, enrich, and deepen the professional practice of designers of the built environment. Direct subjective experience of the site to be designed provides invaluable knowledge for application in the design process. Direct subjective experience of the finished designed product—whether a building, a landscape, a village, a city, or whatnot—is the only way to evaluate the relative efficacy of any given design process: How does it actually *feel* to move through the space so designed? Phenomenology has been integrated into design thinking in scattered cases (e.g., Bachelard, 1958, 1994; Bloomer & Moore, 1977; Cullen, 1961; De Botton, 2006; Hildebrand, 1999; Holl, Pallasmaa, & Perez-Gomez, 1993, 2006; Lynch, 1960; Norberg-Schulz, 1980, 1984, 2000; Pallasmaa, 2012; Rasmussen, 1959; Seamon, 1993; Seamon & Mugerauer, 2000). Yet standard practice in the design professions—as if to emulate the detachment of objective science—has been to disregard direct subjective experience as cumbersome, perhaps even inessential. This objectification of design is exacerbated by the attitude within architecture, queen of the design professions, to treat buildings as individual isolated objects (designed by individual isolated egos) lacking meaningful relationships with their community.[2]

ἐποχή

An essential movement in phenomenological perception, the condition that enables the researcher (or designer) to perceive essence, is the ability to enter successfully the phenomenological *epoché*. *Epoché* (pronounced ep-a-kee) "is the transliteration of a Greek word, which initially/literally meant 'a check or cessation' (as in 'checking an advance'), and later became a technical term used by the early skeptical philosophers [Stoics] to mean 'a suspension of judgment'" (Hammond, Howarth, & Keat, 1994, p. 289). Within phenomenological research, this "gesture of suspension with regard to the habitual course of one's thoughts, brought about by an interruption of their continuous flowing" (Depraz, 1999, p. 99) is precisely what enables the fresh, uncluttered perspective capable of perceiving essence.

Despite the premier importance assigned to *epoché* in the phenomenological literature, this same literature is rather negligent in explaining the explicit process by which this suspension of judgment is to be achieved. For instance, is it to be *willed* into being, as with a firm statement of intention? This leaves too much to capricious chance. The most accommodating explanation I have found for achieving *epoché* was provided as a subjective report in Clark Moustakas' *Phenomenological Research Methods* (1994). In the following passage, Moustakas makes preparation for entering the phenomenological *epoché* sound like *meditation*:

The challenge is to silence the directing voices and

310

sounds, internally and externally, to remove from myself manipulating or predisposing influences and to become completely and solely attuned to just what appears, to encounter the phenomenon, as such, with a pure state of mind...Such an ability to gaze with concentrated and unwavering attention, whether inward or outward, is indeed something that requires patience, a will to enter and stay with whatever it is that interferes until it is removed and an inward clearing is achieved...Every time a distorted thought or feeling enters, the abstention must once again be achieved until there is an open consciousness...This may take several sessions of clearing my mind until I am ready for an authentic encounter (pp. 88-89).

Although Moustakas (1994) never actually comes out and admits that he is referring to meditation, Husserl (1960) himself makes the connection explicit. Consider the following passage from his *Cartesian Meditations*:

If I keep purely what comes into view—for me, the one who is meditating—by virtue of my free *epoch*é with respect to the being of the experienced world, the momentous fact is that I, with my life, remain untouched in my existential status, regardless of whether or not the world exists and regardless of what my eventual decision concerning its being or non-being might be (p. 25).

I do believe that by saying he is "meditating" Husserl (1960) is not admitting to the disciplined practice of an Eastern tradition. No, he is referring more to what we would call "contemplation," for he is attempting to align his philosophy with Descartes' precedent of introspection. It does not take long, however, *within* a study of Eastern traditions, to notice a correspondence of systemic philosophic purpose. This correspondence is most pronounced in Patanjali's *Yoga Sutras*.

Scholar of Yoga Georg Feuerstein (2008) situates the origins of a proto-yoga to the Upanishadic Age of 1500-1000 B.C. Halfway through the Classical Age of 100 B.C. to 500 A.D., a rishi named Patanjali was the first to systematize the various yogic practices into a collection of aphorisms that came to be known as the *Yoga Sutras*. Desikachar (1995) ennobles these *Sutras* as "the heart of yoga," because through them Patanjali gave yoga "a permanent definition and form" (p. 145), a "recognizable philosophical shape" (Feuerstein, 2008, p. 209). The *Sutras* continue to be studied, interpreted, and embellished with exegetical commentary to the present day.

In the second verse of the first chapter of the *Yoga Sutras*, Patanjali offered a definition of yoga that has reverberated down through the ages:

योगश्चित्तवृत्तिनिरोध: ।

Yogas citta vritti nirodah can be translated as "Yoga is the suppression of the modifications of the mind" (Aranya, 1983, p. 6) or "Yoga is the neutralization of the vortices of feeling" (Kriyananda, 2013, p. 17), language which is remarkably similar to that expressing the purpose of the phenomenological *epoché*. Indeed, in my work (2016), I conducted a hermeneutical study comparing the phenomenological literature describing *epoché* with the yogic literature describing *yogas citta vritti nirodah*. The results of this study can be condensed into the following table:

Table 1

Comparison of Characterizations of Two Important Concepts:
   Epoché *and Yoga*

Epoché	Yoga
suspension	suppression
abstention	restriction
abeyance	restraint
neutralization	neutralization

This table clearly reveals a similar purpose underlying the two philosophical systems. This similar purpose was articulated astutely by Depraz (1999) as "suspension with regard to the habitual course of one's thoughts, brought about by an interruption of their continuous flowing." Yet, whereas *epoché* seeks a *temporary* suspension—so that perception may be clarified long enough for the philosopher (or designer) to perceive essence in a given task—yoga seeks a more permanent solution, such that the perception of essence may be a continual and ongoing attribute. Yoga can claim this advantage because it is a *radically embodied* direct subjective experiencing of the mind-body connection whose continuous practice results in neurophysiological conditioning and fine-tuning of the nervous system. What better way, then, to enter *epoché* than through the practice of yoga?[2]

In order to make this all empirically verifiable as methodology for the research program, yoga needs to be qualified a step further. Patanjali's system is called *ashtanga* yoga, which means it has "eight limbs." These are: 1) discipline (*yama*); 2) restraint (*niyama*); 3) posture (*asana*); 4) breath control (*pranayama*); 5) sense-withdrawal (*pratyahara*); 6) concentration (*dharana*); 7) meditation (*dhyana*); and 8) ecstasy (*samadhi*) (from Feuerstein, 2008, p. 244). Of these eight limbs, it is Stage 3, *asana*, that is typically associated with yoga in the West.

These are the postures that can be observed being practiced in any yoga studio. What is not generally realized, however, is that these *asanas* in the *ashtanga* system are intended to prepare the body for Stage 7, *dhyana* or meditation. The somatic effects of postures enable the body to be able to sit for long periods of concentrating stillness, during which time the fluctuations of consciousness may be neutralized and the habitual course of one's thoughts may be suspended, which are precisely the goals of *epoché*.

As a comprehensive system of self-transformation, then, all the limbs are leading up to disciplined meditation. What the *ashtanga* system means for the research methodology, therefore, is that it is wholly consistent to be utilizing and referencing disciplined meditation as a yogic practice, especially when the intention is to influence and condition the nervous system and various energetic centers of the subtle body. This is indeed the approach that was taken during the development of the research *method* that was practiced as part of the initial case study associated with the research program of Designing for Consciousness.[4]

Method

Whereas *methodology* is the study of ways of producing knowledge through research, *method* is the actual technique or procedure used to collect the data that will be analyzed to formulate that knowledge. Within any given methodology an array of methods is possible; specific design will depend on the type and quality of data that is sought. I developed the method that will be outlined here in conjunction with the initial case study representing this research program. The method consisted of two stages: 1) a yogic meditation sequence focusing on brain centers known to be integral to the activity of perception, and 2) conducting "phenomenological walkthroughs" in the resulting meditative state of mind over a topological landscape for the purpose of collecting detailed perceptual data. These data were later analyzed and applied during a phase of Design Studio, at which time I produced a detailed conceptual site plan of the campus. The production of the conceptual site plan signifies a climax stage of the designing for consciousness process.

The yogic meditation sequence had the purpose of conditioning and fine-tuning the nervous system in preparation for the observation stage of the design scenario. I determined the specific sequence from knowledge gained by a study of the neuroanatomy of spatial cognition, particularly the visual perception component (Bear, Connors, & Paradiso, 2001; Connors & Long, 2004; Creem & Proffitt, 2001; Espinosa & Stryker, 2012; Gazzaniga, Ivry, & Mangun, 1998, 2009; Gilbert & Li, 2012; Goodale & Milner, 1992; Grill-Spector & Malach, 2004; Hubel, 1988; Kosslyn, Ball, & Reiser, 1978; Kravitz, Saleem, Baker, & Mishkin, 2011; Livingstone, 2002; Palmer, 1999; Shen, Yacoub, & Ugurbil, 1999). The yogic meditation sequence focused on these organs of spatial perception with the intention of stimulating them, with the underlying hypothesis being that by locating and visualizing these organs in thought, and then concentrating on their clarification and purification, I could achieve heightened perceptual acuity—where "heightened" is understood as a qualitative increase in awareness as compared to the baseline normalcy of the natural attitude.

There were nine stages to the meditation sequence:

Stage 1. *Anapana* meditation: To cultivate sensitivity and to begin stilling the mind and getting centered, preparing for the meditation tasks to follow. My experience has been that *Anapana* alone is enough to commence the suspension of the flow of habitual thought that is the goal of *epoché*.

Stage 2. Moving the attention upward to rest at "the point between the eyebrows," a technique which is said to cultivate "inner vision."

Stage 3: Moving the attention further upward to locate the *Sahasrara* chakra, situated at the center of the top of the head, and an inch or so above the skull.

Stage 4. This stage begins at the *Sahasrara* chakra, then splits the attention into two, slowly moving simultaneously down both hemispheres of the parietal lobe.

Stage 5. With the attention still split in two, movement continues down through the junction of the parietal and occipital cortices. The attention continues to move through the occipital lobe until it arrives at the nodes situated at the very posterior region. This is the locus of V1, the primary visual cortex.

Stage 6. After focusing for some time on V1, the attention resumes, moving bilaterally until it arrives and rests at the two mini-hemispheres of the cerebellum.

Stage 7. At this stage, the attention resumes its singular focus as it converges and crosses the ventricle canal to arrive at the brainstem. After becoming situated along the brainstem, the attention moves ever so slowly upward: through the medulla and through the pons, penetrating ever deeper into the densely-packed interior of the brain called the diencephalon.

Stage 8: The circumnavigation around the brain, concentrating on organs vital to spatial perception, has now reached its destination as the attention arrives at the centrally positioned thalamus: "The thalamus has been referred to as the 'gateway to the cortex' because, with the exception of some olfactory inputs, all sensory modalities make synaptic relays in the thalamus before continuing to the primary cortical sensory receiving areas" (Gazzaniga, Ivry, & Mangun, 2009, p. 82).

Stage 9. After meditating on the thalamus for an extended period of time, the attention adjusts to locate an appendage to the posterior of the thalamus called the *pineal gland*, postulated as the seat of the "third eye" (Hall, 1972). Opening of the third eye is said to increase intution, heighten sensitivity of perception and, according to Gupta (1998), access *saksin*, the "witness consciousness" of Advaita Vedanta phenomenology. The hypothesis here is that *saksin* will be the ideal lens through which to perceive in the process of designing for consciousness.

Introducing meditation into the design process was intended to, as it were, "cleanse the doors of perception" (Huxley, 1963), conditioning and fine-tuning the nervous system for the purpose of producing more valuable, clarified, *neurophenomenological* sensory data. It should be emphasized that I developed this specific method to accommodate the situation at hand, which was retrofit designing for the campus of a yoga college. Within the given methodology, other methods might conceivably be developed to more specifically attune to other scenarios. Upon the close of the yogic meditation sequence outlined, having thus entered *epoché* with sensitized organs of perception, I would step out onto the campus to begin phenomenological walkthroughs of the topological landscape with the intention of perceiving *essence*.

Each phenomenological walkthrough was preceded by preselecting a route through the campus of the yoga college. Routes were chosen so that prominent topological and ecological features could be experienced from varying perspectives. The routes surveyed existing circulation patterns on campus—sidewalks, paths, roads—in order to get a feel for how movement through the campus is currently experienced. Design decisions were based upon *enhancing* existing circulation patterns, where appropriate, or *remedying* circulation patterns that produced uncomfortable experiences or were otherwise dysfunctional. The perceptions gained from "moving through" the campus during the observation stage are absolutely essential; perceptions gained from simply sitting in one spot and observing will not be adequate during the initial design phases, which are devoted to apprehending the site as a whole. This need for movement can be explained from a neurological perspective:

> All areas of cortex have outputs to lower motor centers and...one important characteristic of cortical organization is that the cortex monitors ongoing motor outputs

not only from the phylogenetically older subcortcal parts of the nervous system but also plays a significant role in monitoring itself, with one cortical area receiving information through the thalamus about the motor outputs of related cortical areas...That is, early in the evolution of the cortex, *the areas that receive sensory inputs also had motor outputs* (Sherman & Guillery, 2013, p. 53, emphasis added).

Motility, therefore—or locomotion if you will (locus-motion)—is not incidental or an extra add-on if there is time: *Motility is fundamental to sensory experience.*[5] Sensory and motor surfaces are so intricately interconnected that it is more accurate to speak of *sensorimotor* phenomena (in the same way that body and mind are so intricately interwoven that it is more accurate to speak of *bodymind*). According to Alva Nöe and J. Kevin O'Regan (2002), "Seeing is an exploratory activity mediated by the animal's mastery of sensorimotor contingencies. That is, seeing is a skill-based activity of environmental exploration. Visual experience is not something that happens *in* us. It is something we *do*" (p. 567, emphases in original). Another way of saying this is "perception is not in the brain, but rather the whole embodied animal interacting with its environment" (Thompson, Nöe, & Pessoa, 1999, p. 186).

It is important to remember when speaking of perception and spatial cognition that the nervous system evolved through long eons of this "environmental exploration" or, more accurately, exploration of *specific ecologies.* This evolutionary perspective forms the basis of the embodied or "enactive" approach to cognition (Thompson, 2006a): "Cognition is the exercise of skillful know-how in situated action" (Thompson, 2006b, p. 226). This understanding of cognition as a form of embodied action has implications for consciousness, since "consciousness lies at the operational interface between body movement and the body's surroundings" (Cotterill, 2000, p. 285). We could also say that "consciousness is nothing other than the dialectic of milieu and action" (Merleau-Ponty, 1942, in Rietveld, 2008, p. 342). Designing for consciousness, then, is a matter of masterfully creating circulation patterns that can optimally stimulate the nervous system during the ordinary activity of moving through the built environment.

What Makes This Neurophenomenology?

The intention of Varela (1996) in establishing the research program of neurophenomenology was to articulate a methodology that could approach the study of consciousness bivalently—that is, by correlating both subjective and objective accounts. Such an integrated approach was projected to be far more productive than studying either subjective or objective accounts in isolation: "Neuro-phenomenology is the name I am using here to designate a quest to marry modern cognitive science and a *disciplined approach* to human experience, thus placing myself in the lineage of the continental tradition of phenomenology" (Varela, 1996, p. 330, emphasis in original).

The knowledge produced by neurophysiological studies of the effects of yoga is powerful neuroscience knowledge, *objective* knowledge regarding the functioning of the brain and its nervous system. Applying this knowledge to devise a method for using the *dhyana* stage of yoga to enter the phenomenological *epoché* thus could be considered as an expression of the goals of the research program of neurophenomenology. In fact, I would propose that any time yoga—understood as a comprehensive system for conditioning the nervous system—is used in conjunction with phenomenology, then a *neuro*phenomenology is being invoked.

I also used knowledge of cognitive neuroscience to design a specific meditation sequence to achieve my desired results, so that this was not only *dhyana* in general. This, then, was further application of neurophenomenological methodology: knowledge derived from cognitive neuroscience was "married" to phenomenology to produce a method preparing for a specific perceptual task of spatial cognition. I thought this was a particularly promising application, because Thompson and Zahavi (2007), speaking of the phenomenological reduction, declare: "its purpose is to enable one to explore and describe the spatiotemporal world as it is given" (p. 70). What could be more relevant to an environmental design scenario?

Conclusion: Applying Neurophenomenological Sensory Data to Design Decisions

In this closing section I will provide a sketch of the thought processes involved when translating data collected via phenomenological walk-throughs into design decisions in the studio. The goal is to create a vivid conceptual site plan that may become a meaningful communication tool, relaying through graphic visual media the vision that coalesced via the stages of the design sequence. The site plan may or may not be implemented, or may be implemented only partially; that is not the concern of this phase of the research program. The plan exists as a vision of what *could* happen if there was a commitment to designing for consciousness, and the beauty of the plan itself is an inspiration to move in this direction. The plan was conceived during highly sensitized states that facilitated the perception of *essence*; open-ended creativity was encouraged during its production. Issues such as financing, zoning, coding—or even finding capable, skilled craftsmen—are for another discussion, and should not, like computer-aided drawing programs, limit the imagination at inception.[6]

The campus of the yoga college was situated on 55 acres of a former Seventh Day Adventist college that had lain abandoned for years. By today's standards, there was not a lot of thought put into the layout of the original campus. For example, orientation for passive solar gain was not a consideration. The campus was laid out on a northwesterly facing hill with a highway below, and because priority was given to facing buildings toward the highway, this means that all their backs face sunward. Circulation patterns tend to be blocky, lacking flow, and in some cases are quite dysfunctional. There is a preponderance of long straight sidewalks that seem to extend into the horizon. The buildings stand alone, as individual isolated entities, with only a sea of grass between them, and the grass is everywhere, requiring enormous inputs of energy to keep it looking lawn-like. The buildings themselves are uniformly symmetrical, barracks-like, lacking in imagination or embellishment. No provision was made for outdoor social space or gathering nodes. The overall feeling is functional and austere, the kind of place that might instill conformity and commitment to an authoritarian mandate.

The retrofit conceptual plan emphasizes the flow of *chi* and the containment and storage of that *chi* within the campus. Particular attention is given to reorienting for passive solar gain, and creating opportunities for solar access. Entrances are reworked to facilitate an inviting openness, while other areas are designed to nurture privacy and contemplation. Circulation patterns throughout the campus have been reconfigured to allow free flow and enjoyable locomotion, with particular emphasis on sinusoidal patterns that accent subtleties in topography. Numerous outdoor social spaces have been added, and many of these are used to create meaningful connections between buildings. Particular attention was given to the sequencing of spaces, such that movement enticingly transitions from one event horizon to the next. The sea of grass has been pushed way back, and has been replaced with ubiquitous gardens and decorative groves of trees through which people can meander. The presence of abundant water in this valley has been capitalized upon with the integration of numerous water features, including a sequence of waterfalls that culminates in a collection of quiet, reflective pools. The overall intent was to create a lively and vibrant built environment, oozing with beauty, such that an expansion of consciousness may be experienced simply by walking about the place. This would be a fitting purpose for the campus of a yoga college.

The radically embodied research program of designing for consciousness is ideally suited for adaptation to the scales of campuses, retreat centers, resorts, parks, academies, monasteries, and ashrams, and eco-villages of various persuasions, yet the lessons go beyond that. The typical built environment is constructed without any concern for its effects on consciousness. Indeed, even the possibility that there *are* such effects still would be debatable in many quarters, including graduate schools of landscape architecture. The typical built environment of North America was constructed according to the logic of "real estate" within the dictates of "the market." This financial gain imperative has resulted in a conspicuous nationwide abstraction, and I would be willing to argue that being forced to inhabit and participate in this abstraction is actually dumbing people down. This unwholesome situation is only compounded when design professionals limit their imaginative potential to the abstraction of cyberspace. This current state of affairs, therefore, makes the ambition of designing for consciousness an act of deliberate conscious evolution.

Endnotes

[1] Churchill was speaking on the occasion of a proposal to build a brand new House of Commons. Apparently, the original building was damaged during WWII and the idea was to replace it. Churchill strongly rejected this proposal on the grounds that conducting government in a new building would irretrievably alter the nature of the dialogue that had proceeded for centuries. The House of Commons was repaired instead.

[2] The extent to which this objectification of design has become standardized was exemplified in a recent interview with the Graduate Program Director of the School of Landscape Architecture of a prominent research university, who informed me that it is becoming common practice to "farm out" designs to technicians in India who have become masters of the intricacies of computer drawing programs. These tech-

nicians will never actually experience the locations they are designing for. The design process is happening entirely within the abstraction of cyber-space. The need for a radically embodied design methodology is as urgent as ever!

[3] There has been a variety of studies documenting neurophysiological conditioning of the nervous system through yogic practice. See for example: Goldberg, 2005; Khalsa, 2004; Raghuraj & Telles, 2008; Sathyaprabha, 2010. There are even studies with direct implication for the *design process*, such as by effecting parietal lobe and spatial perception: Jella & Shannahoff-Khalsa, 1993; Madanmohan, Mahdevan & Balkrishnan, 2008; Naveen et al., 1997.

[4] There has also emerged a robust literature documenting studies of the effects of meditation on the nervous system. Leading this vanguard of neurophysiological research is the Waisman Laboratory at the University of Wisconsin. Foundational studies include: Brefczynski-Lewis, Lutz, Schaefer, Levinson, & Davidson, 2007; Davidson & Lutz, 2007; Lutz, Greischar, Rawlings, Ricard, & Davidson, 2004; Lutz, Slagter, Dunne, & Davidson, 2008; Lutz, Brefczynski-Lewis, Johnstone, & Davidson, 2008; Lutz, Slagter, Rawlings, Francis, Greischer, & Davidson, 2009; Lutz, Greishar, Perlman, & Davidson, 2009.

[5] Such knowledge would tend to devalue or raise suspect the sedentary design process of sitting at a desk and flipping through pop-up windows on a computer screen, especially under the all-too-common scenario of the designer never actually going out to experience the site somatically. Such a design process would tend to contribute to a disembodied "virtual" reality in which users of the design will be compelled to inhabit.

[6] Because of space limitations, the following can only be a brief description. A full account of analyses of the transcripts and their translation into design solutions is contained in the doctoral dissertation from which this essay was extracted. This dissertation can be found through Pro Quest or viewed at www.villagedesign.org.

Appendix A

Conceptual Site Plan of the Yoga College (original size = 2' x 3')

References

Ainge, J. A., Dudchenko, P. A., & Wood, E. R. (2008). Context-dependent firing of hippocampal place cells: Does it underlie memory? In S.J.Y. Mizuomori (Ed.), *Hippocampal place fields: Relevance to learning and memory* (pp. 44-58). Oxford, England: Oxford University Press.

Aranya, S. H. (1983). *Yoga philosophy of Patanjali.* New York, NY: State University of New York Press.

Bachelard, G. (1958/1994). *The poetics of space.* Boston, MA: Beacon Press.

Bear, M. F., Connors, B. W., & Paradiso, M. A. (2001). *Neuroscience: Exploring the brain* (2nd ed.). Baltimore, MD: Lippincott, Williams & Wilkins.

Becker, S., & Burgess, N. (2001). A model of spatial recall, mental imagery and neglect. *Neural Information Processing Systems, 13,* 96-102.

Bird, C. M., & Burgess, N. (2008, March). The hippocampus and memory: Insights from spatial processing. *Nature Reviews Neuroscience, 9,* 182-194.

Bloomer, K. C., & Moore, C. W. (1977). *Body, memory, and architecture.* New Haven, CT: Yale University Press.

Brefczynski-Lewis, J. A., Lutz, A., Schaefer, H. S., Levinson, D. B., & Davidson, R. J. (2007). Neural correlates of attentional expertise in long-term meditation practitioners. *Proceedings of the National Academy of Sciences, 104*(27), 11483-11488.

Burgess, N. (2008). Spatial cognition and the brain. *Annals of the New York Academy of Science, 1124,* 77-97.

Burgess, N., Becker, S., King, J. A., & O'Keefe, J. (2001). Memory for events and their spatial context: Models and experiments. *Philosophical Transaction of the Royal Society of London, 356,* 1-11.

Burgess, N., Maguire, E. A., & O'Keefe, J. (2002, August 15). The human hippocampus and spatial and episodic memory. *Neuron, 35,* 625-641.

Buzsaki, G. (2005). Theta rhythm of navigation: Link between path integration and landmark navigation, episodic and semantic memory. *Hippocampus, 15,* 827-840.

Buzsaki, G. (2010, November 4). Neural syntax: Cell assemblies, synapsembles, and readers. *Neuron, 68,* 362-385.

Cohen, Y. E., & Andersen, R. A. (2004). Multimodal spatial representations in the primate parietal lobe. Retrieved from Oxford Scholarship Online. doi:10.1093/acprof:oso/9780198524861.003.005.

Connors, B. W., & Long, M. A. (2004). Electrical synapses in the mammalian brain. *Annual Review of Neuroscience, 27,* 393-418.

Cotterill, R.M.J. (2000). Did consciousness evolve from self-paced probing of the environment and not from reflexes? *Brain and Mind, 1*(2), 283-298.

Creem, S. H., & Proffitt, D. R. (2001). Defining the cortical visual systems: "What", "where," and "how." *Acta Psychologica, 107*, 43-68.

Cullen, G. (1961). *The concise townscape.* London, England: Architectural Press.

Davidson, R. J., & Lutz, A. (2008, January). Buddha's brain: Neuroplasticity and meditation. *IEEE Signal Processing Magazine, 25*(1), 172-176.

De Botton, A. (2006). *The architecture of happiness.* New York, NY: Vintage Books.

Depraz, N. (1999). The phenomenological reduction as *praxis.* In F. J. Varela & J. Shear (Eds.), *The view from within: First-person approaches to the study of consciousness* (pp. 95-110). Bowling Green, OH: Imprint Academic.

Desikachar, T.K.V. (1995). *The heart of yoga: Developing a personal practice.* Rochester, VT: Inner Traditions International.

Dobzhansky, T. (1956). *The biological basis of human freedom.* New York, NY: New York University Press.

Dubos, R. (1968). *So human an animal.* New York, NY: Charles Scribner's Sons.

Ekstrom, A. D., Kahana, M. J., Caplan, J. B., Fields, T. A., Isham, E. A., Newman, E. L.....Fried, I. (2003, September 11). Cellular networks underlying human spatial navigation. *Nature, 425*, 184-187. doi:10.1038/nature01964.

Espinosa, J. S., & Stryker, M. P. (2012, July 26). Development and plasticity of the primary visual cortex. *Neuron, 75*, 230-249.

Feuerstein, G. (2008). *The yoga tradition: Its history, literature, philosophy, and practice.* Prescott, AZ: Hohm Press.

Gardner, D. (Ed.). (1993). *The neurobiology of neural networks.* Cambridge, MA: A Bradford Book.

Gazzaniga, M. S., Ivry, R. B., & Mangun, G. R. (1998/2009). *Cognitive neuroscience: The biology of the mind* (3rd ed.). New York, NY: W. W. Norton.

Gilbert, C. D., & Li, W. (2012, July). Adult visual cortical plasticity. *Neuron, 75,* 250-264.

Goldberg, E. (2005). Cognitive science and hathayoga. *Zygon, 40*(3), 613-629.

Goldman-Rakic, P. S. (1988). Topography of cognition: Parallel distributed networks in primate association cortex. *Annual Review of Neuroscience, 11,* 137-156.

Goodale, M. A., & Milner, D. (1992). Separate visual pathways for perception and action. *Trends in the Neurosciences, 15*(1), 20-25.

Grill-Spector, K., & Malach, R. (2004). The human visual cortex. *Annual Review of Neuroscience, 27,* 649-677.

Gupta, B. (1998). *The disinterested witness: A fragment of Advaita Vedanta phenomenology.* Evanston, IL: Northwestern University Press.

Hall, M. P. (1972). The pineal gland: The eye of God. In M. P. Hall, *Man the grand symbol of the Mysteries: Thoughts in occult anatomy* (6th ed.). (pp. 329-342). Los Angeles, CA: Philosophical Research Society.

Hammond, M. A., Howarth, J. M., & Keat, R. N. (1994). *Understanding phenomenology.* Oxford, England: Blackwell Publishers.

Heidegger, M. (1962). *Being and time* (J. Macquarrie & E. Robinson, Trans.). New York, NY: Harper Perennial.

Hildebrand, G. (1999). *Origins of architectural pleasure.* Berkeley, CA: University of California Press.

Holl, S., Pallasmaa, J., & Perez-Gomez, A. (1993/2006). *Questions of perception: Phenomenology of architecture.* San Francisco, CA: William Stout Publishers.

Hubel, D. H. (1988). *Eye, brain, and vision.* New York, NY: Scientific American Library.

Husserl, E. (1913). *Ideas: General introduction to pure phenomenology* (W.R.B. Gibson, Trans.). London, England: Collier Macmillan Publishers.

-------. (1950/1960). *Cartesian meditations: An introduction to phenomenology* (D. Cairns, Trans.). The Hague, Amsterdam: Martinus Nijhoff.

Huxley, A. (1963). *Doors of perception and heaven and hell.* New York, NY: Harper Colophon Books.

Jantsch, E. (1975). *Design for evolution: Self-organization and planning in the life of human systems.* New York, NY: George Braziller.

Jeannerod, M. (1994). The representing brain: Neural correlates of motor intention and imagery. *Behavioral and Brain Sciences, 17,* 187-245.

Jeffery, K. J. (2007). Integration of the sensory inputs to place cells: What, where, why, and how? *Hippocampus, 17,* 775-785.

Jella, S. A., & Shannahoff-Khalsa, D. S. (1993). The effects of unilateral forced nostril breathing on cognitive performance. *International Journal of Neuroscience, 73,* 61-68.

Johnson, M. (1987). *The body in the mind: The bodily basis of meaning, imagination, and reason.* Chicago, IL: The University of Chicago Press.

-------. (2007). *The meaning of the body: Aesthetics of human understanding.* Chicago, IL: The University of Chicago Press.

Kentros, C. G., Agnihotri, N. T., Streater, S., Hawkins, R. D., & Kandel, E. R. (2004, April 22). Increased attention to spatial context increases both place field stability and spatial memory. *Neuron, 42,* 283-295.

Khalsa, S.B.S. (2004). Yoga as therapeutic intervention: A bibliometric analysis of published research studies. *Indian Journal of Physiology and Pharmacology, 48*(3), 269-285.

King, J. A., Burgess, N., Hartley, T., Vargha-Khadem, F., & O'Keefe, J. (2002). Human hippocampus and viewpoint dependence in spatial memory. *Hippocampus, 12*, 811-820.

Kosslyn, S. M., Ball, T. M., & Reiser, B. J. (1978). Visual images pre-serve metric spatial information: Evidence from studies of im-age scanning. *Journal of Experimental Psychology, 4*(1), 47-60.

Kravitz, D. J., Saleem, K. S., Baker, C. I., & Mishkin, M. (2011, April). A new neural framework for visuospatial processing. *Nature Reviews Neuroscience, 12*, 217-230.

Kriyananda, S. (2013). *Demystifying Patanjali: The Yoga Sutras.* Neva-da City, CA: Crystal Clarity Publishers.

Lachaux, J.-P., Rodriguez, E., Le Van Quyen, M., Lutz, A., Martinerie, J., & Varela, F. J. (2000). Studying single-trials of phase syn-chronous activity in the brain. *International Journal of Bifurca-tion and Chaos, 10*(10), 2429-2439.

Lachaux, J.-P., Rodriguez, E., Martinerie, J., & Varela, F. J. (1999). Measuring phase synchrony in brain signals. *Human Brain Mapping, 8*(4), 194-208.

Lakoff, G., & Johnson, M. (1980). *Metaphors we live by.* Chicago, IL: The University of Chicago Press.

-------. (1999). *Philosophy in the flesh: The embodied mind and its chal-lenge to Western thought.* New York, NY: Basic Books.

Levins, R., & Lewontin, R. (1985). *The dialectical biologist.* Cam-bridge, MA: Harvard University Press.

Livingstone, M. (2002). *Vision and art: The biology of seeing.* New York, NY: Harry N. Abrams.

Lutz, A., Brefczynski-Lewis, J., Johnstone, T., & Davidson, R. J. (2008, March). Regulation of the neural circuitry of emotion by com-passion meditation: Effects of meditative expertise. *PLoS ONE, 3*(3), 1-10.

Lutz, A., Greischar, L. L., Perlman, D. M., & Davidson, R. J. (2009). BOLD signal in insula is differentially related to cardiac func-tion during compassion meditation in experts vs. novices. *Neu-roImage, 47*, 1038-1046.

Lutz, A., Greischar, L. L., Rawlings, N. B., Ricard, M., & Davidson, R. J. (2004). Long-term meditators self-induce high-amplitude gamma synchrony during mental practice. *Proceedings of the National Academy of Science, 101*(46), 16369-16373.

Lutz, A., Slagter, H. A., Dunne, J. D., & Davidson, R. J. (2008, April). Attention regulation and monitoring in meditation. *Trends in Cognitive Sciences, 12*(4), 163-169.

Lutz, A., Slagter, H. A., Rawlings, N. B., Francis, A. D., Greischar, L. L., & Davidson, R. J. (2009, October 21). Mental training enhances attentional stability: Neural and behavioral evidence. *The Journal of Neuroscience, 29*(42), 13418-13427.

Lynch, K. (1960). *The image of the city.* Cambridge, MA: The MIT Press.

Madanmohan, Mahdevan, S. K., & Balkrishnan, S. (2008). Effects of six weeks' yoga training on weight loss following step test, respiratory pressures, handgrip strength and handgrip endurance in young healthy subjects. *Indian Journal of Physiology and Pharmacology, 52*(2), 164-70.

Mare, E. C. (2016). Designing for consciousness: Towards a theory of environmental design using neurophenomenology as methodology (Doctoral dissertation). Retrieved from http://gradworks.umi.com/10/12/10123839.html. (Accension No. 10123839).

Maturana, H. R. (1974). The organization of the living: A theory of the living organization. *International Journal of Human-Computer Studies, 51*, 149-168.

Maturana, H. R., & Varela, F. J. (1987). *The tree of knowledge: The biological roots of human understanding.* Boulder, CO: Shambhala Publications.

Merleau-Ponty, M. (1942/1983). *The structure of behavior* (A. L. Fisher, Trans.). Pittsburgh, PA: Duquesne University Press.

Moustakas, C. (1994). *Phenomenological research methods.* Thousand Oaks, CA: SAGE.

Muller, R. (1996, November). A quarter of a century of place cells. *Neuron, 17,* 979-990.

Nadel, L. (2008). The hippocampus and context revisited. In S.J.Y. Mizumori (Ed.), *Hippocampal place fields: Relevance to learning and memory* (pp. 3-15). Oxford, England: Oxford University Press.

Naveen, K. V., Nagendra, H. R., Nagarathna, R., & Telles, S. (1997). Breathing through a particular nostril improves spatial memory scores without lateralized effects. *Psychological Reports, 81,* 555-561.

Nöe, A., & O'Regan, J. K. (2002). On the brain basis of visual consciousness: A sensorimotor account. In A. Noe & E. Thompson (Eds.), *Vision and mind: Selected readings in the philosophy of perception* (pp. 567-598). Cambridge, MA: A Bradford Book.

Norberg-Schulz, C. (1980). *Genius loci: Towards a phenomenology of architecture.* New York, NY: Rizzoli International.

Norberg-Schulz, C. (1984). *The concept of dwelling: On the way to figurative architecture.* New York, NY: Rizzoli International.

-------. (2000). *Architecture: Presence, language, place.* Milano, Italy: Skira Editore S.p.A.

O'Keefe, J., & Nadel, L. (1978). *The hippocampus as a cognitive map.* Oxford, England: Clarendon Press.

Pallasmaa, J. (2012). *The eyes of the skin: Architecture and the senses.* Chichester, West Sussex, England: John Wiley & Sons Ltd.

Palmer, S. E. (1999). *Vision science: Photons to phenomenology.* Cambridge, MA: A Bradford Book.

Raghuraj, P., & Telles, S. (2008). Immediate effects of specific nostril manipulating yoga breathing practices on autonomic and respiratory variables. *Applied Psychophysiological Biofeedback, 33,* 65-75.

Rasmussen, S.E. (1959). *Experiencing architecture.* Cambridge, MA: The MIT Press.

Rietveld, E. (2008). The skillful body as a concernful system of possible actions. *Theory & Psychology, 18*(3), 341-363.

Rodriguez, E., George, N., Lachaux, J.-P., Martinerie, J., Renault, B., & Varela, F. J. (1999, February 4). Perception's shadow: Long-distance synchronization of human brain activity. *Nature, 397*, 430-433.

Sathyaprabha, D.T.N. (2010). Neurophysiological studies of yoga in health and diseases. *International Symposium on YOGism,* December 21-25, 2010. Retrieved from http://www.arogyad-ham-seva.com/YOGism/GL3.pdf.

Seamon, D. (1989). Foundations of the human sciences: Humanistic and phenomenological advances in environmental design. *The Humanistic Psychologist, 17*(3), 280-293.

-------. (Ed.). (1993). *Dwelling, seeing, designing: Toward a phenomenological ecology.* New York, NY: State University of New York Press.

-------. (2000). A way of seeing people and place: Phenomenology in environment-behavior research. In S. Wapner, J. Demick, T. Yamamoto & H. Minami (Eds.), *Theoretical perspectives in environment-behavior research: Underlying assumptions, research problems, and methodologies* (pp. 157-178). New York, NY: Springer Science+Business Media.

Seamon, D., & Mugerauer, R. (Eds.). (2000). *Dwelling, place, and environment: Towards a phenomenology of person and world.* Malabar, FL: Krieger Publishing.

Selemon, L. D., & Goldman-Rakic, P. S. (1988, November). Common cortical and subcortical targets of the dorsolateral prefrontal and posterior parietal cortices in the rhesus monkey: Evidence for a distributed neural network subserving spatially guided behavior. *The Journal of Neuroscience, 8*(11), 4049-4068.

Shen, L., Hu, X., Yacoub, E., & Ugurbil, K. (1999). Neural correlates of visual form and visual spatial processing. *Human Brain Map-*

ping, 8, 60-71.

Sherman, S. M., & Guillery, R. W. (2013). *Exploring the thalamus*. Amsterdam, The Netherlands: Elsevier.

Smith, D. M., & Mizumori, S.J.Y. (2006). Hippocampal place cells, context, and episodic memory. *Hippocampus, 16*(9), 716-729.

Stinchcombe, A. L. (1968). *Constructing social theories*. Chicago, IL: The University of Chicago Press.

Thompson, E. (2006a). Sensorimotor subjectivity and the enactive approach to experience. *Phenomenology and the Cognitive Sciences, 4*, 407-427.

-------. (2006b). Neurophenomenology and contemplative experience. In P. Clayton (Ed.), *The Oxford handbook of religion and science* (pp. 226-35). Oxford, England: Oxford University Press.

Thompson, E., Noe, A., & Pessoa, L. (1999). Perceptual completion: A case study in phenomenology and cognitive science. In J. Petitot, F.J. Varela, B. Pachoud, & J.-M. Roy (Eds.), *Naturalizing phenomenology: Issues in contemporary phenomenology and cognitive science* (pp. 161-195). Stanford, CA: Stanford University Press.

Thompson, E., & Zahavi, D. (2007). Philosophical issues: Phenomenology. In P. D. Zelazo, M. Moscovitch & E. Thompson (Eds.), *The Cambridge handbook of consciousness* (pp. 67-87). Cambridge, MA: Cambridge University Press.

Tononi, G., & Edelman, G. M. (1998, December 4). Consciousness and complexity. *Science, 282*, 1846-1851.

Varela, F. J. (1996). Neurophenomenology: A methodological remedy for the hard problem. *Journal of Consciousness Studies, 3*(4), 330-349.

Varela, F. J., Thompson, E., & Rosch, E. (1991). *The embodied mind: Cognitive science and human experience*. Cambridge, MA: MIT Press.

Varela, F. J., Lachaux, J.-P., Rodriguez, E., & Martinerie, J. (2001,

April). The brainweb: Phase synchronization and large-scale integration. *Nature Reviews Neuroscience, 2*, 229-239.

White, D. J., Congedo, M., Ciorciari, J., & Silbertein, R. B. (2012). Brain oscillatory activity during spatial navigation: Theta and gamma activity link medial temporal and parietal regions. *Journal of Cognitive Neuroscience, 24*(3), 686-697.

Christopher E. Mare, PhD, completed a doctoral dissertation at Fielding Graduate University entitled *Designing for Consciousness: A Theory of Village Design Using Neurophenomenology as Methodology*. Mare is founder and president of the Village Design Institute, an educational nonprofit seeking a land base upon which to establish an Academy of Design. He has worked internationally with village designers to help them produce ecologically sustainable environments that will enhance the consciousness of those who live in and pass through them.

About the Series Editor

Jean-Pierre Isbouts, DLitt is doctoral faculty in the PhD programs of Human and Organizational Development (HOD) at Fielding Graduate University. A humanities scholar, Dr. Isbouts served as Editor-in-Chief of the *Bertelsmann Multimedia Lexikon*, published in German, and as Editor-in-Chief of the *Standaard Multimedia Encyclopedie*, published in Dutch. He has written on a number of subjects, including American cinema (*Charlton Heston's Hollywood*, 1998, and *Discovering Walt*, 2002); Renaissance art (*The Renaissance of Florence*, 1993, and *The Mona Lisa Myth*, 2013); comparative religion (*From Moses to Muhammad: The Shared Origins of Judaism, Christianity and Islam*, 2010); and biblical history, including two National Geographic bestsellers: *The Biblical World* (2007), and *In the Footsteps of Jesus* (2012). In addition, he has published articles in the *International Journal of the Humanities* and was a contributor to the *Oxford Handbook of Media Psychology*. His most recent publication is a survey of the Christian imprint on Western civilization, entitled *The Story of Christianity*, written with six doctoral students from Fielding Graduate University and published by National Geographic in November of 2014.

About the Associate Editor

Casandra D. Lindell, M.Div., M.A., is a PhD student in Human and Organizational Development at Fielding Graduate University. She is a licensed marriage and family therapist working with people who have engaged in sexual misconduct. She has worked as an editor and writer, and taught psychology and psychotherapy at both undergraduate and master's levels. Her research interests are in understanding spiritual and sexual development, understanding how people make meaning in life, and in creating healing community through restorative justice.

About Fielding Graduate University

Fielding Graduate University, headquartered in Santa Barbara, CA, was founded in 1974, and celebrated its 40th anniversary in 2014. Fielding is an accredited, nonprofit leader in blended graduate education, combining face-to-face and online learning. Its curriculum offers quality master's and doctoral degrees for professionals and academics around the world. Fielding's faculty members represent a wide spectrum of scholarship and practice in the fields of educational leadership, human and organizational development, and clinical and media psychology. Fielding's faculty serves as mentors and guides to self-directed students who use their skills and professional experience to become powerful, socially responsible leaders in their communities, workplaces, and society. For more information, please visit Fielding online at www.fielding.edu

Printed in Great Britain
by Amazon

Printed in Great Britain
by Amazon